BEHIND THE
BERLIN WALL
STEVEN KELMAN

Behind the Berlin Wall is the day-by-day account of life in East Germany by a young American observer.

Steven Kelman entered East Berlin in the summer of 1971, ostensibly to study the glorious successes of socialist democracy in the German Democratic Republic, actually to find out how ordinary people — especially young people — react to the regimentation of a Communist police state. Other inquisitive visitors had landed in prison and he was well aware of the need for discretion. The risks to him might be considered as a little greater than to the average tourist, for he is, in his own words, "a loud-mouthed anti-Communist" who had expressed his opinions in several magazine articles and a book. If the East German authorities had chanced to come across any of the articles or a review of the book, he might be in serious trouble. But nothing was going to hold him back. He had visited East Germany briefly in 1969 with no untoward results, and besides, *The New Yorker* had commissioned him to write a "Letter from East Germany."

When Steven Kelman landed at the East Berlin airport one rainy June day, his application for a visa was still unanswered but this, apparently, was not unusual. Would they accept him as a student of the European labor movement and an enthusiastic supporter of Communism? At first there were difficulties and he wondered whether he would be turned back or even placed under arrest. But before long everything was arranged. Under the auspices of the friendly Herr

continued on the back flap

1072

BEHIND THE BERLIN WALL

by Steven Kelman

Push Comes to Shove
Behind the Berlin Wall

BEHIND
THE
BERLIN
WALL

An Encounter in East Germany

STEVEN
KELMAN

1972
HOUGHTON MIFFLIN
COMPANY, BOSTON

A portion of this book originally appeared
in *The New Yorker*.

First Printing   w

ISBN: 0–395–14003–X
Library of Congress Catalog Card
Number: 72–2279

Printed in the United States of America

For Cesar Chavez
and
Alexander Solzhenitsyn,
who are each
working in their own
ways for freedom
and justice.
And for Mike Kolatch
and Anne Barrett,
who made everything
possible for me.

Some names, places, and minor
descriptions have been changed,
although all important facts
recounted are true.

NOTE TO THE READER

THIS BOOK DESCRIBES what happened to me when I visited East Germany in the summer of 1971 to research a story for *The New Yorker* magazine. The article itself is reprinted at the end of the book. One of the things I have set out to do is to indicate what a journalist's sources are for the statements he makes and the conclusions he draws. Thus, there are some repetitions — especially of quotations — which appear first in the account of my experience in East Germany, and then at the end of the book in *The New Yorker* story itself. My hope in doing this is to make the process of journalism come alive for the reader.

At the same time, there are many facts, incidents, and conclusions which appear only in *The New Yorker* article and not in the main account at all. Thus, while the account stands by itself, I would urge the reader not to regard *The New Yorker* story at the end merely as a sort of academic appendix which can be skipped over without any loss.

Stockholm
April 1972

INTRODUCTION

FROM THE VERY BEGINNING my parents didn't want me to go. The dispute started even before I left the States, and continued via the mails afterward. Every Sunday night my father sat down at the typewriter, which still sat on the desk in my old bedroom, to write his weekly letter. On Thursday, his letters would arrive in Stockholm through the letterbox hole in the door, plopping down onto the hall floor with all the other mail for the corridor. More often than not, the other three students in the corridor had classes when the mail arrived. So it was my job to pick up all the mail from the floor and put each person's letters on the floor outside his door. The plopping sound every morning made me hopeful and expectant. As for my father's letters, the Swedish mail service was so efficient that the letters he mailed Monday mornings invariably arrived Thursdays. That was great. Especially when you're abroad, getting letters from home is one of the best things that can happen. No matter how much you're enjoying yourself, without news, and love, from your family and friends, you could never make it. Without communication, you're lost.

Of course, my prospective visit to East Germany played a relatively small part in my father's letters. But it would surface again and again, like a symphonic theme, with varying intensities and modes. His most common method was just to send clippings. My father liked to send clippings anyway — Tom

Wicker columns, articles on Sweden and Harvard from the papers — as a sort of mental care package. Every once in a while among the clippings there was something like this:

The East Germans began handing out prison sentences to American and other Western students in September. Last week, a closed court in East Berlin sentenced two more students to long terms.

Frank King, 24, a Detroit medical student, was given two years in prison. Michael Woodridge, 25, King's British cousin, was sentenced to 15 months' confinement. Though neither man was known as a far-rightist in his home country, both were arrested in East Berlin last summer for pasting up propaganda posters bearing Nazi swastikas. They joined three other Americans in East Berlin's grim Hohenschönhausen prison: Jack Strickland, 28, who was sentenced two months ago to four years for alleged border violations and supposedly trying to slip East Germans out of their walled-in country; Lyle Jenkins, 30, who drew 2½ years on similar charges; and Mark Huessy, 21, who is serving the longest term of all. Six weeks ago, Huessy drew a 7-year term for slandering the Communist regime.

The son of a University of Vermont professor of psychiatry, Huessy was writing a paper on Communist playwright Bertolt Brecht and living with an East Berlin family. According to his father, young Huessy was "positively impressed" with the regime, but he also clung to his faith in the U.S. Shortly before his arrest, he wrote to his parents, "How can I explain to these people that even though I agree with all their criticism of the American system, the Viet Nam War and racism, that there is still something about America which gives it more potential than any system I know?" Last January, less than a week before he was scheduled to return home, Huessy was arrested in East Berlin. Eight months later, he was charged on three counts: espionage, trying to help East Germans escape, and provocative criticism of the state. Acquitted on the two more serious charges, he was convicted on the state criticism charge. His alleged slander was that the Communist regime would collapse if Moscow decided to pull its 20 divisions out of East Germany.

No extended commentary in the letters was then felt to be necessary. Only something like, "See the enclosed clipping on the D.D.R. Steve, why don't you be sensible and reconsider? How about going to Hungary or Rumania or Yugoslavia instead? They're just as interesting, and not half as dangerous." Then there would be a handwritten P.S. from my mother: "Steve, darling, please don't go to East Germany."

Basically, their argument was that it was insane to go to East Germany posing as a normal student, and expect to be able to meander around talking with ordinary people and gathering material for a magazine article or a book. The authorities would know who I was, and I would be arrested as a spy. Indeed, ran the argument, "by their laws" I would be guilty, since to them normal information-gathering was espionage.

Who *was* I?

Basically, among other things I was a loud-mouthed anti-Communist. Or to put it more precisely if more confusingly, an anti-Communist democratic socialist, in the European tradition of social democracy. I have heard, far more times than I want to, that I belong to a past epoch. What does a rickety and cranky old Menshivism or anti-Stalinism have to do with someone who was born thirty years after the Russian Revolution and was five when Joseph Stalin died? The sixties, they said, was a new age, when anti-Communism stank of napalm-burned flesh and to be with it required a poster of Che hanging from your wall. Still, I refused to curse the age in which I was born. Both going along with the crowd and standing out as a gadfly have their psychological compensations. You adapt to the rewards of your convictions.

Another necessity in the sixties was the poster telling you to love, with two silhouettes of nude bodies ambling along a quiet beach. It was more human, more gentle, more soft, more beautiful than the brightly lit, fleshy plastic pinups of the forties and fifties. Kids sensed the contradiction between Che and the soft, sensuous, beautiful people — the realities of the world did not correspond to our love visions. Many saw the gap between reality and dreams in one light, and kept Che on their walls in spite of everything. I saw it in another light, and opted for America in spite of everything. America appeared so imperfect, it seemed to me, and the gap between dream and reality oh so enormous, until one considered the nations in the other great power bloc which made up the world beyond the beach. Power exists: something which the people who chose Che realized, and something I realized. That was one reality. But power is not just force and cynicism, it also represents ways of life and the ultimate happiness or sufferings of people, including the couple on the beach. That too was a reality that the Che people and I both accepted. But what was the nature of life, everyday life, in those two great blocs? What did the power of the West represent, and what did the power of the Communist states represent? The Che people had their version of that fundamental reality, and it was in search of my version that I wanted to go to Eastern Europe and stay there for a while.

As a child I grew up quickly, looking back I would say without hesitation too quickly. In third grade my favorite reading was *The World Almanac,* and I could hardly think of anything more fun than learning the names of all the countries in the world and their capitals. I also gave a speech to the class, as part of a mock election campaign, for Adlai Stevenson. Our class voted for Eisenhower anyway, and I remember my father sighing to my mother, "They vote just like their parents will vote in November."

A few years later I was a young radical. By young I mean twelve or thirteen. Maybe that's not so strange today, with pot in the playgrounds and the mass media pushing revolution on tots. But then it was definitely young. It was good in some ways for one side of you to develop so young, but you got dizzy with success, you ignored the concrete and unpretentious things in life for the slogans, only to come back to what you missed earlier when others had first discovered the shouting. That gives advantages now, because you've been through it before. But you realize now that you were less happy then than you fooled yourself into thinking.

When I entered junior high, the big theme was Cuba. Well, it wasn't exactly a big theme for everybody in our class, but two of us were strongly interested in defending, at the greatest possible length, the view that Fidel Castro, bless his heart, had gotten a raw deal from the United States. But in the end it was Cuba which put an end to it all. As Fidel increasingly transformed himself into a Soviet puppet, all the ideas about Cuba I had defended when I was thirteen suddenly seemed ridiculous.

In the middle of my sophomore year I agreed, just for the fun of it, to take an anti–Communist China position in a debate the class had arranged; by the time I had finished my research I had convinced myself of it. Then I gobbled up some wonderful things by Theodore Draper on "myths and realities" about the Cuban revolution. There followed a lot of books about the crimes of the Stalin era, and the betrayal of the Russian Revolution. It was all a completely intellectual changeover, but it was still from abstract intellectual arguments and debater's points that I gathered my emotions. So during those months I felt joyous, and liberated — liberated from the obligation to shout for freedom of speech for students at the high school while supporting those abroad who crushed it. During those months I found out about democratic socialism, an ideology both anti-Communist and on the Left. That was crucial: I could never think of abandoning the Left. But democratic socialists could tell the truth and still be on the Left.

Great Neck, New York, was probably one of the few, if not the only, communities in the country where such truths might, early in 1964, be unpopular, for a relatively large number of old Communists had settled there. They had climbed up the economic ladder but still maintained an affection for the old "progressive" causes. They were far from a majority in the community, but their children controlled the political life of Great Neck South Senior High School, and that was my world. Before Berkeley, before the New Left came to dominate the campuses, before Weathermen and radical chic and America seeming to fall apart — in 1964 the type of people whom most Americans got to be familiar with only as the decade dragged on already controlled my high school. Or at least its discussion clubs and political activities, and that was what mattered to me. They were big on Cuba, China, the military-industrial complex, and, already, Vietnam. They went unchallenged.

At South there was a girl named Lori, who was a member of the intellectual group, but sort of cynical and never really in with the politically active kids. She was in my social-studies class back in seventh grade, and she followed our arguments about Cuba, but she either didn't participate or else made small comments that seemed to side with the teacher.

She read a little magazine called *The New Leader*, which she thought was absolutely the best thing around. That year, tenth grade, she persuaded me to subscribe, but I waited until a discount offer appeared in the Sunday *Times*. My father at first didn't want me to. He said *The New Leader* was still fighting the battles of the thirties. That sounded O.K. to me, and only made me more anxious to begin seeing it. One thing

I noticed was that when you cited *The New Leader* in discussions with the other political kids, it would get a rise out of them. They were still fighting the battles of the thirties too. It was only that they were on the other side.

It's funny, I can't really remember exactly what possessed me to do it — maybe it was summer-vacation boredom — but one day I sat down at my typewriter and began writing an article to send to *The New Leader*. It was about politics at Great Neck South, about the dangers of young people accepting wide-eyed a double standard in judging democratic and totalitarian countries. I titled my article "Youth and Politics: Headed for A Fall?" The idea was that, in the thirties, many former Communists had become disillusioned by the revelations of the stark reality of Soviet Russia, and turned into right-wing extremists in reaction. A simliar fate, I wrote, could befall my generation unless we were careful.

It was too good to believe: they accepted the article. My life, I thought, was made the day I got the letter from *The New Leader*. A great future stood before me. And you know, I was more right than I knew. The article came out. The local paper took it up, and William Buckley wrote a column about it. The political kids at school went insane. Nobody had ever questioned them before. But I wasn't mainly thinking about the hatred then, because other things were happening. Out of the April 1965 march on Washington, the first big anti-Vietnam demonstration, out of that grew a long article on an organization relatively few people had heard of, the Students for a Democratic Society. After that came letters from *Harper's*, *Commentary* and *The Saturday Evening Post* in orgiastic succession. They wanted me to write for them. It was as good as going steady with the best girl in the school. And easier. I was only a senior in high school.

It just got better and better. The next fall I went off to Harvard, and wrote an article on the freshman class for the Sunday *New York Times Magazine.* Other pieces came out, mostly on students and the student movement. And finally, in my senior year, a book on the student movement and the 1969 Harvard strike. For three years I had been working on a magnum opus diary of my freshman year, an unwieldy work which I am convinced never would have seen the light of day. But sections of it got incorporated into *Push Comes to Shove,* which was my definitive showdown with the political extremism which, through a quirk of fate, I had been facing, not just for a year or two like most Americans, but ever since my sophomore year in high school.

I think I had grown up somewhat. Politics was still important to me, very important, but I realized that politics made itself felt for everyday people in small ways, ways having to do with their everyday lives. Also, I think I got an understanding of the limits of what politics can or should be expected to achieve. I became distrustful of those who wanted to politicize and sloganize everything. People don't like it. People have a need to be left alone, to pursue private things with their families and friends, and there's nothing wrong with that. Life isn't a revolution, and revolution's no life.

I remember when I was younger, my mother sometimes used to yell at me that I loved the People but didn't give a damn — she must have said "darn" — about people. That summarizes growing up too fast. And her words come back every time I hear something about the "People's Coalition for Peace and Justice" or "People's Park" or how "the streets belong to the people." Revolutionaries, with their glowing faith in the People, usually dislike or even despise real, live, in-this-world people. They hide their hatred by arguing that people have become evil and horrible because of bourgeois indoctrination and capitalist economic relations, and that when their revolution imposes a new system of indoctrination in selflessness and righteousness, people will become like saints. Bullshit. The important thing is that they think people right now are pretty despicable, pretty horrible. I don't believe that anymore. I think most people are O.K. I've grown up a little.

I had in the meantime decided to go to Eastern Europe. About thirty years ago a woman left money to Harvard in her will so that each year two Harvard seniors would get a sum of money to travel abroad for a year with no conditions attached. It's the type of prize which is so unbelievable that you would probably never bother to apply if you had to go through a long procedure — the chances just seem too small. But all that is necessary is to tell your house master that you wish to be considered. If you are lucky, a few months later you're told that you are one of the thirty-six finalists. Then all you have to do is write a little two-page essay saying where you want to go. In April, I found out I won.

Everybody who wins goes to Asia, of course. How else could you get the money to visit Asia before you turned too old to be able to take the strain? I had written in my essay that I also planned to visit several countries in Eastern Europe, especially East Germany and Czechoslovakia. I had already visited both places, for about a week each, in 1968 and 1969. My interest was partly academic. My field of study had narrowed down to the industrialized societies of Europe, and I thought it was unfortunate that few scholars in the field ever bothered to include the industralized countries of East Europe in their research. I had already taught myself Swedish through a combination of the Harvard language lab and two summer visits to the country, and I hoped to use the same method with Czech. So in January of my senior year I bought a textbook and began going to the language lab about every other day. Czech was much harder than Swedish, but I hoped that with three months or so in Czechoslovakia I could pick it up.

With the tight employment situation for academics, I joked with a young professor one day, I felt I ought to take advantage of the area where my abilities lay. And I knew I was good at languages. But of course it wasn't just that. In the back of my mind was that question: what is it like for ordinary people day after day, month after month, year grinding on after year, borders guarded with men and guns and barbed wire, to live in a totalitarian society? How do people adapt to it, make their compromises with it, get along in it? Is freedom just a luxury item without much meaning for the man on the street, as some claimed? An outsider could never know exactly. But living there for a while, talking with people, and trying as far as possible to subject myself to the conditions the people underwent there would give more than a few clues. Speaking the language (I already knew some German) would help, because it was above all a question of talking with people, not about high politics or power struggles, but about their lives.

To be sure, most of the attention of politically active American youth had been going to the underdeveloped countries, and many of those who admired the likes of China and Cuba professed little love for "revisionist" East Germany or Czechoslovakia. But if the question is revolution for America, it's just there you should look, for it is those countries which most resemble America. They have a complex industrial structure of the type easily ruined by overly centralized direction. They possessed all sorts of independent institutions — clubs, political parties, mass organizations — which had to be cracked to make way for utopia. And the people there were used to speaking their minds.

About a month after I heard about the traveling fellowship my book, *Push Comes to Shove,* came out. About the same time a piece I had written for *Foreign Affairs* appeared, and the editor-in-chief at Houghton Mifflin, on reading the article, asked my editor whether I had another book in mind. All along I had vaguely thought about a possible book on Eastern Europe, but his words crystallized my reveries. It would be a book on youth in Eastern Europe, and it would be a manifesto of my reality. There would be conversations and portraits and above all an attempt to describe what it was like to be caught in a totalitarian state. It would be a *livre de combat.*

By this time I was plastered over the *Reader's Guide* and the *Book Review Digest,* and anyone in authority in Eastern Europe who wanted to look me up would find a lot of things he wouldn't like. It was thus not even especially certain that they would let me in. And, my parents argued, if they did let me in, as likely as not the purpose would be to trap me.

My argument the whole time was that, sure, they could find all these things if they looked, but why the hell should they look? Why, right off, should they suspect me? Just a kid, a student, why should I be dangerous? My parents were far from so sure. The East Germans would get suspicious if for no other reason than because I wanted to stay so long. Who goes to East Germany for two months and Czechoslovakia for three months? Normal countries are, of course, happy to have tourists stay as long as possible. The longer you stay, the more dollars they get. But to these countries, a long stay means that you must be a spy.

When I left for Sweden in August to study there for a semester, the whole question was still up in the air. In my mind, however, I was determined to go. I would tell the Czechs that I wanted to learn their language, as part of my academic studies

— which was true in and of itself. As for the East Germans, I would tell them of my (genuine) interest in the history of the German labor movement, and even request to incorporate a *Studienbesuch* (study visit) in my trip, meeting with local labor officials and such. In November I dutifully wrote my first letter to the offices of the Youth Travel Agency in East Berlin:

> I graduated from Harvard University in June 1970, where my field of study was the history of the European labor movement. During my visit to the D.D.R., I would be most interested in visiting various museums and monuments of the German labor movement, such as Karl Liebknecht's home in Leipzig or the Museum of German history in Berlin. It would also be a great privilege to see library or archive material.
>
> Would it be possible for me to arrange a study visit in connection with my trip to the D.D.R.? In particular, I would be interested in meeting with
>
> 1. local trade union officials and grassroots members of the Socialist Unity Party;
> 2. professors whose field is the history of the German labor movement;
> 3. activists, especially students, in the German movement for Vietnam;
> 4. members of local German-Soviet Friendship Societies.
>
> I hope to visit the D.D.R. for 6–8 weeks next summer. Could you please send me information on the location of different youth hostels in the D.D.R.? Also, if you are not in a position to arrange a study visit, can you tell me whom I should contact?

What I got back, after three weeks, was a printed sheet with information on youth hostels. The agency explained the procedure for arranging a stay in East Germany, which I already knew about from 1969. The itinerary must be announced in advance, and all hotel reservations confirmed and paid for. Then

you receive a series of vouchers to present at the hotels. On
presenting the vouchers at the border a visa is granted. At the
bottom of the two-page form letter, one line was typed in. "The
Youth Travel Tourist Agency is unfortunately not in the position to arrange study visits."

I wrote them another letter, asking again if they could tell me
who might be in a position to arrange study visits. I didn't get
any reply, and at this point I thought up a new strategy. It was
obvious that I couldn't present myself as a journalist, because
then a hop over to the *Reader's Guide* was a certainty. But perhaps if I presented myself as a writer for a *college* newspaper,
things would go O.K. Even my parents liked the idea. They
assumed that the application for a journalist's visa would be
turned down, which was fine by them, but reasoned that if I
actually got a journalist's visa, the worst that could happen
would be that I'd be thrown out of the country, rather than
arrested.

My stakes in making it into East Germany had increased.
Before I left America in August, I had succeeded in getting an
assignment from *The New Yorker* to write an article on Sweden.
Normally, *The New Yorker* does not bring in outside people
because their own staff is so big. Apparently, I got the assignment because I had been there before and spoke Swedish. It
was an honor, a challenging honor. I sweated on that "Letter
from Stockholm," and I felt very good early one November
morning when a telegram boy woke me up to deliver a message
from William Shawn, the editor-in-chief, that he liked what I
had written.

I had a suspicion that, in spite of that, I was perhaps asking
too much when I wrote Mr. Shawn from Stockholm telling him
of my plans to go to East Germany. As a young kid, I wrote, I
would have much more opportunity to talk with ordinary peo-

ple than would an older, official journalist. I hoped to do a piece on everyday life in East Germany, and wondered if maybe I might be taken on once more. Within a week came a telegram.

> OUR PROBLEM WITH OUTSIDE PEOPLE REMAINS   YET IN
> THIS SPECIAL CASE GO AHEAD   IT SHOULD BE VERY INTER-
> ESTING   REGARDS   WILLIAM SHAWN

It was now February, and I was in Japan. I wrote to a friend on the *Yale Daily News*, asking for a letter of introduction to forward to the East Germans. He came through in record time with letters for the East German and Czech authorities, identifying me as a student journalist, and asking that all help be extended me.

During the next month I went over my well-fingered East German map, and my list of youth hostels, and prepared my proposed itinerary in the D.D.R. It included a week each in East Berlin, Leipzig, and Dresden — cities I had visited in 1969. Leipzig is an industrial town that was a traditional source of Communist Party strength before 1933. Dresden also has a fair amount of industry, but is special both for its artistic treasures and as a victim of Allied terror bombing during World War II. Then I hoped to visit Weimar, the university town; Rostock, a port in the north where a university is also located; Eisenach, a smallish place where the East German automobile, the Wartburg, is manufactured; and a youth camp located on the vacation island of Rügen. There would also be a few days visiting a schoolteacher I had met last time in Dresden. He lived in a small village about forty miles from Dresden, and the visit to him would require getting permission through a special bureau set up for the purpose. I hoped the itinerary would give me a chance to talk with a lot of young people, and also to see industry and town planning.

My final letter to the Youth Tourist Travel Agency took up two tightly packed single-spaced typed pages, with exact dates and hotels desired and requests for train reservations. There was also a letter of introduction from the *Yale Daily News*. I repeated my requests for meeting with various people, and added knowingly that I was aware that the Youth Tourist Travel Agency was not in a position to arrange any of this, but could they pass on this request to the appropriate agency. With the letter I enclosed traveler's checks to pay for all the hotels.

The problem was mailing the letter. Posting it from, say, South Korea was impossible — the South Korean government at first didn't even want to give me a visa to their country because I had the East German visa from 1969 stamped on my passport. Hong Kong wasn't really completely safe either, an outpost of British colonialism and Chinese as well. Indonesia hadn't been too friendly with East Germany since the coup against Sukarno. Part of the question of where to mail the letter concerned what the East German authorities would think of my having visited the country in question. But there was the even more basic question of whether the letter would get there.

I arrived on April Fool's Day in the island republic of Singapore and posted the letter, air-mail registered, right after checking in to my hotel. Singapore was neutral, relatively "progressive," and her bitter anti-Communism limited itself mainly to China, something which the East Germans wouldn't mind. Singapore had even, I had read in the papers while in Hong Kong, received a visit from the East German foreign minister. The Youth Tourist Travel Agency was supposed to write to me in care of one of three American Express mail pick-up addresses in Calcutta, New Delhi, or Bombay.

There was nothing waiting for me at American Express in Calcutta a month later, or, three weeks after that, at American

Express in Delhi. I was beginning to get nervous. Why hadn't I even gotten an answer from them? Also, of course, I still knew nothing about my visa application for Czechoslovakia. Since the Czechs, unlike the East Germans, had diplomatic relations with most countries, you could apply directly at Czech embassies instead of through the mails. Originally I had wanted to apply from Singapore, but it turned out the Czechs had no embassy there, so here too I had to wait for New Delhi. Finding the embassy, and finding a time when the visa section was open, presented problems. But one Monday morning in May I made it over to the embassy's consular annex. After nearly an hour's wait, with frequent interruptions from the plump and saried Indian secretary assuring me that the consul would soon arrive, the consul arrived.

"You would like a tourist visum?" he said with a high voice and a heavy lilt. He was thin, of medium height, bespectacled, and looked scared.

"Well, I'm not sure exactly what kind of visa I want, but I've written down here the purpose of my visit to Czechoslovakia." I handed him a typed page that explained that I was interested in studying the Czech language in connection with my academic studies and would also be writing an article for the *Yale Daily News*. I said I realized three months was a long time, but added that I would be happy to submit to a preliminary interview if they wanted. "I'm mostly interested in studying the Czech language. I have already studied one semester at university."

I realized abruptly that I was speaking too fast for him to follow. He looked confused for a while, and then haltingly got his forces together. "Study Czech language, yes, study Czech language. For this, you become enrolled at the Charles University. When you become enrolled at the Charles University, you show to me the letter from the Charles University, and then I give you a visum."

The problem was that I had already written Charles University twice about their Czech-language course for foreigners, without getting any reply. I had given up on them, and it was certainly too late to start with them again now. I wanted to get into Czechoslovakia in August. Unfortunately, the consul's English was obviously too poor to explain any of this in detail — I had experienced similar problems with Czech officials in New York and Stockholm, post–1968 purges of the Czech diplomatic corps having deprived it of any competent English-speaking personnel. So I answered him simply, "Sir, I want to study myself. I can read newspapers and talk with people. I have already studied one course in grammar."

He read over my typed explanation. "Yes, yes. I must send telegram to Prague. Foreign Ministry. They will decide whether I can give you visum or no."

I swallowed nervously. Send a telegam to Prague? It disintegrated my hopes that things would be easier from New Delhi. It wasn't encouraging altogether.

"When will you hear from them?" I asked.

"Within one month."

"I will not be in New Delhi then. Can you send me a letter to Bombay as soon as you hear from them?"

I gave him the address at American Express in Bombay. He took it and promised he would. Two weeks later I arrived in Bombay, and the only letter waiting for me was from my parents. Nothing from the East Germans, nothing from the Czechs.

On June 5 I took a taxi from my hotel to the Consulate of the German Democratic Republic, on a street right off the beautiful palm-treed *maidan* in downtown Bombay, where boys played soccer and Pope Paul met the Indian masses. The taxi driver had trouble distinguishing between the consulates of the German Democratic Republic and the German Federal Republic, but finally we got there. I was directed upstairs to Herr Horst, vice consul. He was young, and Germanic-looking, but somehow sympathetic. I explained that I had sent a visa request two months previously but had heard nothing since. "Yes," he assured me, "these things can often get caught in the bureaucratic grindstones." He meant the bureaucratic mills, but that was O.K. He promised that he would telegraph Berlin, but that if neither of us had heard anything by the time I was ready to leave Bombay, he would write a note for me which I could show at the border, and which, he said, would help out. I felt very relieved.

But my happiness didn't last, because I went every day to American Express — the Bombay office was more pleasant; there were no lines and it was cooler, for the monsoon had begun — and all sorts of letters kept arriving, but nothing from the East Germans or the Czechs. The time was nearing when I had to leave Bombay. And still I didn't know a thing. After leaving Bombay I was going to be spending a brief week in the Soviet Union, and then submerge myself for six whole months behind the Iron Curtain, without contact with the outside world. And I still didn't know whether I'd be able to go.

Finally I determined to telephone the Czech Embassy long distance. It had been well over a month. Getting the long-distance connection went surprisingly quickly — it was even possible to dial direct — but the embassy phone must have been broken, because for over an hour on two consecutive days, the line was busy.

The third day I got through. The secretary told me the consul was on another line, could I call back in five minutes? I was calling long distance, I said. After a minute's pause, the consul came on the line. First he didn't remember me or my story. I repeated it again, with the circumstances of my application and the fact that he had promised to send me a letter within one month. He looked through some papers and then said he didn't see any passport in his office with my name. I told him, speaking slowly, that I couldn't leave him my passport because I was leaving New Delhi. He murmured something indistinguishable, and there was at least ten seconds' silence on the line.

"Yes, Kelman. Mr. Kelman, American," he finally came out. "I am sorry, but it will not be possible for you to visit Czechoslovakia this autumn."

"This autumn?"

"It will not be possible for you to visit Czechoslovakia this autumn."

"*Not* possible?"

"I am sorry. Not possible."

"Any reason?"

"I am sorry, what do you say?"

"Reason. Explanation. Why can I not visit Czechoslovakia this autumn?"

"No reason. Foreign Ministry says this is not possible this autumn."

I felt like asking how it would be in the winter, but deep-going repartee was hardly possible linguistically, so I merely said, "Thank you."

"Mr. Kelman?"

"Yes?"

"Mr. Kelman, you may come and take back the thirty-rupee visum fee at the embassy whenever you like." Four lousy bucks. My present to Czechoslovakia.

In a strange way, I felt relieved. It was hard to tell how much of this was over at least having *some* answer, some certainty, and how much because, inside, in spite of everything, I was afraid that my planned trip behind the Iron curtain was more than I could handle. But one thing was certain as I hung up the phone: it was curtains for any book. There wouldn't be enough material just from a visit to East Germany, even if I got to visit East Germany. So my goal was now more modest: to get into East Germany to do a piece for *The New Yorker*.

In pursuit of that goal, I tried to ring up Herr Horst that same afternoon. The receptionist told me to come around the next morning. The next morning, my last day in India, I dropped over to make a final stab at American Express. There was in fact one letter there, from a Harvard friend. From there, I walked over to the East German consulate.

"Yes, Mr. Kelman, I am sorry that you have not heard anything as of yet from our travel agency, but everything will be all right with this letter, I assure you. Do you read German? It asks the border officials to give you all possible assistance in getting your visa."

"Thank you very much. I really appreciate your help."

"Enjoy your trip in the D.D.R."

I walked downstairs. The receptionist, smiling, stopped me. "Oh, Mr. Kelman, I saw the article about you in the paper." She beckoned in that beautiful Indian singsong English. "It was very good."

My heart skipped at least one beat. In connection with some talks to students I had given in Bombay, there had been a few articles in the local press, of at best partial accuracy. I had been presented as a "vocal opponent of Marxism" and such. In the back of my mind I had been afraid that somehow Herr Horst might see one of those articles.

It wasn't just paranoia. For the first time during this whole thing I was genuinely frightened. But it was too late to stop the ball. I left India on June 16, bound, with some brief stops, for East Berlin with a letter in my hand and an assignment in my head. My parents had been informed of a warning system. If I began my letters with *afternoon* on the top, I thought I might be in trouble. If they began with *evening*, I was in trouble, and they should immediately start alarming all sorts of people, from a man who knows Willy Brandt through the Prime Minister of Sweden. I promised to write every two days, although I told them that there would be nothing controversial in my letters, and they should write nothing controversial in theirs. Basically, I'd be cut off from real news for two months. I promised to be very careful, not to listen to Western radio, and not to utter one word critical of the East German government. I remembered Mark Huessy, who got seven years for one remark. I listened to my father's warnings against provocateurs, and the danger that those who posed as my best friends could be the ones who turned me in. My fears would be forcing me to live as East Germans do.

I was hopeful, but not sure, I'd get into East Germany; and hopeful, but not sure, I'd get out. For the East German authorities, what I was hoping to do — getting the story — is a crime. The planning of the crime was far from perfect — I was a kid who never even stole anything from the candy store. There was reason to be worried, and I was. But I didn't have the slightest dream about what I turned out to be in for in order to get my story, and certainly the readers of *The New Yorker* could have no idea of what lay behind that week's "Letter from East Germany."

CHAPTER 1

EARLY THAT MORNING in Moscow I put on the jacket and tie
which had become my standard gear for difficult border cross-
ings. To get into puritan Singapore in April I had worn a
jacket and tie in the ninety-degree heat, because my hair, even
after being cut quite short in Hong Kong, might still strike the
officials as overly long, unless I clearly showed by my dress I
was no hippie. Three months had passed since my Hong Kong
haircut, and I remembered what some East German kids had
told me in 1969 about policemen stopping kids on the streets
and taking them to the stationhouse for a free clipping. I
combed my hair straight back and under my ears before I left
the hotel in Moscow, and I took a comb onto the plane to brush
up before landing at Schönefeld in East Berlin.

I needed the jacket, for the cold if for no other reason. It was
chilly and raining mist as we arrived, ideal Eastern European
gray. All the other passengers were Russians or East Germans.
(The morning Moscow–East Berlin shuttle — who else would be
on it but trusted bigwigs? The flight had been, in fact, a sort of
"new class" special. For breakfast we got cold chicken breast
and genuine Russian caviar. You never saw that even in Moscow.) Amidst all these people, I wasn't sure which line to go
on at the airport. Finally, I decided for the window ARRIVING
PASSENGERS WITHOUT VISAS. Nobody had lined up there, and
the window was deserted by border officials as well. There

were two more flights that day, but I took the earliest because I was supposed to catch a train at eight that night for Grosspostwitz, the little village outside Dresden where my friend the schoolteacher lived. The next morning, Friday, I was to visit his school. Without a visa, and in possession only of an official-looking letter from Herr Horst in Bombay, I viewed any trip to Grosspostwitz that evening as quite unlikely. But at least with an entire day to work things out the idea was not completely utopian.

After all the others were gone, a man shuffled over from the passport window to the counter where I was. I showed him my letter.

"And you sent the money for your hotel reservations already, it says in the letter."

"Yes, I sent them the money in traveler's checks."

"Youth Tourist Travel Agency?"

"Yes."

"Herr Kelman, we will call up the Youth Tourist Travel Agency and see what they say. In the meanwhile you can go sit over there." The man pointed to a sofa over in the corner, still on the arrivals side of the passport counter. I hadn't crossed the border yet. "Don't worry. We will make sure your luggage doesn't get misplaced." The official smiled in a friendly way. The luggage was on the other side of the passport window.

I was left there a long time, or what seemed like a long time, sitting there alone on that sofa. The airport was empty, but modern and efficient-looking. I could see pictures of the newly rebuilt sections of East Berlin, towering larger than life, dominating the hall on the other side of the passport window. When I was in East Berlin in 1969 all that was still under construction, but I had read something about it in India in issues of *Democratic Germany*. A few customs officials whirred around

occasionally, going in and out peephole doors and around coun-
ters, walking up small metal flights of stairs like out of a science
fiction movie. It was quiet, and it was the type of occasion
which led you to reflect on your past and future life. Would
they know who I was? Would they, could they, really arrest
me? I thought about sitting in prison. I thought about reading
the complete works of Marx, in German, in prison. I thought
about working on my Czech, something I had given up on after
the Czech visa had been turned down. Maybe I could write a
novel — you never have time otherwise. Maybe being in prison
wouldn't be so bad. I didn't think about any bright lights or
brainwashing.

Then I thought about walking around the streets of East Germany. How would I meet people? It had been easy last time,
but maybe I wouldn't meet any this time. Last time I had been
a bit more reckless, hadn't put so many limitations on myself
or promised myself to be suspicious of everybody and not to
utter a word of criticism. What would people on the street look
like? I couldn't remember from 1969. Obviously, people can't
go around crying all the time. They have to adapt. How do
they do it?

Of course I might be flying home tomorrow from West Berlin. The whole thing might be over, harmless but resultless.
Anyway, I would know within minutes, yes or no.

Two outcomes appeared equally unlikely. One was making
it through the two months and getting the story. The other was
not.

"Herr Kelman, we are sorry for the delay. But you understand it is not nine o'clock yet. The Youth Tourist Travel
Agency hasn't opened yet." The man from behind the counter
had come over to the sofa. Before, I hadn't really gotten a good
look at him. Now I could see he was wearing a gray and green

policeman's uniform. He was youngish, and had a sort of happy-go-lucky steel smile on his face. "You come from America, right? What do you do there?"

"I'm a student."

"Yes, well we read a lot about America. Is it true all the problems we read about?"

I stiffened up. "Yes, well, uh, America has many problems. You know about Vietnam, and racial discrimination. But many students are working to change these things, you know."

"Do you think Angela Davis will be freed?"

"Angela Davis?" I wanted to say that I hoped she would get a fair trial, but I couldn't think of the word for *trial* in German. All that came to mind was *rättegång*. That was Swedish. It was already becoming more and more difficult to express myself in German. Finally, with the policeman's help, I remembered the word. *Prozess*, of course, *der Prozess*. Stupid of me, that was the title of Kafka's novel. "You know, she has very good lawyers. Also, I think people are watching to make sure that she gets a fair trial. Some of the other trials against black revolutionaries have been fair. There was the trial against Bobby Seale, and people agree that was a fair trial." He looked blank. I don't think he knew who Bobby Seale was. But he knew Angela Davis. She's a member of the American Communist Party.

"Why are you coming to the D.D.R.?" He was asking in a light, noninvestigative way.

"Well, I was here in nineteen sixty-nine, and I enjoyed my stay very much. People were very friendly. So now this time I hope to write an article on the D.D.R. for a student newspaper. I think that if American students knew more about the D.D.R., they could work to change the policy of the American government."

"So you were impressed during your last stay?"

"Yes, I enjoyed it very much."

He mused for a while. "Yes, you know, people are always complaining. They say they want a car, and they want this and they want that. But I think we have it pretty good here. Everybody has a job. I work and my wife works. We have a day nursery for the children."

"How many children do you have?"

"Two."

"Boys or girls?"

"One boy and one girl."

"How old are they?"

"Two and five."

"That's very nice."

He nodded easily. "Yeah, people complain. But I guess they complain in every country, don't they?"

Somebody called the policeman over. When he came back he told me that the Youth Tourist Travel Agency had told them that, since my letter had included a request for a journalist's visa, it had been immediately passed on, without any attempt to arrange the hotel reservations, to the Press Section of the Foreign Ministry. They were now trying to reach the right person there.

I was left sitting alone again. Suddenly, I realized clearly that I didn't actually *want* to get this official journalist guided tour. Not that it wouldn't be interesting to talk to officials. But if the Press Section took care of me, I'd probably never be able to get out to talk with ordinary people. The whole time I had gone through this request for a journalist's tour as a formality, in the expectation that it would never be granted for a college newspaper, but at the same time would provide an excuse for a long stay and for talking with people. But they had sent my request to the Foreign Ministry! What if it was granted? I might spend two months in East Germany and still not get the story. I froze.

"Herr Kelman, we have just spoken with the Press Section. They have told us that it will be impossible to grant your request for a journalist visa."

I gulped, that was all.

"An official from the Foreign Ministry will come here to the airport to give you back your money."

All the fine plans, all the letters, all the waiting and worrying — and now I would be flying back home to New York within a few days. I thought how I was homesick after all the time in India. But simultaneously I realized that what I had just heard was undoubtedly disastrous. My plans were ruined. Fishing out, trying to reestablish some order in the confusion created by the jovial border guard's one-line message, I stumbled, in broken German, for an explanation. "It would be impossible to grant me a — journalist's visa. Yes — well, you know, I'm not surprised. I'm not a real journalist, you know. Only a — student journalist. They should not have sent this to the Foreign Ministry." Finally, mumbling: "What about a — tourist visa?" Somehow it didn't seem very likely. The Press Section could have sent my application back to the Youth Tourist Travel Bureau; they didn't have to refund my money.

"Tourist visa? Yes, they told me to tell you to address yourself to the Youth Tourist Travel Agency with a request for a tourist visa, giving your desired itinerary, and maybe they could arrange something."

"But I already sent my application to them two months ago."

"Yes, I know. But they sent it on to the Foreign Ministry."

"So I must — start over again? From the beginning?"

"Unfortunately, yes." He paused. "One more thing. We

cannot give you a visa to enter the D.D.R. right now, because you have no hotel reservations. We can only give you a transit visa to take the bus from here to West Berlin. Then you can return to the D.D.R. over the Friedrichstrasse border crossing on a one-day visit pass, and go to the Youth Tourist Travel Agency from there. Good luck."

I remembered about D.D.R. transit visas from 1968, when I flew from Prague to East Berlin. There's a bus straight from Schönefeld to West Berlin, but in addition to the bus fee one is obliged to pay $1.25 — in hard currency, no East German money accepted — for transit privileges. This gives the East Germans the opportunity to affix a huge official document onto your passport, larger than the tourist entry stamps of most countries. I remembered a brief moment of absolute terror on arriving at Schönefeld then. It was late at night, and there was a long line of passengers going through an exhaustive customs check — they were coming in from preinvasion Prague. Suddenly I panicked. In Munich a month earlier I had picked up some election posters of the Neo-Nazi Party as a sort of joke. I hadn't thought at all about anyone searching my luggage . . .

In the midst of the terror I saw a border guard motion over to a window, and announce that transit passengers need not go through customs inspection, but could proceed directly to the window to pay their transit visa fees. Since then three years had passed and I was much more worldly wise about these things. Every book, pamphlet, or piece of printed matter not officially issued by the East German government, except for an English-German dictionary and two empty notebooks planned for notes, had been thrown out or sent home. Even the most minute search of my baggage would produce nothing anyone could question.

I also recalled from previous visits the East-West Berlin

border crossing system. Foreigners from West Berlin could visit East Berlin for twenty-four hours, without a visa, on presenting their passports at either Checkpoint Charlie or the crossing at the S-Bahnhof Friedrichstrasse elevated subway station. One was required to exchange a minimum of five West German marks at the official rate of one to one into East German marks.

Bewildered and uncertain about whether I would be in New York or the German Democratic Republic within one week's time, I slunk mechanically through passport control and picked up my baggage. Except for the guards buzzing around, I was alone in the airport. It felt surrealistic trudging out surrounded by the towering photograph of rebuilt East Berlin like "Big Brother Is Watching You" posters. The exit door looked tiny in comparison. Everything had come so suddenly. I was just following orders.

Quickly I was in West Berlin, let off by the transit bus on Uhlandstrasse. I didn't know where I was exactly but I felt happy to be there. Everything was bright and glad, despite the drizzle. I hadn't expected to get to West Berlin during my stay in East Germany, because I had heard it would make the East Germans suspicious you were passing over spy information while you were there.

I couldn't get to a bank to get West German marks because my luggage was too heavy to move any distance. I remembered the name of the hotel where I had stayed in 1969 — Pension Schiff. A friend had recommended it because a nice old Jewish man ran it. But I didn't know the address anymore. The taxi driver helped me locate the address and accepted my dollars — at a discount — and by 2:30 I was composed and ready to take the S-Bahn in the direction of Friedrichstrasse.

Friedrichstrasse is the last stop on the train from the West. Before the Wall, the train went further, and, in fact, the line still does. For East Berliners, Friedrichstrasse is the first stop, and the lines go eastward from there. You see a section of the Wall from above as you travel over the border on the S-Bahn, long and sandy and desolate. And guards along the train tracks. The train chugs along, and you've come into East Berlin. Just a few blocks in was a long red banner, hung onto a long gray building on an empty street. LONG LIVE THE PARTY. You could see the banner clearly from the train.

The procedure for border crossing was the same as last time. The hall was incredibly, almost purposefully, dirty, cold, and depressing. A first man looked at you, and at your passport picture, paying special attention to your nose, ears, and chin. He asked you to take off your sunglasses. Then the passport disappeared behind a mysterious window. Meanwhile, you went to another counter and exchanged your Western currency. You also filled out a currency form declaring how much foreign currency you were taking with you. You guarded that form with your life: if you lost it, you didn't get out. Then you waited, with the other tourists, on some shabby leather-type couches if there were enough seats, or else just stood up, until they called your number. You went to another window to claim your passport, they pored over you and your picture again, and then you went through customs, which might be nothing or might be a body search for currency stashes or forbidden books, depending on your luck. I had gone through both. The whole thing makes most one-day tourists despise East Germany before they get out on the streets.

I was waiting, sitting on the leather couch. It had been a long time, longer than usual I thought.

"Herr Kelman, could you please come with me?"

Within a split second, every nightmare welled up into a tidal wave of fear. *It was a policeman,* and he had come out from behind that mysterious cubbyhole, and he had my passport, and he was telling me to come with him.

He walked with me, holding the passport, not holding me. Things whirred and blurred around me; I didn't know where we were going. Just a few doors, corridors; who ever knew this fucking building was so big? Nobody but the policeman and me. Yeah, there was one person somewhere along the way, sitting behind a desk, whom he saluted. Darkness at noon.

Finally, we came into a room. "Herr Kelman, please wait here." He shut the door and left. A few teardrops appeared. My throat dried to sandpaper. The room was smallish and painted a lightish green. I stared at the window, stared for what seemed like forever. It was a fake window; in back of it there was only a wall. The room had a flimsy wooden table with a newspaper lying on top.

Would they let me study Czech or write a novel in prison? How much would people in America care about my case? Would I get sick from losing too much weight? Shit, I'd starve if I had to live on the disgusting *Wurst* that Germans eat even when they're not in prison — how would I survive prison food? They had escorted me into a little green room with a fake window and told me to wait. I wanted to go home, go back to New York.

I went through every permutation of theory about why I was in that room, and started reading through the newspaper on the table. That would be a point in my favor when they came in and saw me engrossed in a newspaper.

But they didn't come in. Finally, I reached the end of the newspaper and was forced to leaf back artificially to the middle pages, so when they came in they could see me reading. But now it was artificial. They were taking so long.

"Herr Kelman?" A man had walked in. "Bach is my name.

I am sorry I took so long. I was out when the message came you had arrived here at Friedrichstrasse. How long have you been waiting?"

"Oh, not more than a half-hour or so," I blurted out, seemingly instinctively. "No problem."

"No, no. It must have been much longer than that." I glanced at my watch. He was right. It had been an hour and a half. That was dumb! I was going to have to tell enough lies without adding an unnecessary one.

"I am from the D.D.R. Travel Bureau. I understand you want to apply for a visa."

With that sentence, I lightened up immediately. Within seconds, I could even feel my stomach churning. The knots had untied; I felt hungry.

"Yes. Do you have my original application, sir?"

"No."

"Do you know about it?"

"No, I was only asked to come here. Why don't you tell me about it?"

"Well, you see, the problem was that I sent my visa application to the Youth Tourist Travel Agency, but they forwarded it to the Foreign Ministry because I had sent a letter from a student newspaper that I was going to write an article about the D.D.R. The Foreign Ministry said I couldn't get a journalist's visa, and that I would — have to apply again. I'm not surprised, I mean, because I am not a real journalist of course. I just asked a friend if he could give me — this, uh, letter, so that maybe I could meet with some trade-union officials or professors, maybe visit some factories. I was thinking of the Wartburg automobile factory at Eisenach."

"What is the purpose of your visit?"

"Well, you see, my field of academic study is the history of the European labor movement. So I was hoping to be able to talk — with some people who have studied this field in the D.D.R. Also, I could visit various museums. I know there are many good museums on the history of the German labor movement in Leipzig. When I was in Leipzig last time, I wanted to see the Lenin Museum and the Karl Liebknecht Museum. But I was only there for one day, on a Monday — and all museums were closed that day. So I — I couldn't see anything. I was very disappointed." I laughed, a pitiful, tinny laugh. I was doing O.K., but my voice sounded strained to me. My throat muscles were still tight, and my German wasn't flowing freely.

"You have visited the D.D.R. before?"

"Yes, I was here for a week in nineteen sixty-nine. I — I enjoyed myself very much. I hope to visit some of the friends I met then. I am supposed to visit a schoolteacher I met last time. I hope to visit his school classes. Actually, I am supposed to arrive tonight, but it looks like that will be impossible. I should telegraph him soon to tell him I won't be coming yet."

"You can do that when we're through here."

"Yes, fine. Anyway, the purpose of my visit is to study the German labor movement and observe the construction of socialism in the D.D.R., and also to visit my friends from my last trip."

"When was it you were here?"

"Nineteen sixty-nine, August — the early part of August." He opened my passport and inspected the East German visa from 1969. "Anyway, I do also hope to write this article eventually for the student newspaper. I hope that American students will become more interested in the D.D.R., maybe help start a student movement for the diplomatic recognition of the D.D.R. You know, American students have concentrated on

Vietnam up until now. You can understand why, I know. But there has been too little interest in questions of — European security." I consciously brought up the question of diplomatic recognition, which I knew to be a major East German goal, and used the standard Soviet term *European security,* which roughly means shielding their bloc from any Western influences. "Maybe my article on the D.D.R. could help change things." I was sort of looking into the distance, but not seeing anything much but the wall, the whole time I delivered this speech, during the whole conversation in fact. Now I gulped briefly, caught my breath, and glanced toward the man next to me. I had forgotten his name already. He was taking notes, almost furiously. "Yes," I concluded, "and by the way, I also wanted to spend a week at the youth camp at Binz on Rügen Island, just taking a rest and swimming. I hope the weather is nice."

"Why don't you tell me something more about your studies at university?"

I explained to him my major, and my work on Sweden, and Swedish compared with German history, going into great lengths about my senior thesis at Harvard. His notetaking became more sporadic as I got into the details of historical theories. The idea, I thought to myself, was to present myself as a little of the absent-minded professor. The more rambling about the thesis, the more childlike delight at obscure academic topics, the better.

"Herr Kelman, this has been a most enjoyable discussion. I will do everything I can to see you get your visa."

"When do you think you'll know if hotel reservations and things are taken care of?"

"We can meet tomorrow at four P.M. at the Neptune Fountain."

"Neptune Fountain?"

"Yes, it's right in the center of town. Do you know where City Hall is?"

"Yes."

"Right opposite there."

"Fine. But wouldn't it be more convenient to meet at your office at the travel bureau?"

"Yes, well, you see, the travel bureau has so many offices all over the city. This is easier."

"And you will have an answer already tomorrow?"

"Well, I should have more information."

We shook hands, and walked together through the labyrinth that had gotten me into the green room. "Your passport has been found to be in order, and you are free to spend the rest of the afternoon in the capital. There is a post office off Friedrichstrasse, two blocks past Unter den Linten. You can telegraph your friend from there. *Auf Wiedersehen,* Herr Kelman."

I came out into the chilly afternoon, onto Friedrichstrasse. There were two new signs since 1969, color posters. BROTHERLY SOLIDARITY WITH THE ARAB PEOPLES came first. Then FREE ANGELA DAVIS AND OTHER PATRIOTS IN THE CAPITALIST COUNTRIES. I passed along by the old entrances to the subway to West Berlin, now closed with iron doors. And then to the post office. As I walked along, I realized I would have trouble recognizing the man from the travel bureau the next day. I had never really looked at him. I was in my own world during that whole hearing. I didn't remember what he looked like. But I had gotten out my story, under short notice and hard conditions. Now I felt relaxed and good.

*

He waved at me, and smiled from the distance. I ran toward him, and he increased his pace until we were together right near the fountain and shaking hands. He was smiling and relaxed, and this time the first thing I did was to take a good look at him. He had thick lips, pushed up against his face as if he were a kid leaning against the windowpane of a candy store. Mostly, he looked very German, sort of Bavarian beer-hall variety: curly receding hair, almost middle-aged, rosy cheeks. It looked as if there should be a beer mug raised high from his hand instead of the black leather bag drooping down.

"Well, do you have good news for me?" I began hurriedly.

"Come, let's take a drive in my car. We can go someplace and talk about it."

We got into his car and drove away from the border area, first a little through the new modern Alexanderplatz. I thought of the pictures at the airport. There was a blue skyscraper, and then a not-yet-completed one, which, he said, was to be the new House of Travel.

"What is your job in the D.D.R. Travel Bureau?" I asked, sort of to pass the time.

"I work with foreign tourists to the D.D.R."

"Foreign tourists only?"

"Yes."

We quickly passed the new construction, and drove through some older, but wide, streets. We kept on driving, the streets got less populated and less wide, and for the first time since he came into the green room the day before, I began to become afraid again. Where was he taking me? Finally we reached a small one-way street, almost an alley. My heart began pounding hard. I was afraid he would be able to hear it, but I couldn't stop.

"Why are we parking here?" I asked, trying not to seem either scared or accusative.

He looked jolly and unconcerned. "Come! I'm treating you to an ice cream. Right around the corner."

We arrived at a quiet place and sat on a terrace outside. We were the only ones there.

"Herr Kelman, I have some good news for you."

"There will be no problems with the visa?"

"Well, I don't know yet about the hotel reservations. That will take a few more days. However, by coincidence it happens that I am driving to Dresden over the weekend on business, and I will be happy to drive you tomorrow to Grosspostwitz to visit your friend."

"Gee, that is really very nice of you."

"It will be pleasant for me — to have a conversation partner in the car. It's a three-hour trip, and it can be pretty dull otherwise. It's so rare that one gets to meet an American, especially an American student. We will have many things to talk about."

"Yes, we will. I hope maybe you could teach me the German words to 'The Internationale.' I know them in English, French, and Swedish, but only a few lines in German. I just know it starts with *Wach auf, Verdammte dieser Erde!*"

"Yes, of course I could teach you the words. I would also be most interested in hearing your viewpoints on the American student movement. We hear so much about it, you know."

"Yes, well, as I — said yesterday, part of the purpose of my visit here in the D.D.R. is to make the American student movement more aware of the achievements here."

"It will be quite an interesting discussion. And I will then be able to pick you up on Tuesday, after you've spent the four days you were planning to spend in Grosspostwitz, and drive you back to the capital."

"You mean, I don't have to take the train back?" I thought he had said he was going for the weekend. Wouldn't he have to be back at work on Monday? Maybe I just hadn't understood his German right before. "What about my visa, though?"

"I will take care of that. We will get you a visa now up to July first, and hope we have the hotel reservations in order by then."

The ice cream had just arrived, and we ate it without speaking. I reflected that I felt happy and, politics aside, friendly toward this man who was going out of his way to help me. He didn't have to drive me to Grosspostwitz or invite me out to ice cream. He was being friendly, and helpful, and maybe I was overly suspicious in my approach to this whole trip to the D.D.R. Maybe it wouldn't be nearly so bad as I expected. I liked this man who looked as if he should be in a beer hall except for his black leather bag, even while I still knew for certain that no kindness he could show would get me to let down my guard. The only thing I wondered about as he drove me back to Friedrichstrasse was why he would be able to pick me up on Tuesday.

*

I was jolly, and doing everything to show it. "Let me tell you this, Herr Bach: you will be able to see how my German improves during the time I'm in Grosspostwitz. It's just a matter of time. Now it's still pretty slow, but I just have to speak more, and get more practice. Watch, you'll see."

But I was still being careful. I had to stick to my story, and I had to remind myself that one wrong word — one criticism of the D.D.R. — could mean arrest. More than one mistake you're not allowed. Herr Bach was a nice man, and only a bureaucrat at the travel bureau, but he could pass along anything I said to others. Friendly Herr Bach, kind Herr Bach — *es tut mir leid,* but I have no choice but to regard you as the functional equivalent of a cop. Curly-haired and thick-lipped as you are, I will have to keep my distance and not open up even a crack for you. If you don't — God forbid — already know who I am, you're not going to find out anything now. You'll get friendly conversation, and lies. Sorry, but it's the only way to get the story. I wish I could tell you the truth, and argue it out, and then go freely and just look around. But your system doesn't allow that.

"You'll have to be tolerant of my car, it's an oldie." Herr Bach beamed as we got in. "You know, it's five years old already, so it doesn't work so well anymore. Heats up too fast, you know." I looked at the blue *Moskvitch* and thought to myself about the criticism of planned obsolescence. What this was, was unplanned obsolescence. Too bad I couldn't share the witticism.

Gradually we made our way out to the *Autobahn*. It was silent in the car, and I was intently observing things passing by us. We passed some ridiculous exit marker for East Berlin, which did not regard it as sufficient just to point the driver in the direction of "Berlin," but instead, in big white letters on green: BERLIN, CAPITAL OF THE DDR. That was their clumsy way of emphasizing at every small occasion the official East German position that while West Berlin should have no connections with West Germany, East Berlin has been incorporated into East Germany. What's mine is mine, what's yours is negotiable. I chuckled to myself, not only at the few cars on the road, but at the many cars at highway resting stations off the road, hoods up and smoking from overheating. I repeated silently the points I wanted to remember to write down in my notebook that evening.

"So, my friend," bellowed Herr Bach, interrupting my ruminations. "Tell me something about the student movement in your country! And what about its relationship to the Negro movement and the Black Panthers?"

My first real test. I was pretty confident that I knew what kind of analysis I could give that an East German Communist would find relatively orthodox. It would be all right to say some things that I believe, such as that the student movement had isolated itself from the American people, spiced with words about the "bourgeois class origins" of most students, which isolated them from the working class. I could even *indirectly* say that the student movement had become extremist as long as I used the word *Maoist* instead of *Communist*. And I could talk about *Abenteuerer* ("adventurists") in the Black Panthers. It wasn't too hard. Moscow-line Communists don't like the New Left very much either, and if you blame everything on lack of contact with the working class, you can't go too far wrong.

"How does my view correspond with your own on the subject?" I asked cautiously as I finished my remarks.

"Yes, very similar to the view presented in our theoretical journals on the subject. It is the Marxist view that no student movement can succeed alone, without the working class."

"Are you especially interested in student movements?"

"Yes, you know, I studied for some time at the Institute of Marxism-Leninism. During our final year there we each chose a special field of study within Marxism-Leninism. I studied the history of student movements."

I laughed to myself. A bureaucrat at the D.D.R. Travel Bureau has to go to the Institute for Marxism-Leninism! Gee, how they trust their people! Just to come in *contact* with foreign tourists is such a sensitive position that you have to be completely reliable.

The car had meanwhile overheated, and we had stopped on the side of the road. In front of us was a Skoda with Czech plates. Herr Bach looked toward the plates, and looked toward the sky, musing, "They gave us a lot of trouble a few years ago, the Czechs. They really did." I looked closely at him, wondering whether he was checking out my reaction to his words. But he appeared to be almost talking to himself, or to the sky. "But now it's clear who has the power. We haven't won over all the minds there. But it's clear who has the power."

"Yes."

"I'm going to have to send this car for repairs. It just doesn't work right at all. What I really need is a new one." Czechoslovakia was over. Herr Bach's hands were oily and filthy from fooling around under the hood. He had a towel to clean himself with but it too soon became filthy. I offered him my handkerchief, and he took it. "You know," he offered suddenly, "I like you. Unfortunately, not all your countrymen are like you."

"You mean the government."

"*Ja wohl.*"

"But the people are good."

"Yes, of course, the people are good."

The ice had been broken in a certain sort of way, I felt. I decided to ask him about his family background.

"My parents were both active Communists before Hitler."

"What about during the war? Did the Communists have any illegal activity?"

"I remember that the comrades used to have secret meetings. Sometimes they were in our house. But I was very young. Mostly I remember the suffering of the war — the bombing of Dresden. Horrible, horrible."

"What about after the war?"

"It was also very, very difficult. It was a struggle to get food for the next meal."

"Yes, but at the same time there must have been a feeling of joy at being able to participate in the first years of the building of socialism of the D.D.R.?"

"No, it was mainly the suffering. There wasn't time to think about much else."

There was a long silence. I was wondering, thinking. Occa-sionally, I'd sing out loud some Bertolt Brecht song, in German. He'd like that, I hoped. I thought about seven years in prison for Mark Huessy. I wanted to ask Herr Bach a question, a critical question. Did I dare? It would be critical, but it would be just a query, not my own statement. Was this all a trap? A question, a critical question, but not a statement. Just asking.

"Herr Bach? The SST? You know, the supersonic airplane? The Left in America — worked against that plane. They said it was a waste of money and that it damaged the environment. Why is the Soviet Union building a supersonic plane? Couldn't the money better be spent on other things?"

"The Left? I don't understand what you mean. The capital-ists wanted to keep the Soviet plane from the New York airport, so they used the excuse of noise. It is just a question of wanting to stop the Soviet competition, that's all. Why is the Soviet Union building the SST? A great technological advance. We are very proud of it, you know. The plane stopped in the capital recently on the way back from the Paris air show. We are very proud. The plane makes it much faster to fly. Time is money, you know." He winked at me. "Yes, time is money." This time he said it in English. "An old business expression, you know."

"No, but Herr Bach, the capitalists didn't try to close the air-ports to the SST. It was the Left. The capitalists wanted to go ahead with the construction of the American SST."

"*American* SST? Was America going to build an SST too? Then why did they try to close the airports? All I know about is the closing of the airports. Believe me, it was the people with money behind that. In America, it is always the people with money."

＊

I had met Günter Schwer only briefly at the Weimar youth hostel in 1969, when he was leading a bunch of eight-year-olds on a trip to see the Goethe Museum and so forth. We were both stamp collectors, and during the succeeding two years we sent each other nice stamps, with letters inside. From his letters, I got the impression that he supported the government. Once, in response to a question about whether I could write freely what I wanted in my letters, he cited a "Law on Postal Secrets," which seemed a particularly bad joke because the very same day I had received another letter from East Germany, with a phony return address, from a kid I had met. The letter might not get through, the kid wrote, but he had to tell me what had happened to him. The rumor had spread around East Germany that the Rolling Stones were going to give a concert on the West Berlin side of the Berlin Wall for the twentieth anniversary of the D.D.R. Kids had come to East Berlin from all over the D.D.R. But the morning after my friend arrived the police raided the house where he was staying. He was arrested and held in jail for two days, during which he was made to stay standing up the entire time. Then they cut his hair and packed him on a train back home. He had no idea how the police even knew he was in Berlin.

As I decided to try to return to East Germany, my letters to Günter Schwer became increasingly written directly for the censors. I filled them with accounts of my participation in support of the grape strikers and the auto workers, interspersed with words of praise for the German Democratic Republic.

As things turned out, the entire visit to Grosspostwitz was more of a vacation interlude of hiking and wallowing in the great outdoors than in learning anything about East Germany. I was out after everyday life, and the little village of Grosspostwitz was after all part of it. True, it was no great revelation that governments couldn't possibly force politics into *every* nook and cranny, prevent people in a little village from having some unpolitical fun. No matter how bad things might be, people can't keep crying all the time, either.

"Only a Moskvitch?" Herr Schwer smiled as I appeared at the door of his little home, back off a side road near the main street running through Grosspostwitz. "When we got your telegram saying you'd be arriving today by car, we thought you'd come with one of the big American cars! Too bad."

"No, I don't have any car. But Herr Bach from the D.D.R. Travel Bureau was nice enough to drive me."

Waiting inside for me was cold beer and some cheese. The cheese, unfortunately, was tasteless, but helped sustain my thirst throughout the beer, so I ate some. "Steve, let me just get the bad news out of the way first. You had asked if you could visit my school. I'm sorry. I tried, but it was impossible. The principal said that the decision was not up to him, so we sent the request to the regional school officials in Bautzen. They sent it on to the Education Ministry in Berlin. But they said no."

He showed me a copy of his request. Indeed, he had used material from all those letters — the ones written for the censors.

From the time I first met Steven Kelman in Weimar in 1969, I noticed that his political viewpoint was extremely progressive. This impression was confirmed by our subsequent correspondence. Thus, he wrote me of his participation in demonstrations against the Vietnam War and for the struggles of the American working class. From Japan, he wrote that many aspects of Japanese society clearly show the failures of capitalism. From Indonesia, he expressed feelings for the starving children there. Honorable Minister, I am convinced that the visit of Steven Kelman to the Grosspostwitz Elementary School will not have an endangering, but rather a positive, effect on the social-political education of our pupils.

But the letter wasn't enough.

"Don't take it personally. The rule is not to let anyone in our schools unless they are part of an official delegation."

The next morning we were scheduled to engage in some Germanic *Wanderlust* through the Saxon Alps. I put on my loosest hiking gear, including an orange guru shirt I had picked up in India, only to be given the friendly reminder by Herr Schwer that the police wouldn't approve if they saw my shirt sticking out of my pants. As ridiculous as it looked with the guru shirt, I stuffed it into my blue jeans. I wasn't going to a fashion show, I guess.

The train ride took a long time. I kept on trying to find the right occasion to raise political questions, but it never seemed right. So I just read through *Neues Deutschland*. Herr Schwer got *Neues Deutschland* with the mail every morning, but read only the sports section. When I arrived the afternoon before, he had asked me whether I had any newspapers with me. I showed him the copy of *Neues Deutschland* I had, and he looked disappointed. "I have that too," he said. Each train station had those long red banners along it, with the slogan LONG LIVE THE DDR, and banners still up from May Day informing the workers of their "obligations in socialist competition" in honor of the holiday.

We got out of the train and looked into the distance. There was a steep hill. "On top of that hill is a restaurant. That is our goal for lunch."

"How far away is it?"

"About six miles."

"*Six?*"

"Don't worry. It's not so far."

It was a little misty and cool, the way that makes mucous flow down your nose and onto your face. But when you blow your nose to clear it, it feels good. It was nice countryside, and just about no other people around.

We were climbing up the forest-covered hill. "This is beautiful," I said. "I'm so glad we came."

"Yes. But you know, I'd really like to visit your country sometime."

"Well, let me tell you — you have an open invitation."

*

The Schwer home was how one imagines a German village home to be. A garden around it, a few chickens in a pen. Always take off your shoes when you come in, and put on felt slippers. No modern toilet, but at least you didn't have to go outside the house. Small porcelain figures, glassware, and now the Indian bronze vase I had brought them. An old-fashioned mammoth radio, with four bands including short wave. In the kitchen, a transistor radio hanging from a nail near the sink, always tuned to Bavarian radio in West Germany. Near the bookshelves hung medals with the state shield of the D.D.R., for the twentieth anniversary in 1969 and the twenty-first anniversary in 1970. And on the hearth two empty bottles of Cinzano, something which is not normally for sale in East German stores.

"Here is the proudest possession I have," began Herr Schwer Monday evening, as we all sat in the living room after dinner. He took out a certificate on bond paper, with a D.D.R. seal, proclaiming him as an outstanding teacher. "There were only nine teachers in the whole Bautzen area who got the award this year. I am the first teacher from Grosspostwitz ever to receive it. You know, in West Germany they say that only Party members can get ahead. That's not true. I'm not a Party member, and I got this award. Then they gave me this book — "

"Let me see," I said, in an excitement at least half-feigned. It was a huge picture biography of Walter Ulbricht.

"Do you mind if I ask you about prices of different things in America?" Herr Schwer asked. I said of course not, and he inquired what a good industrial worker earned in America, what it cost for meat, bread, refrigerators, automobiles, housing, and so forth. He wrote everything down in a notebook, and then put the notebook away. "Your workers earn four times as much as ours, and your prices are mostly lower, you know."

"Oh."

"So why did those workers at General Motors strike?"

"They wanted better conditions. And they deserved them."

I liked the Schwers. But I was looking forward to getting back to Berlin. Herr Bach would probably have the hotel reservations for me, and the next day, I hoped, I could really begin getting the story, getting out and looking at East Berlin.

"My car has been left for repairs," he began. "This time I have an office car. I think things will go much better." The first thing we had to do out on the road was get gas. At the first place we stopped, ten cars were lined up at each of the two tanks. From my brief experience at seeing the service proffered by East German gas stations, such a situation was far from unheard of. But after around five minutes of waiting, honking, and trying to cut ahead on the line, Herr Bach put up a good show of disgust at the long wait. We would leave and find another station, he exclaimed. We proceeded toward the only other gas station in Bautzen. It was almost equally crowded. "I don't know why there are so many people today." It was a Tuesday noon. This time we waited patiently, but Bach appeared to be looking somewhat nervously at me.

That was the last thing I wanted. To get our minds off the

long wait, I asked him how he had reacted to the storm over the Pentagon Papers, which was then making a lot of headlines. *Neues Deutschland's* account had gone to great lengths to point out that the publication of the papers did *not* mean that any great "freedom of the press" existed in America, and anyway Nixon's court would no doubt stop continued publication. But for poor Herr Bach of the travel bureau such self-confident assurances did not reassure.

"I don't know *why* the American papers published it. I just don't know why. I can't imagine what their motives were. It hurt the American government, and yet they published them. It's a mystery. What do you think?"

That put me in a spot, and the easiest thing was just to avoid the question by saying I'd been away from the country too long to make any judgment.

We had gotten our gas — it cost $1.50 a gallon for an octane level below that sold in America or Western Europe, prompting a silent reflection over what benefits the East German consumer had obtained from his country's having broken loose from the international oil cartel — and it became silent in the car for a long while. I wanted to ask about the hotel reservations and the visa, but at the same time not appear too pushy. Why hadn't he said anything? I was trying to get up the courage to say it, and I felt that Herr Bach was also trying to get up his courage to say something.

Finally, he took his glance briefly away from the road. He looked straight at me for a few moments and bit his big lips. "Steve, I would like to clear up a misunderstanding."

"A misunderstanding?" My stomach instinctively tightened.

"I do not work for the D.D.R. Travel Bureau."

I wanted to jump out of the car.

"I work for the Academy of Sciences."

I stared at him, and swallowed.

"I used to be a dean at Humboldt University in Berlin. Now I am part of a research group which is trying to see how socialist society will look in the D.D.R. in the year two thousand."

"Futurology?" I stammered.

"That is what it is called in the West. Of course, our societies, America and the D.D.R., are very different. They have different forms of ownership; we are socialist and America is capitalist. Yet despite this we have certain problems in common. Take the problem of crime in an affluent society. Now, here in the D.D.R. we have eliminated the social basis of crime. Yet we still have young people, often from very fine families, with all the comforts, who go out and vandalize and steal. This is the kind of problem I am thinking of."

"Yes, of course there are common problems in all industrial societies," I replied lamely.

"The unfortunate thing is that our two countries do not yet have diplomatic relations. So we have very little contact with American scholars. This hurts us, particularly in a research group like ours, because we have these common problems about the future to discuss. That is why we are interested in you."

"How did you know to seek me out?"

"I have left a standing message at the Airport that every time an American scholar enters the D.D.R., I should be contacted. They called me up about you."

I thought to myself desperately with what coordination the trap had been sprung. Not only had Herr Bach been informed, but the border station at Friedrichstrasse knew to wait for me. Everybody had been informed. But did they know what I was really like? Would they just question me and throw me out? Or had I passed the first test, and did they believe me and want to find out more from me?

"It is my hope that we can discuss further our common problems during the next few days. Such a scholarly interchange will be equally interesting for us both, I am convinced."

"Does that mean that the hotel reservations are set up and the visa is clear?"

"No, we don't have any answer yet. Nothing is settled beyond July first. But up until then I have arranged a room for you at the home of the mother of a colleague of mine. She will take good care of you."

CHAPTER 2

FIRST I HAD TO CHECK whether I was being shadowed when I left my room Wednesday morning. A friend who had spent a good deal of time in the Soviet Union had previously told me techniques to use if you suspect something. You can go to a bus stop where several different lines come. When the first bus arrives, you just stand there as if that's not the one you're waiting for. Then you jump on the bus at the last moment — and look if someone else jumps desperately on after you. Or you can walk up a deserted street, turn around after a while, and see if anyone's in front of you.

Outside the door of the apartment house where I was staying I looked around, as if to survey the surroundings. But nobody was there, at least nobody standing still waiting for me. So I started walking cautiously down the street, maybe a hundred yards up till the corner. I stopped to look at the window of a store, and glanced backward through the reflecting glass. Nobody. After turning the corner onto a busy street, I stopped and looked at the first store window, waiting to see if someone would turn the corner and then stop when he saw me. Nobody. I waited down in the subway station to see if anybody would come following and then wait for me to go in. People streamed through, but they passed without looking at me.

I bought my subway ticket and got into the train toward Alexanderplatz. Finally I was on my own in East Berlin. My first free day!

But there was a bitter taste in my mouth from the day before. Herr Bach's innocent helpfulness turned out not to be particularly innocent, and I could no longer regard him as, politics aside, a nice friendly guy. I still didn't know exactly what he wanted from me, what he knew about me, or what he was planning to do with me. But my mistrust had returned to maximum level, and I was looking for people shadowing me on my first trip into the center of East Berlin.

Herr Bach had put me in a room in Pankow, a part of East Berlin where high Communist officials once lived — there was very little destruction there during the Battle of Berlin in 1945, and most housing remained undamaged. Konrad Adenauer made Pankow famous by using it as a curse word to describe the East German regime. I was on a quiet, tree-lined street called Binzstrasse, in the home of a quiet widow named Frau Koch. Frau Koch's son, Herr Bach told me, worked for Radio D.D.R., and he and Herr Bach were friends through some connection. But he had only met Frau Koch once before. It was, I had to admit — even with my suspicion — nice of Frau Koch to put me up for a few days until the hotel reservations were cleared up. And she made me a nice, filling breakfast that Wednesday morning. Normally I don't like eggs, but I accepted her offer and took a hard-boiled one. That's the only type I can stand, and I felt it was silly to say no to good protein-filled food. My visit in 1969 had taught me that, in general, one leaves an East German restaurant hungrier than when one enters, the interminable waiting time before getting a table, getting waited on, and finally getting served acting to increase hunger pangs more than the tiny portions you receive act to quench them. My 1969 East German week had been an utter nutritional catastrophe, and my parents had not failed to use in their arsenal of arguments against my trip the point that I might not survive two months of East German food. This time, I assured them, expense would be absolutely no object in getting decent food, that I would try to keep eating constantly, and that I would be certain to take my vitamin pills every day. Thus one of the first things I wanted to check out when I got off the subway at Alexanderplatz was whether the new modern city center perhaps contained at least one new modern restaurant. For what I hadn't told my parents when I promised that cost would be no object in my search for good and filling food was that, as far as I could tell, you couldn't find a decent-sized portion of food anywhere in the D.D.R. no matter how much you were willing to spend.

But I was curious, incredibly curious, about much more. How did the new center look? Did it really mean things *were* getting better in East Germany? I wanted to find out something about the new housing they had built in the center. East German propaganda booklets I had seen, playing up to those in Western Europe who have complained about long distances from homes to work places, emphasized that, in East German city planning, "people can live in the center of town, near where they work." But which people?

God, maybe it isn't so bad after all! I stood in the middle of Alexanderplatz, a large cement-paved plaza. In front of me were a fountain, a department-store building with a textured beige façade, and then the tall blue skyscraper I had seen before. Staring at it I saw the large block letters reading INTER-HOTEL STADT BERLIN. In front of it I could make out a sign reading GRILL BAR and some outdoor tables. What struck me first was that the letters spelling out GRILL BAR were genuine, full-color plastic, like the ones you see in modern shopping centers in the rest of the world, rather than the sickly sort of lettering which is normal for Eastern European stores. In fact,

I had never seen happy, shining letters anywhere in Eastern Europe before.

I turned around, and looked at the apartment houses in back of me. Not especially bright, not especially attractive, not especially anything, but standing there at any rate. Not bad places to live. I have to find out who lives there before I leave this place, I reminded myself. Are things getting better? Alexanderplatz was just a huge building site in 1969. Sure, you see new and fine city centers all over Western Europe. It's nothing unusual. But before, the entire Communist world didn't have a single one.

I had to meet some people and talk with them! But I didn't really know how to go about it at a big place like Alexanderplatz. I walked over to the bench around the fountain and started reading the copy of *Neues Deutschland* I had picked up in Pankow. There were a good number of people sitting around the fountain, but reading *Neues Deutschland* was probably not the way to start a conversation. So I put it down, and just sat there looking. People were walking around, no special expressions on their faces. I started tapping my hands on my lap to relieve the frustration of not knowing how to proceed. People came and went at the fountain.

O.K., it was only my first day. Today I can just look around, I reassured myself. Of course, today was also the last day of my as yet unextended visa, and I didn't really know what my future was. Herr Bach had mentioned something about going to West Berlin the next day and coming back immediately to East Berlin, when he'd probably have a new visa for me and my hotel reservations. It seemed like a strange procedure, but they would extend my visa, I was rather sure of that.

But if I didn't meet any people today, what was to say I would meet people any following days? Maybe I wouldn't meet *any* people this time. For the first time since arriving I was worried about something that didn't have to do with my making it through without getting arrested.

I couldn't just *sit there* around that fountain, though. Over there, right inside the entrance of the department store, was a newsstand, and I determined immediately that I would perform my first official duty in pursuit of my story. One of the tasks I had promised myself to undertake was a check on a busy newsstand to see what, if anything, people buy there. In 1969, nobody ever appeared to read newspapers or magazines. At that time I often had the feeling that my daily purchase of *Neues Deutschland* caused a statistically significant sales spurt at whichever stands I honored with my patronage.

This time I wanted to make a scientific investigation. At 10:15 I began my observations, positioning myself at the postcard rack right next to the newsstand. The postcard and letterpaper area was in fact far more popular than the newsstand, and there was a line of about fifteen or so the whole time. Not surprisingly nobody bought the postcards with portraits of Walter Ulbricht or Erich Honecker. Originally, a half-hour seemed enough for my test. But at 10:45 I decided I was in no rush — why not wait for a whole hour? I glanced at a few magazines myself, and then read through the typed sheet of paper on the wall, listing the obligations of the newspaper and stationery divisions of the Centrum Department Store in "socialist competition." The division, the sheet said, was "struggling for the state title 'Collective of Socialist Labor.'"

As I suspected, not many newspapers were sold — only five copies of a local Berlin paper, one of *Neues Deutschland*. The most popular magazine was something called *Wochenpost,* which I had never heard of before: five copies.

I took the escalator up to the second floor. The department

store was certainly nicer than any I had seen in East Germany in 1969, but it was better from the outside — the façade was quite striking — than the inside. The walls were plain, dirty white. The selection of clothes on the second floor was horrible. No variety, no colors, but prices almost as high as in America. Why can't they have *deep* blue as well as off-blue, *deep* green as well as pale green? Twenty bucks for a pair of Dacron pants, six bucks for a really pitiful shirt. There was a corner of the store called Boutique '70, which I wandered into — following the crowd — and discovered it contained fashions imported from the West: Austrian suede jackets, Italian pullovers, Swedish shoes. The prices, though, were from another world. Surprising numbers of older people were wandering through Boutique '70, also loads of boys with their girl friends, and pairs of draftees in uniform. I mused: this is like an exhibit, nobody can buy these things, people come to look the way you go to visit a museum. Teen-agers went out on a date, probably: "Hey, would you like to go to Boutique '70 today?" I stood by a suede jacket marked 1275 marks — over 300 dollars — and watched people feel it lovingly, like a mink coat. Then I moved over to the exit to Boutique '70 for a while, and counted. Of a hundred people leaving, two had made purchases. I was getting the story.

Instead of looking around some more, I went back down the escalator and over to the post office near Alexanderplatz to mail a letter home. It was strange. I hadn't put my return address on the letter and the lady behind the counter told me to put one on. In line I could see that when people sent packages they had to show their identity cards, and their identity card number was put on the package. The officials must get suspicious of what's inside if you don't have a return address. And with packages, I guess, they make double-sure through checking your identity card that you haven't lied about the return address.

I was now hungry, and I was curious to see if the food at the grill would be decent. The joint was, I saw on entering, impressively fancy. Basically, it was a lunch counter, newer but not much different from a New York coffee shop. But look at the red leather swivel seats! Never saw anything like that before in Eastern Europe. And it was spotlessly clean and bright.

Of course there was a wait. Some people were seated on a sort of low Formica counter which stretched along the window, probably designed for people to sit on while they were waiting. But most of the people were just standing up. I had remarked to a Russian in Moscow what a large proportion of people's lives appear to be spent standing waiting.

I sat down on the Formica counter and looked around for a minute. Then I began to unfold my copy of *Neues Deutschland*, but before I could start reading it, a kid next to me interrupted. "You know, you'll have to wait a half-hour here for a seat. Come with us, we'll show you a place that's cheaper and where you don't have to wait."

I was surprised and caught off-guard, so I just said what first came to mind. "Did that restaurant hire you to bring them customers?" I laughed out loud. Somehow that seemed unlikely since both restaurants were state-owned.

The kid just said, "Come with us." There were two of them. One was tall, with a blue polo shirt and long reddish hair. His friend was of average height with short hair. As soon as they got up, they started poking at each other in a friendly way.

"You're a tourist, right?"

"How did you know? I didn't even say a word to you."

"Your shirt. Your shoes." I looked down at my shoes; to me they looked pretty shabby and worn.

We were in the middle of Alexanderplatz. "Do you smoke?" the tall one asked me.

"No."

"So you don't have an American cigarette?"

"No, sorry."

"That's too bad," said the other one.

"Let me tell you where the restaurant is anyway," the tall one continued. We had been walking in the direction away from the hotel and the department store. "See over there, that low building right on the other side of the S-Bahn?" The shabby elevated S-Bahn line from Friedrichstrasse ran right through the new construction. "There's a cafeteria there on the second floor. Go there." I didn't really want to, actually. I would have preferred to wait, and to pay extra, for what I had the feeling would be much better food at the Grill Bar. But I said thanks, and started walking in the direction they pointed. They began walking back the other way.

Suddenly, on impulse, I called out to them. "Stop! Come here!" They turned around. "Hey, excuse me, could you do me a favor and answer a question for me? See all those modern apartments around here?" I pointed straight ahead and around. "Who lives in them? Can a normal person live there, or do you have to have connections?"

More or less simultaneously, both of them broke out in paroxysms of laughter. They looked at each other, like stand-up comics, and laughed again. Then the tall one looked at me. "What do you think? You need money, lots of money. And friends. You have to have everything going for you." He pointed toward an old rundown building we could just barely see in the distance. "See that over there? That's where people like us live."

I wanted to laugh myself, not because what they had said was funny, but because they had just let the cat out of the bag.

"Hey, what do you guys do?"

"We are high school students. We just finished ninth grade, so we have one more year to go."

"What are your names?"

"Rüdiger. Call me Rudi," said the tall one.

"Karl," said the other.

"Hey, why don't you come have lunch with me? Is that place really as good as you said?"

"Yeah, sure it's good," popped up Karl. "But we don't have enough money to afford to go there. We'll just get ourselves a beer."

"O.K. My name is Steve, and I'm an American."

"An *American?* Did you hear that, Karl?" said Rudi, playfully roughing up his friend's hair. "America is the greatest place in the world. We love America. But we get to meet so few Americans here. And of course we can't get out. The Wall, you know."

"I know."

We had arrived in the cafeteria they recommended. There was a wait there also, and it was incredibly crowded, but we made our way through the line relatively quickly.

"Another question. Do you know the magazine *Wochenpost?*"

"Yeah," said Rudi. "Sure. The one with the marriage announcements. They have people who put in ads to get married."

"Is that why people buy it?"

"Yeah, that and the crossword puzzle. It's a little less political than the others."

"What about your school? What is it like in your school? Do kids believe what they're taught about your country and about other countries?" That was perhaps a daringly direct question, but I had thought it through while we were walking toward the cafeteria. These kids were only sixteen or so, and nobody had followed me to Alexanderplatz, so the chances for a trap were small. And it was, after all, just a question.

"Sh-h-h!" Karl said, glancing around. "Don't talk so loud."

"In my class in school last year," Rudi started, "one day the teacher was babbling away with hate propaganda against West Germany. That's mostly what we get in social studies, hate propaganda against West Germany. We were all sick of it, but when the teacher blabbed something about how rents were higher in West Germany, a boy got up and yelled out that wages were higher also, why didn't she tell us *that*. And then he said that in West Germany they can go where they want to and see a lot of movies they want to and not just dull ones. Well, then two days later two policemen came into the class and arrested him."

"*Into the class?*"

"Yeah, to scare the rest of us. They came right in the middle of class and took him. He was there in jail for six weeks for investigation, and then they let him go."

"I can't believe it." I sighed. It's funny how you oscillate between reconciliation and hate: first Herr Bach is nice, and then it turns out he has some ulterior motives. First you see the new Alexanderplatz, and then you hear about sixteen-year-olds arrested for saying the wrong thing at school. What I had just been told really shocked me, and I stared at them for a while as they sipped their beers. I wondered to myself if kids didn't learn earlier than that what they weren't allowed to do in an East German school.

I went on. "What about the other kids in the class?"

"We were mostly for him, but we didn't dare say anything. Ten percent of the kids are for the government, ninety percent are against."

"What about the parents? Do the kids have the same opinion as their parents, or a different one?"

"Ten percent of the parents are for, ninety percent against. The kids who are for, their parents are members of the Party or something like that. So those kids become F.D.J. leaders in each class, and work with the teacher." F.D.J. — *Freie Deutsche Jugend* (Free German Youth) — I remember the reports of how angry their representatives got when Czech youth compared them to the Hitler Youth at a conference in 1968.

"Is there an F.D.J. in every class?"

"Yeah, they're supposed to get kids to love Ulbricht."

"Are most kids members?"

"Yeah, you have to be. Rudi and I are members. But after next year we won't have to be anymore because we're leaving school. Only the kids who are going on to *Gymnasium* have to keep in the F.D.J."

"Hey, Karl, remember Rudi asked me if I had a cigarette before? I'll tell you what, we'll go to one of the foreign currency shops and I'll buy you a package of American cigarettes."

"Really?" Karl burst out. "Steve, you're an angel!"

"Where can we pick them up?"

"There's an Intershop pretty near here, we can even walk there. It's at the Hotel Neva. You can see how people live on the way, and there's also a good view of the Wall."

We started walking and passed what used to be a pub — now it was boarded up and closed down — with a sort of painted glass sign for Berliner Schultheiss beer next to it. There was a hole in the sign from a rock thrown at it, but otherwise it looked like the signs for Schultheiss that you see in West Berlin. "You don't have Schultheiss beer here in East Berlin, do you?" I asked. "Is this sign just from before the Wall?"

"*Was trinken wir? Schultheiss Bier!*" crooned Karl, rollicking and clapping his hands. That was an advertising slogan from West Berlin — he must have heard it on West Berlin radio or something.

"Yeah, we have something they say is Schultheiss beer," replied Rudi. "But my parents say it's not nearly as good."

"Did you ever visit West Berlin?"

"Sure, before the Wall. But I don't remember anything. I was too young then."

"Steve, look at how much everything costs here!" interrupted Karl. "In West Germany, everyone has a refrigerator. Look at the prices in the window." It was 350 dollars for a small refrigerator with three shelves.

It was a long walk, and Rudi and Karl started talking with themselves. I couldn't understand everything they were saying, but our political discussion seemed to have gotten them onto politics. They were telling jokes to each other — and urging me to listen and laugh — about Ulbricht. But their jokes had a special stamp: about how fat Ulbricht's wife was, about the funny way he talked. It is hard to avoid politics in East Germany, hard to be just "not interested." So these kids, red-blooded types who in less politicized conditions would probably spend all their time on football, were interested, in their way, in politics.

There was also a line in the Intershop. We got our cigarettes and a pack of chewing gum. It was like something out of Western Europe around 1946: an American cigarette, a nylon stocking, a pack of chewing gum. People at the Intershop were buying lots of coffee.

"Steve, why don't we meet again tomorrow?"

"Yeah, except the problem is that I won't be home most of tomorrow. You see, my visa runs out tomorrow, and it's probably going to be extended, but I have to leave East Berlin and go to West Berlin and then come back here. It's very strange, but you know that — "

Just then, Rudi pushed me into the lobby of the building we were passing by. It all happened so fast I didn't know what to think. He and Karl ran into the dark, unlit hallway. I just gasped, and kept quiet. What was this? After around twenty seconds, they motioned to me to step out into the light again.

"It was a policeman. When they see kids coming out of an Intershop, a lot of times they come up and take away the things we bought there. They like to smoke the cigarettes themselves."

I went on to tell Rudi and Karl that I'd like to see them again, but that I had a friend — as I called Herr Bach — who was a supporter of the government and perhaps wouldn't want me to associate with normal kids. But if they came over the next morning, and presented themselves to Frau Koch as old friends from 1969 whom I had called and asked to come over, that would be all right.

That night at Frau Koch's house I watched a little East German television. There was a reportage on a police judo exhibition for ten-year-olds at a summer camp featured on the evening news. "Even when they don't have weapons," the announcer said, "the police aren't defenseless."

✿

As far as Herr Bach was concerned, I had only one duty in West Berlin. He asked me if I could buy a package of pills for raising blood pressure. I could get them at any drugstore in West Berlin, he said, and Frau Koch would be very grateful to have them. Whether such pills existed at all in East Germany, and if not, what Frau Koch did to keep her blood pressure up, I didn't know, and felt it impolitic to ask. Herr Bach told me to put the bottle of pills in my pocket, and if they asked me any questions at the border crossing, I should say the pills were for personal use.

I had with me my camera, my typewriter, and a copy of *Neues Deutschland* for the morning which I hadn't finished yet when Herr Bach came to pick me up around one. The camera and the typewriter I had declared on my currency declaration when I arrived in East Germany; I had to show them when I was leaving, even if I was coming right back. Herr Bach asked me whether it was safe to take *Neues Deutschland* into West Berlin; it turned out he thought it was illegal there.

Rudi and Karl had come over that morning, and suggested that we go see a movie that night — an English film called *Privilege*, which was advertised as dealing with "the rise and fall of a pop idol." I said I hoped I could go, but was not completely sure because Herr Bach had implied that he might have something planned for me when I returned from West Berlin — he had mentioned something about introducing me to a colleague of his. I told the two to call me up again later.

The way the kids spoke in front of Frau Koch worried me. She was an old, grandmotherly-looking lady, but obviously connected in some way with Herr Bach, and thus I knew I had to be careful with her. But the happy-go-lucky pair didn't seem to know, or care, and they let slip lines like that they wanted to continue school but weren't willing to go along with the short-hair regulations which went into effect for *Gymnasium*. After they left, Frau Koch sort of took me aside and said motheringly, "Steve, your friends are very nice, but don't believe them when they say they can't go to *Gymnasium* because they won't cut their hair." Maybe they *were* making up excuses; I made a mental note to check it out.

I was supposed to meet Herr Bach and his colleague in front of the Museum for German History on Unter den Linden at four. In West Berlin I read the day's *International Herald Tribune*, had some delicious pizza and Löwenbräu beer on the pulsing, wonderful Kurfürstendamm in West Berlin — and got Frau Koch's pills. I was afraid that I took so long I might be late back, but things went unusually quickly at Friedrichstrasse, and I actually came a few minutes early. Herr Bach and his friend didn't arrive for over a half-hour.

"Steve, I'd like to present to you my colleague Doctor Waack."

I looked him over and smiled inside. He was *sympatico:* young, maybe about thirty, with a walrus mustache and sort of long, though well-trimmed, sideburns. He reminded me of Günter Grass, I thought. He looked so much more accessible than Herr Bach. You could have a conversation with him, maybe even a little bit critical one. He was probably more open-minded. You wouldn't have to be on your guard quite so much, maybe.

It was windy out, and my hair was blowing all over. I had been sitting on the doorstep of the museum, a model of American informality, waiting for them. I didn't think Herr Bach would appreciate that, but Dr. Waack wouldn't mind, I told myself.

"Herr Bach, what is going on with the extension of the visa?"

"We still haven't heard about the hotel reservations."

"What does that mean?"

"It means that no formal visa extension can be granted yet. However, we have told the police authorities you are here, and since we are taking care of you, they will let you stay temporarily for another five days — through next Monday. You had mentioned something about wanting to visit a friend of yours from nineteen sixty-nine in Dresden. You can go down there and do that on Saturday and Sunday. We should have an answer for you by Monday. Meanwhile, Doctor Waack is interested in having some discussions with you. See you Monday!"

He was gone and I was left with Dr. Waack. He hadn't said a word yet, but it was a relief to be alone with him.

"Well, would you like to go for an ice cream?"

"Great!" I exclaimed.

"How about the place on Karl Marx Allee?" Karl Marx Allee was the first showpiece street in East Berlin, built already in the fifties, right near Alexanderplatz. Previously its name was Stalinallee. "We can talk there," he went on. "Please feel that you can answer all my questions freely. Don't hold anything back."

An interesting viewpoint, I reflected to myself, but I thought of the Americans in prison.

"Let me tell you right off the bat," Dr. Waack continued. "I am going to be provocative."

"Provocative?"

"Yes. I'm not going to ask you just easy questions."

"What do you mean?"

"Like about this traveling scholarship that you told Herr Bach you have. That's a very impressive award. It seems to me you'd have to be in pretty well with the powers-that-be in America in order to get that award. Isn't that right?" He snickered.

There went Günter Grass and mustaches and sideburns and idyllic visions of man-to-man bull sessions over ice cream! Dr. Waack was like the rest. And he had just posed a question which I never conceived I'd be asked and for which I had not the slightest reply prepared.

"Well, uh, no, uh, it's not right. Not necessarily, you see. There was, uh, in fact, you know — the last two years the people who got the award — the last two people were members of the student movement. They had been active in demonstrations." As I was trying to get all this out, I was rattling through my brain for more things to say. "It's not — it's not the powers-that-be in America that — that give the award. It is Harvard University. It is several professors at Harvard University who sit on a committee. The powers-that-be in America don't even know about the award."

"Oh, really!" he parried meanly. "So you claim that a critic of American society can get this award!" The kid gloves were off.

"I am a socialist, and I got the award."

"Look, every society in the world favors those who support its ruling institutions."

"But many universities in America have gotten — a great deal of independence from the ruling institutions in American society. The universities have been a center of the student movement and of critical thought against American society."

"The student movement! Critical thought!" he spat out contemptuously. "We know the student movement from West Germany. Mostly anarchists and Maoists! That kind of critical thought they'll allow. But what about Marxism, genuine Marxism?"

"Certainly. When I studied German history, for example, we read many interpretations of different periods, including those by Marx and Marxist historians."

His voice softened. "Yes, you read many interpretations. Very good, you think. Many interpretations. But only one of those interpretations is true."

"Only *one?*"

"*Natürlich.* How could more than one be true?"

"And — "

"And they didn't tell you that Marxism was the truth, did they?"

"No, but — "

"But, but, but! Look, we'll continue the discussion some other time." We were already at the café, and seated. "Look at the menu and decide what you want."

My mouth was dry — all the water had flowed to my tear ducts, poised to come out, the muscles in my eyes holding it back. He stayed quiet for a while, and then perked up to ask me whether I'd like to go to the movies that night. Obviously I would have preferred to go with Rudi and Karl, but equally obviously I couldn't say no. We went and looked at a film schedule for all of Berlin in the window of the enormous Kino International next door to the café. It was mostly Soviet World War II films, which I had no desire to see, so with some hesitation I finally suggested *Privilege.* I wasn't sure why the East Germans were showing a film about a pop star, or whether Dr. Waack might object. In fact he had seen it already, he said, but he raised no complaints against seeing it again. He said he would pick me up around six at Frau Koch's. We could have dinner and then go to the show.

He came with me the short distance to the subway stop at Alexanderplatz, and down to the ticket window. "So tell me, Steve, how have you been impressed with the D.D.R. during your short time here?"

That was a nice, easy, jovial question, and I showed not the slightest hesitation in answering it jovially and with a smile. "Oh, not bad. People seem to have it pretty good here."

"Seem? *What do you mean by 'seem'?*"

I froze and shivered for a moment. Then I had my ticket punched, and walked down to the subway tracks. Dr. Waack walked away in the other direction. I took a few deep breaths, and stared straight ahead.

*

At dinner, the *Wienerschnitzel* tasted horrible. There were about two bites of meat on it, and in what I regarded as a brave display, I showed all the fat to Dr. Waack. I had wanted to order *Berliner Weisse mit Schuss,* a special sweet Berlin specialty beer, with dinner, but no go. "Don't even bother, they won't have it," Waack told me.

"How do you know they won't have it? This is Berlin, isn't it?"

"I know our restaurants well enough to know that they won't have it."

Frau Koch had mentioned that Rudi and Karl had called up on the telephone while I was gone. She hadn't told them anything, she said, because she didn't know what my plans were. When we arrived at the theater, Rudi and Karl were standing out front. Karl ran up to me.

"Steve, hi! We tried to call you! We bought you a ticket!"

I should have made believe I didn't know them, but that was impossible. I hadn't mentioned anything to either Herr Bach or Dr. Waack about them, and I also realized that if Dr. Waack thought things through he would realize that I had known about the film *Privilege* before seeing it on the film schedule at the Kino International. That would be only a little lie exposed — but with him, who knew?

"Doctor Waack, these are two friends of mine whom I met when I was in the D.D.R. in nineteen sixty-nine. Rudi and Karl, this is Doctor Waack, another friend of mine." Fortunately, there was no time for further explanations — or questions — because it was already a few minutes after the film was supposed to start.

It was obvious why the East Germans had decided to show *Privilege*. The film presented the superstar Steven Shorter as a capitalist tool, launched by big businessmen in order to take people's attention away from their problems. Shorter is called upon by his masters at the end to lead a fascist, hero-worship cult, revolving around loud music and strobe lights, which would head off increasing strike waves and student unrest. At a monster rally, with torches, posters, and semihypnotized masses, Steven Shorter was supposed to speak to announce the new cult — but he breaks away, and cries that he can't, he won't. "I am a man. I am a man," he exclaims. I was disgusted that the East Germans were showing the film, but wondering at the same time whether anyone else was making the same unintended associations as I was. I thought of East German monster rallies, with banners and torches, and of the day when an East German Steven Shorter would get up and say just those words to the Communist masters.

"What do you think of the film?" Dr. Waack asked as we were leaving.

"I liked it."

"It was good social criticism. The problem with it was that it gave no answer. It didn't tell the alternative to the pop hysteria."

"Socialism, you mean?"

"Yes, *natürlich*. At the same time, of course, we have a problem with young people in the D.D.R. who are attracted by this pop hysteria. They've even begun to bring drugs into the D.D.R."

"Yes, well drugs have become a problem in all industrial societies now," I said sympathetically.

"*Wrong*," he replied bitingly. "A problem in *capitalist* industrial societies. Drugs will never be a big problem here. We have strict punishment for crimes like that."

I sighed. I had made what I thought was a pretty safe statement, especially with regard to Herr Bach's earlier talk about the common problems of America and East Germany which his research group was dealing with. Dr. Waack was like a steel trap.

It was cold out in the night outside the theater, especially since I had only a T-shirt on. So far, Rudi and Karl hadn't said a word, and somehow I had to get them not to shoot their mouths off. Would they get a hint I passed to them, or were they too innocent, too uninitiated in the world of higher politics?

"Doctor Waack," I began, speaking almost ceremoniously, "I have been genuinely surprised by the high level of political consciousness of D.D.R. youth. When Rudi, Karl, and I met each other again, one of the first questions they asked me was, 'What will happen to Angela Davis?' I was very impressed." I smiled paternally and hoped, prayed, they would understand.

"Yes, Angela Davis," began Rudi, looking solemn for the first time since I met him. "We learned about her in school, and we wrote letters that she should be freed. And Miki Theo-d-d-d —"

"Miki Theodokoris," Dr. Waack helped along.

"Yes, him too. We wrote letters for him too."

"What grade are you in?"

"We just finished ninth."

The kids got on a tram going home, and we kept walking. We were going to walk the whole way back, well over a mile, despite the chill.

"Why are those two little kids interested in you?" Waack blurted unexpectedly.

"What do you mean by that? We're just friends. We met each other."

"No, but why should they want to know an American?"

"I don't know. Why not?"

He was silent for a good while as we walked on. "The young people in our land, many of them follow fashions, you know. Nothing serious, of course, but they follow fashions. They become enchanted with America."

I tried to cut short his musings. "They are interested in politics. They want to know about the antiwar movement in America, among other things."

He didn't look convinced. We kept walking. He was thinking to himself. I was thinking about what he might be thinking about.

"I hope that in our discussions we can treat the question of idealistic versus materialistic philosophies," he uttered, all of a sudden. "I am interested to know whether you believe in a materialist or an idealist philosophy."

"What do they say?"

"Idealism believes that the world was created and is ruled by supernatural powers, while materialism believes that the world is ruled by certain explainable natural laws."

"Well, it doesn't sound to me like much of a dispute then. I don't think anyone with a scientific education believes in the world being ruled by supernatural powers."

"No, in fact many great scientists were idealists, not materialists."

"Who, for example?"

"Einstein."

"Einstein? You mean he believed the world was ruled by supernatural powers?"

"Well, I have simplified somewhat. Another part of the philosophy of idealism is that the existing social order cannot be changed."

I didn't see what that had to do with his first definition, but I kept within his boundaries. "But that's not true about Einstein. He was politically active. He believed society could be changed."

"But he didn't see the laws which govern the change of society. He didn't believe in the inevitability of Communism." He stared at me steely-eyed, his mustache looking like a knife clasped in his mouth, the way pirates used to do.

My mouth gaped open involuntarily. "But — but — I don't see the connection. Do you mean — do you mean that the inevitability of Communism is a natural law like the law of gravity?"

"This is the materialist view, as opposed to the superstitious."

"But surely there's a difference between human society and the universe?"

"One cannot separate the natural scientific and social scientific parts of science."

*

That night in my bed I shivered. I was afraid of Dr. Waack, not the sudden flash of panic that I had felt when escorted into the green room, but a gnawing fear. He was so hard! He interpreted as slips even statements made innocently. He painted Einstein as an ignorant believer in the occult because he didn't see Communism as inevitable. How would he paint *me*? And why was I being allowed to stay a few days without a visa? Why was there not a word on hotel reservations yet? I wanted to cry into the pillow of my bed, but there was no pillow. So I cried right onto the sheet.

CHAPTER 3

"THERE ARE ALWAYS long lines on Friday, you know," Dr. Waack rattled off. "People are traveling for the weekend." I was by now getting used to his excuses. He had come to accompany me to Ostbahnhof, the main railroad station in East Berlin, from which I'd be traveling alone to Dresden. At each of the ticket lines there were at least thirty people waiting. The people wove around in line like snake-dancing Japanese students at a demonstration.

Ostbahnhof was as decrepit, inconvenient, dirty, and cramped as it had been in 1969. The station had one newsstand, a wretched Mitropa cafeteria — I had been forced to eat lunch there once in 1969 — and an Intershop. The walls were a dirty beige. There was no air-conditioning, and, although the temperature was reasonable outside, in line it was sweaty hot.

Under these conditions, I had no patience with Dr. Waack, but I had to nod my head meekly anyway. The lines had been just as bad in 1969, at the Ostbahnhof and at every other East German railroad station I used. To assure myself that he was lying, I spent the time in line trying to recall which day of the week I had been at Ostbahnhof in 1969. Let me see: I had been in Leipzig on a Monday, I knew that because that turned out to be the day all the museums were closed. Before that I had been in Weimar for three days and Dresden for three days. So that meant I took the train from East Berlin to Dresden on a — Tuesday. People weren't traveling for the weekend then, Dr. Waack! The trip was horrible. For the entire three and a half hours, the train was as crowded as the New York subway during rush hour. I had to stand up the whole way, not in the corridor, where you could at least look out the window, but in the entrance to the car. Ten or so of us cramped together in that narrow entrance compartment, and every time we stopped at a station and people had to get out or in, chaos resulted. There was hardly enough room to open the door to the bathroom, which was located right next to where I was standing. I first tried to read, then to doze off standing up. At least I had a handle — an iron bar on the door separating the two railroad cars — to hold on to.

A guy my age named Manfred, whom I had met in 1969 — he had a job working at a restaurant I visited occasionally — would be meeting me at the train station, or so I hoped. I had originally written him that I'd be coming to Dresden right after leaving Grosspostwitz. He had written back that he wasn't sure whether he'd be back from a vacation in Bulgaria yet, but hoped he would. I had written him from Grosspostwitz that I'd be delayed, and then sent him a telegram the day before that I'd be coming for the weekend.

What I would have liked to do most when I finally arrived in Dresden was to lie down and fall asleep. I waited almost an hour for Manfred, and finally gave up. I felt depressed. I had no place to stay. I wondered whether Manfred was still away, or whether he was just still at his job. I had no idea how to get to his house. First I checked the telephone book in the hope he might have a number. No luck. Finally I decided to ask for the tram in the direction of Radebeul, which was the part of Dresden where he lived. Once I got on the bus, I hoped, someone would be able to help me find the street.

After almost an hour on the bus, I imagined we might be getting there. A man I asked told me we were only two stops away. The street where I got off was quiet and deserted, but finally I saw someone from whom I could ask directions. An old man in a beret, in front of a little house and garden, was painting his fence.

I asked him if he knew where the street was.

"Are you visiting Dresden?"

"Yes, I am, sir. I am visiting a friend whom I met when I came here in nineteen sixty-nine."

"What do you think?"

"Well, there is some new building here in the D.D.R. since I came the last time. I've heard there's a new town center in Dresden, but I haven't seen it yet. I'm just arriving from the station. Are people proud of the new center?"

The man had a slow, comforting voice. "Proud? Son, everything goes so slowly here. It took them twenty-five years to finally build something."

"Oh."

"We must be creating a great deal in this land. Both men and women work here. The question is why we have so little. Where does it all go?"

"What is your opinion?" I asked.

"It can't be proved, but many people believe that it is what is called 'international socialist solidarity.'" He pronounced the words without contempt, more like a pedantic schoolmaster. "This means that we send a factory to a country like Mongolia." He looked at me in a kindly way for a few moments. "Which country do you come from, son?"

"America."

"Ah, America! A fine land. You speak German very well, very well."

"Thank you, sir."

His voice was still slow, but became suddenly more insistent. *The worst thing is that we can't travel.* They won't let us out of here, you know."

"I know."

The man gave me instructions for Manfred's street. He lived in an old building in back of another building. Dark and cold.

"Welcome, welcome. You must be Steven. Manfred told me you would be coming, and then your telegram came this morning."

"Manfred isn't here now?"

"No. He is very sorry, but he did not get his vacation until Monday, and he just left for Bulgaria two days ago. He won't be back for three weeks. He's taken all of this year's vacation and part of next year's for this big trip. He needs the rest, God knows. But Manfred says you are welcome to stay here while you are in Dresden. You may stay in his room."

We had meanwhile come out of the cold hallway into the apartment. Manfred's mother had a worn, wrinkled face but a warm, motherly expression on her lips, harried but with an inner strength. We sat down in the small kitchen, which had a few pieces of pleasant old porcelain on the rickety wooden mantelpiece.

"I just came back from a trip myself. I was in West Germany for three weeks, visiting relatives in Frankfurt."

"Are you a pensioner then?" I was aware of the supremely cynical rule according to which pensioners are permitted to leave East Germany — in the unexpressed hope that they will defect, thus saving the government pension costs.

"Yes, but I work part-time anyway as a cleaning lady. Even with the money Manfred brings in, we can't live alone on a pension."

"Frankfurt — Frankfurt was bombed out during the war just about as badly as Dresden. How would you compare the reconstruction?"

"Compare?" she answered with a startled voice. "There's nothing to compare. They are not even in the same class."

"You mean they've done much more in Frankfurt?"

"Yes, yes, much more. But, you know, I think that for me as an old person life moves too fast in Frankfurt. We have gotten used to it being quieter here, very quiet. We have been through so much, we need quiet now, a little bit of rest. Manfred's father, you know, he was a prisoner of war in Russia for ten years. When he came back, he could no longer function as a human being. It was horrible for Manfred to grow up with, his father sick and bedridden. Manfred and I had a strong bond of love, otherwise we could never have made it through those years. It was almost better when Manfred's father died. The suffering for him was over, at least." I was staring at Manfred's mother during her story. You rarely hear of the sufferings of war from the German side. "We are a small country here. Life is quiet. We make no great claims for ourselves."

"I understand."

She put on a smile. "Well, would you like some coffee? I must apologize for not asking you before. We have lost the habit here. Coffee is so expensive. It's not like before the war, when you invited anyone who came in to have some coffee. Now it is more of a luxury. I have some cakes too. Home-baked."

I smiled. As she warmed up the coffee, she took out a little cardboard carton of cream and put it on the table. I picked it up and played with it. It was from West Germany and the price was stamped 55 pfennigs — about 15 cents — on the top.

"Did you bring this back from West Germany?"

"Yes. We can't get coffee cream here."

"How much are you allowed to bring back with you when you come back from these visits?"

"You are not allowed to bring anything back. But Manfred would never have forgiven me if I didn't get him some Tabac cologne while I was there, so I hid a package in my pocketbook. And I put the coffee cream in my overcoat."

"Just for some cream that costs fifty-five pfennigs?"

"Yes, they are very strict here, very strict." She took her glance away from me, and looked toward the stove. She spoke quietly, with a serene resignation. "No, life isn't as good here as you might think. The newspapers all write that things are fine, of course. But last winter we had no electricity, you know. In the middle of the winter, the darkest time of year, they turned off the neon lights downtown, and many of the streetlights too. Dresden was like a dead city. Our Dresden!" Her voice cracked just a bit. "And then a lot of the homes did not get their coal delivered, and they had no heat. We, who have coal right nearby! No, life is not as good here as you might think. The Wall . . ."

"Were people surprised when the Wall was built, or did they expect it?"

"Everyone was completely surprised. Nobody expected it to come. We just woke up one morning and it was there." She shrugged. "You know, when I was in Frankfurt, all my relatives told me to stay and not come back here. But a mother can't just stay and leave her son behind."

✿

The next morning I slept late, but right after breakfast I took the tram into the city. I wanted to see the next town center. I didn't remember the geography of the city very well — only a big main street that was wide and had no traffic on it. But I had seen the lights of the new center already from the railroad station, and we passed by its edges on the tram ride to Radebeul.

The center basically consisted of a street for pedestrians called Prager Strasse, about a hundred yards long, flanked by a long, five- or six-story apartment house on one side and a couple of snappy new Interhotels on the other. There were two small, square fountains, which were the center for photo-taking. The far end of the street was flanked by two construction areas, at one of which a cylindrical concrete block stood. A neon sign on the façade of one of the Interhotels bore the symbol of Meissen porcelain, which is manufactured right outside of Dresden but is unavailable — except for the lowest quality production — anywhere in East Germany. (It is all exported to hard-currency countries.) On the ground level of Prager Strasse were a few large stores — a clothing store, a supermarket, a toy and souvenir shop, a café. I recalled the cafés and restaurants I had seen on Kalanin Prospekt, Moscow's modern street, a few weeks earlier. They were absolutely cavernous, well over a thousand seats. The notion of small specialty boutiques doesn't seem to have made it to the Communist bloc yet. Their conception of modernity is hugeness. Another neon sign, spanning over several of the stores, read MUSICAL INSTRUMENTS FROM THE DDR — RECOGNIZED AROUND THE WORLD. It struck me as pathetic. For whom was it meant? Foreigners, to encourage them to buy these well-known D.D.R. musical instruments? Or the East German people, to convince them that the products of their industry had gained international status?

I looked at all this, and made mental notes. But, I reminded myself, I shouldn't be too critical. Basically Prager Strasse was pleasant, and certainly an improvement.

I meandered around, looking for an angle. In the supermarket stood two employees behind the meat counter, selling sausages. A whole counter was reserved for big slabs of meat, just like an American supermarket, but it was totally empty. The aisles looked so dull, and instinctively I longed for something all my righteous ideas taught me to believe was worthless or even insidious — bright American packages. Unfortunately, the store was about to close. I'd have to look at some food stores again.

The other stores were also closing, so I looked at windows instead. There was an announcement about a man who had won the prize for "best innovator" by coming up with a plastic coin album. They seemed to be quite proud that he had taken the initiative of manufacturing the thing, and turned in a profit — which they called "usable surplus" — of about 50 percent of invested capital. I grinned; back home we call that capitalism. Interesting to know it is being rewarded with prizes in East Germany. I copied down the announcement.

I had accomplished a lot that past hour. This was how I had hoped it would be, wandering around with eyes wide open and observing. I looked forward to my lunch, at last in a new Interhotel. I came into the grill on the second floor of one of the hotels — the restaurant was jacket and tie only — and saw that all the tables were occupied, but that there were some empty seats at a lunch counter in the back. As soon as I sat down there, though, a waitress came up and told me that I'd have to go check my little leather jacket at the *Garderobe;* it wouldn't do to sling it over the chair. They were going overboard.

I had a decent meal, my first ever in the D.D.R: a smallish beefsteak somewhat overcooked, far from fantastic. But it was a steak. I saw all the food being prepared, in rapid mass production method, on the grill in front of me — the two cooks had their hands more than full. But at least an East German luxury restaurant had made its way up to the level of Frederick's luncheonette in Great Neck, New York.

Almost everyone had ordered the steak, not, I think, for the usual East German reason — that none of the other items mentioned on the menu were actually available — but simply because you could actually *get* a beefsteak at the grill. That's not something an East German sees very often. I noticed on the way out that a German-speaking party asked for a receipt for the cost of their meal. The waitress went over to a small table and brought back a pad of papers marked *receipt*. Maybe they were West Germans, or perhaps some East Germans can also have lunches that somebody else pays for.

The sun had come out when I came outside to sit near the fountain and digest my food. It seemed rather silly to be carrying around the umbrella I had taken with me from Radebeul when it was still cloudy and misty that morning. My next mission would be to look around inside the new apartment houses and see if I could dig up anything interesting. I only hoped nobody would notice my presence.

I went up each floor one by one. It was eerie, 1984 without the deprivation. Right next to the elevator on each floor was tacked up a little display — differing a bit from floor to floor — with color photos of Ulbricht and Honecker, and pictures of mass demonstrations and the Eighth Party Congress. Each floor had a big Party seal, in bright blue and yellow colors hanging there proudly, and most floors also had an imitation parchment document, like the one Herr Schwer got for being a good teacher, that praised the floor for outstanding contributions to the upkeep of "the Center of socialist Dresden." The corridors on each floor were long, seemingly endless. But still, even if these apartments were nothing at all special by Western standards — indeed, big apartments have been criticized by the Left

in Western Europe as "depersonalizing" — it was clear that anyone who lived in a place like this belonged to the privileged
in Dresden. On the entire one-hour trip from Radebeul we
hadn't passed a single dwelling nearly this modern. Those who
lived here must be grateful.

I had hoped to see the mailboxes. It was already the middle
of the afternoon, and most people would probably have taken
any newspapers in already, but it would have been interesting
to see how many of those who lived in this nice monstrous place
got *Neues Deutschland.* If they did, that alone would indicate
they were atypical. But I couldn't find where the mailboxes
were hidden. There was another newer apartment, a high-rise
just off Prager Strasse, probably a few years older. This time,
though, the door was locked. I waited for two old ladies to
come in and went through with them. A large row of mailboxes
stood right at the entrance. A fair number of newspapers were
still stuck in the boxes. There was only one *Neues Deutschland,*
but about ten or fifteen copies of *Die Union,* the daily organ of
one of the puppet parties in the National Front, the (East German) Christian Democratic Union. The C.D.U. has no importance whatsoever, and since *Die Union* does not even have
the advantage of being required reading — literally — for important people, it is even less read than *Neues Deutschland.*
That there were so many copies in this apartment house implied
to me that a place here was the reward C.D.U. big shots got for
their fine work in the National Front. No way to check the
hypothesis, unfortunately, and in fact I left the apartment
quite soon because somebody about twenty-five yards away
seemed interested in the fact that I was tarrying so long in the
lobby.

Yet further away from Prager Strasse, away toward that wide
deserted street I remembered from 1969, was another block of

apartments built adjacent to a warehouse, across which unfurled the banner TWENTY-FIVE YEARS OF THE SOCIALIST UNITY PARTY OF GERMANY — TWENTY-FIVE YEARS OF THE SUCCESSFUL CONSTRUCTION OF SOCIALISM. Facing toward the street from both the warehouse and the apartment block was a spacious, weed-filled lawn. The apartment block had three main entrances, two of which were locked.

At the entrance to all of these newer apartment houses — I hadn't seen it either in Frau Koch's apartment house or where Manfred lives — there is a sign which has OWNER printed at the top with a space to be filled in. Next to that space was written "Property of the People" in the apartments around Prager Strasse, but for this one the owner was the VEB Röntgenwerke, a factory which, I guessed, must make x-ray equipment. I would have to try to ask someone about this — why did just *this* factory get to have an apartment building, and obviously one built even before the new city center, right in the middle of Dresden?

This building was not nearly as glamorous as the new Prager Strasse apartments. None of the floors had the parchment citations, and only about a third had any pictures or party seals. (They can't enforce this politicization down to the apartment-floor level everywhere, thank God. I bet *none* of the older houses, where most people live, have anything like it.) An announcement on the wall next to the ground-floor elevator complained about people putting beach umbrellas on their balconies. The balconies faced the streets and thus, the notice said, disturbed the proper appearance of a balcony in downtown Dresden. The sign also complained about people throwing garbage out the windows onto the lawn. In preparation for May Day, read the conclusion, the residents should stop their bad habits, but if they failed to follow the spirit of May Day, unrepentant tenants would be brought to the VEB Röntgenwerke. It was the third of July, and the sign was still up, so perhaps it didn't do enough good. Or perhaps nobody had bothered to take it down. I took out a sheet of paper and copied down the entire notice, furtively glancing over my shoulder constantly to see if anybody was coming in. Two people did; I stopped writing. Then I went outside and around the building to look at the balconies: there were a few umbrellas, but not many. I felt happy, like a good reporter.

In back of this block was another somewhat older block of low-rise apartments. I didn't find much there: the apartments had only four floors with only two families on each floor at each entry, hardly enough to make pictures or party seals worth it. There was, however, a typed letter on the ground floor of each entryway reminding people to sign up for "Clean Up Dresden Streets for the Spring" volunteer brigades. It was dated last March, but not down yet. The letter said that "unfortunately, many citizens did not yet have the socialist consciousness to realize why they should participate in these brigades. This makes it all the more important for people in your position to participate to the fullest."

Remembering my mother's advice not to spare any expense in getting food, and thinking about getting myself an ice cream, I headed back toward Prager Strasse. Maybe afterward I'd go to see the older parts of the center of the city. The weather was beautiful now, and there were lots of people strolling along Prager Strasse when I returned. Someone asked me the time, and when I uncovered my sleeve to look, a little boy next to me, who stood not much taller than my waist level, screamed out, "Look at that watch!" It *was* a nice watch, a Japanese Seiko I had bought in Tokyo the previous winter.

"May I see your watch too?" the man who had asked me the time said.

I extended out my arm to him.

"Where are you from?"

"America."

"America!" cried out the lady who accompanied the man. "Hans, did you ever think we would meet an *American?*" Her eyes and mouth and whole face exploded with joy.

With a childish look of wonder, the man blurted out: "We have never met an American before. But we would like more than anything to be able to come to your country. Unfortunately, they won't let us go. I have President Kennedy's speech in Berlin on my tape recorder, and also President Nixon's. America is a fine country. I am only afraid that it is forgetting about people like us under Russian control. Is it true that America is going to leave Vietnam?"

I was taken aback by how strong he came on.

"Well, the Vietnam war has become more and more unpopular. Many people feel we have spent billions of dollars to support a corrupt and unpopular government in South Vietnam."

"That's too bad. If America doesn't stop Communism, who will?"

It was incredibly strange to hear those words on the streets of Dresden, in the midst of the D.D.R., from a man exposed all his life to barrages of East German propaganda. I suggested that the three of us go to the ice-cream bar nearby and have something to eat. Hans was, surprisingly enough, exactly my age — he didn't look like an old man, to be sure, but he certainly looked several years older than I. He had a neat round face, clipped hair, and a serene smile. The girl with him was his wife, Käte, and she was blonde and jolly.

"We came in today to place our order for furniture for the apartment we just got. But they told us we'd have to wait. We can't place our order now."

"Why not?"

"There are only certain days a year when you can order furniture. Very few days, really. Then you must wait a whole year for most furniture, sometimes two years for kitchen things. It's horrible. Our house is just about completely empty now. And it probably will be for another year."

I could hardly believe what Käte was saying. "But what about the new furniture stores like Intecta that I saw in Alexanderplatz in East Berlin?"

"Just for show, like everything in this country. Just for show." For the first time, Hans' voice was not merry. "Most of what they have is just floor models. You can't see what you like and buy it, like in the West."

We had sat down at a little table outside and were eating ice cream and cake. It was O.K. Hans and Käte refused to let me pay for them.

"The only decent store in all of Dresden is the Exquisit shop at the Altmarkt," said Käte.

"Which one is that?"

"Oh, you can't miss it if you look. It's the one with all the people there. They sell Western clothes."

"But can anyone afford to *buy* those Western clothes? They're so expensive, aren't they?"

She gave me a sort of "sure, what do you think" expression. "There are no prices in the window at Exquisit. You know what that means. But you save up for a few months anyway to buy something there, so you can at least have *something* nice to wear. Hans bought this turtleneck sweater at Exquisit. He wears it every Saturday when we go out." She smiled, and pointed to his dark green Orlon sweater.

"How much did it cost?"

"One hundred and sixty marks." That was forty dollars. "How much would it cost in the West?"

"Probably around thirty marks."

We kept eating.

"Let me ask you," began Hans. "Is life in America really as good as we all believe it is?"

"Well, you know, America has many problems. We have always had the Negro problem. And we have problems with urban planning, and the cost of medical care. A doctor is very expensive in America. Also we've had an unemployment problem the last two years. But we can talk about our problems, and put pressure on the government to solve them. That makes me optimistic."

"Yes, I guess every country has problems. But it's much better in America than it is here."

There was an elderly lady in a black dress and granny glasses also sitting at our table. She nodded her head.

"May I ask *you* something?" I said after a while. "When they built the Berlin Wall in nineteen sixty-one, did people expect it was coming, or was it a surprise?"

"It was a shock," Käte replied. "Everyone asked themselves how they could do it in one night. People couldn't believe they would ever dare."

"Were people angry?"

"*Angry?* They were furious."

"I was in West Berlin at the time," Hans came in. "I was only eleven, and I was staying at a youth hostel. One morning they announced to us that all the East Germans should come into a room after breakfast for an important announcement. They told us about it then. They said we could stay if we wanted or else go back, but I didn't know anything about politics then. My parents went back home, so of course I went home. When I think back now that I had a chance to escape."

"Well, then you would never have met Käte." I tried to be

consoling, but it didn't look as if I had impressed him. Even Käte didn't seem to believe this a strong enough reason not to have stayed.

"Let me ask you another question. You know, you see these signs everywhere — like there's one hanging out on to the street from the window of the restaurant at the train station — that this or that group of workers at a workplace is 'struggling for the state title Collective of Socialist Labor.' And you read in the papers about 'socialist competition' in factories. What does it mean? Does anybody pay any attention to it?"

"No, nobody. It's just a lot of words they're constantly throwing at us. The idea is to get us to work harder. But nobody listens."

"I don't understand it, though. You see these posters and slogans and signs everywhere, but it doesn't seem that anyone pays any attention to them. Why does the government put them up when they know nobody cares about them?"

"It's advertising for them, like advertising for Coca-Cola or something. This is advertising for the government."

"But Coca-Cola advertising gets people to want to buy Coca-Cola."

"They have a better product to sell."

"So is what you're saying that this socialist competition doesn't mean that workers have to work harder — that they are exploited more. Because nobody listens."

"Yes, mostly. But they do make us work extra on weekends every once in a while. Without pay. They call it 'volunteer labor' because some Party big shot volunteers all his fellow workers, and you have to come in. You waste your Saturdays, you waste your Sundays working for nothing."

"How often?"

"Must be at least ten times a year. They call it voluntary!"

Both of our voices were getting loud, and suddenly Hans noticed the fact. "We'd better leave here, right now." The three of us got up and started walking away. "You know, you really shouldn't talk like this in a public place. They have spies everywhere. And they pay people to turn people in."

"What could happen to you?"

"A long time in jail. It's not impossible."

"I'm sorry."

"I am sorry too. That we are not in a free land. You always must watch out who is sitting next to you here. We don't know who that old lady was."

"But she nodded at something you said."

"Still, we don't know."

We continued walking along Prager Strasse toward the railroad station. Toward the end of the street we stopped, and I started fiddling with my umbrella, tapping it against the ground. "I am really sorry that I might have caused you problems."

"No, no problem. It is so wonderful to meet an American."

"Let me make it up to you. I hope to come back to Dresden sometime during my stay in the D.D.R. When I come back, I'll bring you some coffee from an Intershop."

"No, no. It's really not necessary."

"Well, I will anyway. Let me just ask one more question. What about Willy Brandt? Is he popular in East Germany?"

"I don't think he is as popular here as he is in West Germany."

"Why not?"

"I think many people feel he is making too many concessions to the Communists."

It was unusual. Hans was like a stranger in his own country.

"What about recognition of East Germany? Should the West set up diplomatic relations?"

"No, absolutely not. Never." His voice was insistent.

"What about you? Here you are, living in a political system you oppose, yet unable to do anything about it. How do you find out about things going on in the world?"

"My personal source is RIAS from West Berlin. They have a very strong radio signal which you can hear well on FM. I listen to them all the time."

"What about the Dresden newspapers?"

"Oh, occasionally I look at them for some local news. But anything else is mostly lies. Most of it is a complete waste of time to read. The problem is, though, that here in Dresden we can't get West German television. Most people in the D.D.R. can, but we are in a valley and the signal isn't strong enough. That is my biggest wish — that they build a more powerful television tower in West Berlin. Once I wrote a letter to Axel Springer and asked him to donate the money for it. A West German I met smuggled the letter out for me." I chuckled to myself: Axel Springer, the newspaper millionaire.

I got Hans and Käte's address before I left, and told them I hoped to meet them again if I got back to Dresden during my trip. I want to get to know them better, I thought to myself. What fascinates me is how people get their political consciousness in a totalitarian country, whether people oppose the regime from childhood, or whether they first get their ideas when they get older. And what is it that upsets people most — how much does that abstract idea of freedom mean? What does it mean for a person that the little old lady sitting at your table might turn you in?

*

To get to the older central parts of the city which I remembered from 1969, you walked from Prager Strasse through the wooden pathway built through the area still under construction, in the direction away from the train station, past the spherical concrete shell on your right and the big hole on your left.

The old square, the Altmarkt, was now dominated by an enormous enlargement of the Party symbol, over fifty feet tall and rising from a grassy area at the open end of the square, going toward Prager Strasse. Below the circular symbol stood the text SOCIALIST UNITY PARTY OF GERMANY — 1946–1971. It was scary. I walked along the square, my back turned to the huge sign. It had bulbs and no doubt lit up at night. I trembled inside. Today was the fourth of July. I missed America. I walked past the Exquisit store; there was a large shoe shop right next to it, with Leonid Brezhnev, Nikolai Podgorny, and Aleksei Kosygin in the window. LONG LIVE THE TWENTY-FOURTH CONGRESS OF THE COMMUNIST PARTY OF THE SOVIET UNION. At least it was black and white instead of white on red, and it wasn't a long banner unfurled along the street. On my tram ride in from Radebeul there must have been at least ten banners, probably more. PRODUCE ACCORDING TO THE PLAN, RATIONALIZE INTELLIGENTLY, DON'T LET ANYTHING GO TO WASTE! MARXISM-LENINISM — THE IDEOLOGY OF THE VICTORIOUS WORKING CLASS! HE WHO IS ALLIED WITH THE SOVIET UNION IS ALLIED WITH THE VICTORS OF HISTORY! That one I thought was particularly disgusting. Just an appeal to bandwagon emotions, particularly unfortunate given Germany's past. Shit, this place is nothing but a damn *colony* of Russia.

The façade of the Centrum Department Store dominated the small street which led from the Altmarkt to the long boulevard. They were mainly displaying household equipment, plus radios and record players. They had a large, bulky table radio selling for ninety dollars, which didn't seem so bad, but then there was a small size, a portable transistor thing, which cost almost as much —eighty-five dollars. I pounded my fist against the window pane. It was maddening: once it gets to anything involving modern technology, they are *hopelessly* behind. Everywhere except, of course, *military* technology. *There* they keep up with the latest. But take anything designed for people: maybe they can imitate what Western countries have come up with, but have they ever come up with a consumer innovation themselves? An invention, a discovery, a technique? Never. Never. Maybe they could build a nice Prager Strasse or Alexanderplatz ten or fifteen years after Western Europe did it, but have they *started* anything? What if the whole world were Communist, could you imagine *that*? There wouldn't be any sources of new ideas for the Communist countries to cop. They'd have to allow at least one country to continue to be free, so that they could have some progress to imitate. To the people back home who curse progress and say technology is oppressive, have the people here become any freer or better because they *don't* have progress and improvement? They are not only worse off materially, they are also *more* oppressed. There was a cassette tape recorder in the window also. It cost one hundred sixty bucks and looked pretty primitive. Cassette tapes cost four bucks apiece. Imitation, and not even a quality imitation. No wonder they worship hard currency here. They can't sell any of their junk in any markets where people actually have a choice about what they are going to buy, yet their *wants* from Western production are limitless. And their problems certainly don't come from paying their workers especially well. The workers here get paid no more than in Japan. Curse the bastards! And those new radios — at least the old ones had all sorts of Western stations, Paris or Zurich or something, listed on the shortwave band. These new ones have only Prague, Moscow, Budapest, and Radio D.D.R. three places on the band. Their only Western marking is Göteborg. In Sweden!

I wanted to return to an old watering hole from 1969 for lunch, a giant cafeteria compound which was probably new maybe ten years ago but was now in a state of dirt and rapid decline. It was at the head of the long boulevard, Ernst Thälmann Strasse, named after the prewar German Communist leader. On one side of the wide boulevard a sort of brick roof ran over a portion of the sidewalk, with thin pillars running along, separating the sidewalk from the street. The pavement was cobblestone even though this was the main street. The building façades were grubby and grimy. As I started along I thought that if you took a picture with a low-quality black and white camera, you could think you had gotten a photo of a city scene from the turn of the century. Except that then there would have been at least horses and buggies on the streets. In the distance, at the end of the boulevard, stood a multistory building, also uncleaned but more recent. On top of it was a neon sign stretching across: SOCIALISM IS WINNING.

The vinyl floor of the restaurant was wet and covered all over with track marks, wearing thin in parts like a pizzeria on around 9th Avenue and 45th Street in New York. But on the door was a printed sign:

> WELCOME TO AM ZWINGER. THE LARGEST RESTAURANT
> COMPLEX IN THE DDR. CAFETERIA, COFFEE BAR, RESTAU-
> RANT — MODERN AND CONVENIENT.

Only two main courses were available that day; I got some goulash with red cabbage and potatoes and sat down. I also got some blackberry juice, which was good, so I went back and bought another glass. The goulash was mostly fat.

There was a park and amusement area past the big building with the sign about how socialism was winning. Just as I had remembered it from 1969, two ice-cream stands stood right at the front entrance. As before, the one on the left had a line of perhaps forty or fifty people waiting to get ice cream, while the other stand had two or three. Obviously the left stand had something the right stand didn't, but in the world of total planning it takes a little while to get the message. The amusement area was shabby, with little mud hills everywhere, but the people looked happy. The prizes the shooting gallery offered were strange — canned fruit or a bar of chocolate. I sat down amidst the huge throngs of people on a bench to read *Neues Deutschland*. It was no doubt out of place for me to read something there, and after about five minutes a middle-aged man with an old-fashioned worker's cap and graying stubble came up and looked at me strangely to ask what I was reading.

"*Neues Deutschland.*"

"That's too bad."

The man looked just a wisp drunk, but not too much.

*

Dr. Waack came to meet me at the Ostbahnhof in East Berlin. I was exhausted from standing on the train for over three hours. On the train this time I finally got a seat for the last half-hour of the trip. But what I most wanted to do now was to go back to Pankow, take a shower — Manfred's house had only an old-fashioned little tub in a woodshed outside the house — and shave, then take a nap. But when we got back, Frau Koch informed me there was no hot water on Mondays. As dirty as I felt, I wasn't up to taking a shower in cold water, so I just soaked my face enough to more or less prepare it for shaving off four days' whiskers. Damn, the shaving hurt. Dr. Waack said I could sleep for an hour, and then he would come to pick me up to take me to visit the memorial to Soviet soldiers in Treptower Park.

The only other people around in the huge park when Dr. Waack and I arrived were from a tourist bus out of West Berlin. "Countrymen of yours," Dr. Waack spat out somewhat disdainfully, as we walked into the park and got our first sight of the enormous monument. I could hear Midwestern accents in the group ahead of us, and the plump ladies in Bermuda shorts looked ridiculous.

We had, on my suggestion, sat down in the shade: for the first time since I had arrived, the sun was uncomfortably hot, and I was thirsty. I felt dirty and tired; Waack was well-shaved and fresh. He didn't seem to be sweating at all, in spite of the sun. He was strong. But the afternoon was not going to be just simple tourism mixed with Dr. Waack's side commentary about the heroic Soviet soldiers.

"Steve, why don't you ask me some questions?"

I had trouble thinking. "What kind of questions?"

"Well, you've been in the D.D.R. for a week now. Don't you have any questions about what you've observed?"

"Well . . . Well, what about blue jeans? It seems that the young people want to have blue jeans. Is there an ideological objection to blue jeans? Why can't you make them if they want them?"

Waack glared at me, as if that were not the quality of question he wanted. "What do you care about blue jeans for? I don't know. Probably you need some special material, and we can't get a hold of it. It's unimportant."

"Why is it unimportant, what people want to have?"

"Next question." Waack looked at me for a few seconds, then began again.

"You have told me you are a socialist. What countries were you thinking of as socialist countries? There are many people who call themselves socialists . . ."

I bit my lips. "Well, no one country completely represents

my concept of socialism. I think something between Soviet and Yugoslavian socialism —"

I had assumed that it would be all right to express some sympathy for Yugoslavia. They were, after all, a Communist country. "*Between* Soviet and Yugoslavian socialism? There is no such thing as something *between* Soviet and Yugoslavian socialism. What do you think is so good about what you call Yugoslavian socialism?"

I had to struggle hard to keep my mind from going blank, to keep awake, to forget about how thirsty I was. We had been in the shade, but the sun had moved a little already, and was now beginning to shine on us again. "Well — I — I — think — you have to take a theoretical look at — at a problem in a socialist society. There is a tension between the interests of a single factory, even under socialism, and the society as a whole. The workers in each factory usually want a slower pace of work, better working conditions, and so forth, at the expense of maximum production, while society, consumers, want maximum production. I think that the system of self-management in Yugoslavia allows greater expression of the interests of workers at the plant level than a completely centrally directed socialist system. At the same time, of course, it creates problems."

"Problems! Yugoslavia has gone so far in abandoning socialism that it is hardly a socialist country anymore. The state has lost control over the development of the economy. They have unemployment. They have had to send their surplus workers to West Germany. President Tito himself admitted in a speech just recently that the Yugoslav economy is in a crisis. I'll get you a copy." I hadn't heard of the speech, but thought to myself about how, in analyzing what is really happening in Communist countries, it is often useful to refer to what one Communist land says about its enemy Communist lands. Thus I have always attached great weight to Chinese analyses of developments in the Soviet Union, and vice versa. "No, it's horrible in Yugoslavia. Not socialist. Do you know that in Yugoslavia individual firms can actually enter into agreements with foreign firms — that the state doesn't even know about?"

He obviously thought this would shock me.

"Just a second," I replied. "Sure, I don't deny that a more decentralized socialist system has disadvantages. That's why I said *between* Soviet and Yugoslav socialism. I just think you have to recognize the advantages also."

"*What* advantages?"

"A greater feeling of participation by the workers in the running of the factories, for example."

"*Feeling?*" He looked amazed. "What do *feelings* have to do with socialism?"

"Well, isn't it obvious that people have to feel that socialism is better for them? Otherwise, they won't be convinced that socialism is a good system."

"Ah, but to *convince* the people to believe in socialism, that takes a very very long time."

I felt I had to say something, he was getting me so angry. But I was scared of slipping past the point of no return. "What do you mean, it takes a very very long time to convince the people? Shouldn't they be convinced already *before* socialism is introduced?"

"How can you expect to convince the whole people?"

"Of course, well, I mean a majority of the people."

He hemmed and hawed in a grandfatherly way. "Ah, my friend, if you wait to convince the majority of the people before you introduce socialism, then you will never introduce socialism. There has never been a socialist revolution that had support from the majority of the people."

"But —"

"Yes, perhaps you are going to say Chile. No, but Chile is not a socialist revolution. It is a bourgeois-democratic nationalist government that has come to power."

Actually, that was not what I had in mind when he interrupted me. "But what right do socialists have to take power if the majority of the people don't support them?"

He looked upward toward the sun and laughed. "It is *always* a minority which makes a revolution. A minority, but one that is determined and united. How can you convince the masses of socialism before the revolution? They have no ideas of anything like that." He paused. "The masses are very easily influenced, swayed, like a mob. They have no ideas of their own, no will, no force. One day they can think one way, the next day another way." His expression was excited, almost exalted. "They have no will! We convince one group, and go to another, and we come back and the first group has become unconvinced. They listen to anyone and everyone. They have no will!"

"Why do you have such a negative picture of the people? You sound almost like a conservative."

"No, no! Remember, I am a representative of the masses. But the masses have received a reactionary education, they come from reactionary homes. They are misled. They do not know."

"But that view is directly contrary to Marxism. Marx believed that political opinions are primarily the result of workers' concrete economic situation, not ideological influences. What you are saying is contrary to Marx."

"Says Marx! But look at realities. The majority is never convinced of socialism."

"Well, how are you going to make your revolution then?"

"With the convinced. Those who are united and strong! And then, with adventurers, thrill-seekers, people who enjoy battles and blood. With anyone who will join."

"You're willing to use people like that?"

He came back without a second of hesitation, as he twitched his mustache. '*Natürlich!* What do you think?"

I hated him.

*

Karl and Rudi had called twice on Monday, once in the morning before I had come back from Dresden and once again around dinner when I wasn't back yet from Treptower Park. The next morning, they arrived around nine, even before I had gotten up.

"Hey, you guys, you want to come with me out to some place to get some shampoo for my hair? I haven't had any for a month, and I really need some." Frau Koch told us there was a place on the main street around the corner.

As soon as we got outside, I looked around just to make sure and then spoke to the kids in a low voice. "Look, be careful! The people I'm with are very much for the government. You've really got to be *very* careful what you say. Understand?"

"Yes, we understand," said Rudi.

"Frau Koch even got upset when you said that you couldn't go to *Gymnasium* because you had long hair. So watch out."

The kids suddenly stopped walking. "Hey, look at this," the little one cried. It was a new dark green Swedish Volvo. "A Western car with Eastern license plates! You know what that's used for, they say?"

"No, what?"

"To go to West Germany and track down people who have escaped! I don't know if it's true, but that's what they say."

I was a little skeptical. Sounded like a cops-and-robbers story.

"Hey, can I ask you two a question? You know that film *Privilege* we all saw the other night? What did you get out of it?"

"Well, it was mostly the music."

"But don't you think the film tried to present a negative picture of rock and roll stars?"

"Yeah, sure. But no kids care about that. Kids go to hear the music."

"Hey, one more thing. When we get back from buying this shampoo, you guys better leave. This Doctor Waack guy is coming over around eleven. I think he's suspicious of you two, you know. That night we saw the film he said something like, 'Why would they want to know an American?' "

"Yeah, O.K. But we've got to get some time when we can spend some time together without Doctor Waack. We want to have a party where you can meet our friends."

"O.K., we'll try to do that." I agreed.

Dr. Waack, as it happened, did not arrive at eleven. Just a few minutes before twelve he called to say he had been delayed and that he wouldn't be coming before three. That was happy news; it meant I could slip into town for a while before they came. Even have lunch at the grill bar at Alexanderplatz finally.

I got my piece of beef at the grill bar. I had to wait around twenty minutes for a seat, mostly standing up, but the beef was good, better than in Dresden. One aspect I've noticed of East German restaurants, I thought to myself: they don't have salt or pepper on the table, you have to ask especially. And many of them don't give you napkins. The grill bar at least didn't.

I wanted to check the Intecta furniture store in Alexanderplatz whether there was any indication of a waiting time for furniture. I didn't really learn much. Large numbers of people were looking at the display models, and the area for placing orders was empty the whole time I was there. The furniture was surprisingly nice, though, even if the prices were extremely high. Deep green cloth upholstery, richly padded chairs, varnished wood. New and improved. The books put on the shelves of the sample rooms were, however, odd — all political propaganda, not even a volume of Goethe or Schiller. I wanted to ask someone at the counter about waiting times, but I couldn't get up the courage.

There was a loud argument going on right next to where I sat down for a rest near the fountain at Alexanderplatz. Two long-haired kids, one in blue corduroys and the other in red dungarees, were arguing about East Germany. One of them was defending the East German government, the other one was sighing about every two minutes, saying, "I don't believe that you can really *believe* that." First I assumed it was two West Germans, but after a while it became apparent that the one defending the East German government was actually an East German.

I just sat looking toward them and listening for a while. They went through much of the standard stuff — the Wall, the dictatorship, the Ulbricht cult. "We have built everything up from nothing here in the D.D.R. You just sold out to the Yankees. But still, look at all we've done that you still haven't done. We have more young people going to universities than in West Germany, and most of them are children of workers. And we have free health care."

"Most of our health care is free too," replied the West German. "And you're forgetting the basic question. Where are people *happy?*"

"Everybody is content here," he returned, deadpan.

I came in. "You know, this is the second time I have visited the D.D.R. I have talked to a lot of people while I've been here, and you are the first one I've met who's defended your government."

The East German with the blue corduroys — Lee's Sta-Prest —

and the long curls of brown hair, looking like a hippie, looked at me. "Where do you come from?"

Instinctively, I don't know why, I answered, "Sweden."

"Sweden. You speak German very well. Sweden, that is a very good country, better than us. My father was in Sweden last year. He liked it very much. But we're better than West Germany."

"Your father was in Sweden?" I smelled a rat. "What was he doing there?"

"He works in foreign trade. He was visiting a Swedish trade fair."

Well, it was interesting to see that, as Rudi and Karl had said, there was little conflict of generations in the D.D.R. Like father, like son.

"May I ask you where you live?"

"In that apartment house over there." He pointed to one of the new apartments.

"It's no wonder you support the government. You have a pretty good life."

"Oh, those new apartments aren't so good. The walls are so thin you can hear the neighbor's radio all the time."

"Look, I'd like to continue in this discussion, but just let me call someone I'm supposed to meet in a few minutes and tell him I'm going to be a few minutes late. Where is there a phone?"

"We can go into Centrum. They have public telephones. I was going to show my West German friend here that we have high quality clothes in the D.D.R. too."

"If you have such good clothes, why are you wearing Lee's corduroys, and why does every young person you meet in this place want blue jeans?" the West German interjected.

I got a busy signal on the telephone after dialing Frau Koch's first three numbers. We looked at some clothes for a few minutes — horribly dull — and I tried again. Still busy. I waited and tried again. The exchange was busy. I called over to the East German kid with a disparaging, but joking, comment. He said he couldn't believe the *exchange* was busy, I must be making a mistake. He tried to dial the number and the busy signal came after three numbers. I remembered how we had had problems in New York City with busy exchanges for a while. We thought it was the definitive sign that the city was collapsing totally. East Berlin has only a million people, and only a tiny fraction of those people have telephones. The West German kid laughed at the still-smiling figure in the blue corduroys.

It was already after three and I was getting nervous. Dr. Waack would wonder where I had been — of course, it was a good explanation to say that I had been listening to a "West German" argue with a "citizen of the D.D.R.," as it is called officially. (One is not allowed to say "East German" or even just plain "German," the way West Germans speak of themselves.)

We went over to look at the Boutique '70 with Western clothes. "It's like a museum here," I said. "The prices are too high for anyone to buy anything."

"I think it's an intelligent policy on the part of our government to make the prices high for these clothes," he answered. "People who can afford to pay for quality *should* have to pay a lot."

"But *anyone* can get these clothes in the West!" the West German kid protested. "Your government has *made* them into a luxury article. And poor people save up to buy them too, because the clothes you make yourselves are so bad."

We took the escalator downstairs. I told them I'd really have to go. "One more question, though. About your newspapers here. They're so dull, just propaganda. Even you have to admit that nobody reads them."

"Well, I'll have to say that it's hard to get through *Neues Deutschland.*"

I made one last try on the phone — no luck — and started sprinting toward the subway station.

I was going to be an hour late. I sprang out of the subway at Pankow and jogged, sometimes ran, all the way back to Binzstrasse. "Frau Koch, I'm so sorry I'm late." I didn't see anyone else there. "Has Doctor Waack left already?"

"He hasn't arrived yet."

"Hasn't arrived? I was really afraid I'd come too late. I tried to call, but the telephone exchange was busy. I couldn't get beyond the first three numbers. You weren't on the phone, were you?"

"No. There are often problems with the telephones when it gets too hot like it is today. It's not good for the machinery." She looked at me kindly.

I went into my room and sat down to write notes on the day's experiences. I was prepared to hide my notes quickly when Dr. Waack came, but he still hadn't arrived even when I had finished. I lay down and shut my eyes, and around fifteen minutes later I heard a knock on the door. Both Dr. Waack and Herr Bach had come, Bach with a briefcase. They came into my little room and shut the door.

Herr Bach took out a paper. "We have received an answer from the Youth Tourist Travel Agency. Unfortunately, they have no hotel reservations for the remainder of the summer in any place you requested."

"What about the D.D.R. Travel Bureau?"

"Nothing."

I sat up on my bed and stared at both of them. Bach had plopped down on a chair he had taken out from the small writing table in the room; Waack was lazily, but arrogantly, propped up on the cabinet on which stood an old radio and looked as if he should have had a toothpick in his mouth. Bach was stone-faced; Waack had a tiny grin.

"Does — does that mean my visa cannot be extended?"

"Normally, no visas are granted to foreign tourists for longer than two weeks," he began deliberately. "But there is one alternative. As you know, we are quite interested in scholarly exchanges between American scholars and ourselves. I have been authorized to invite you to be a guest of the Academy of Sciences for the period of your stay in the D.D.R. We will be in a position to show you various of the sites of historical interest you wanted to see, and answer questions you might have about the construction of socialism in the D.D.R. Doctor Waack's vacation begins next week, and he has been kind enough to agree to sacrifice it to travel with you to Leipzig, Dresden, and Rostock, as you requested. He will be an excellent guide, you will have a travel companion, and he can keep you busy and — and watch over you a little bit, right?" He chuckled in a burst of artificial laughter.

"Thank you, Doctor Waack."

He smiled like a weasel, and nodded his head briefly up and down. "Yes, watch over you. Watch over you. But don't worry, we won't keep you prisoner!" He laughed again. I shuddered.

"We have arranged for you to leave for Leipzig next Monday, and stay there for three days. Then you will go on to Dresden for four more days. Then you will come back to the capital. A few days here, and then you will go to Rostock for five days, to get a little swimming and rest on the Baltic Sea. Then you will return back here, and at that time I will have returned from my vacation. I unfortunately cannot stay, because I have already made plans to visit Bulgaria. But I only ask that you save your last few days for me. You had originally requested to stay until August fourth. We request only that you stay until the tenth."

"What about Weimar and Eisenach?"

"You cannot do too much at one time. You will be quite busy as it is."

"I had hoped to visit the Wartburg factory at Eisenach."

"Oh no, that would have been impossible in any case. Factories are never open to the public. We can't just let people go in and see them. I'm sure it is the same way in your country. A private person could not just go and visit General Motors."

"Yes they can. People can go and visit General Motors."

There was silence, and I realized I shouldn't have said that.

Bach recovered his tempo, and began with his speech again. "We ask only one thing. In connection with our research project on the year two thousand, we are interested in scholarly reports on various American social phenomena. We would like you to write a report on the American student movement before you leave for Dresden next Monday. We would want general background information on its history, but then above all specific details on the various groups, particularly the Maoist and terrorist groups." His voice became more grave. "How many members and what influence do they have? What are their sources of funds? What is their attitude to various other nations like the Soviet Union and China? What are their relationships to other groups? We don't want primarily an ideological analysis of the student movement on your part. Ideological analysis is of course important, but what we want from you is *facts*, without ideological interpretation. Details about each group: members, influence, financing. After you do this paper for us, we can have further scholarly discussions. How does my offer sound to you?"

He knew I had no choice. I smiled. "Fine, wonderful. I accept."

"You accept? That's splendid!" He grinned at Waack. "And now, just one more request — no visits. You have already had the chance to visit your friend Herr Schwer, and your friend

Manfred in Dresden last weekend. Normally, you know, a foreign tourist is not allowed at all to make private visits to people's homes. You have already been privileged in this respect. From now on you will be *our* guest. We will keep you quite busy."

*

I had planned to go out again that night, but I was so frayed that I just stayed home in my room and tried to think through what had just happened. They had me on a string now. Every time I went out alone now I'd have to sneak out. The whole trip, until I left, they'd be watching me! Waack being *nice enough* to give up his vacation! God, they must think I'm naive. And a scholarly work for their research on the year 2000 — on the financing of the American student movement. These guys are probably from the secret police.

I hadn't really thought about my little cell room much before, because I assumed it was a very temporary home. But now it appeared this would be my permanent residence in Berlin. That meant that Frau Koch, nice lady, was more than just the mother of a friend showing some kindly hospitality to a foreign guest for a few days. How would I get along all this time without a bed with pillows, I wondered. And that horrible feather cover was just making my hay fever worse. I had sniffed and sneezed in bed every night. I'd have to start listening regularly to a Western station over the old desk radio on top of the bureau in my little room, at least when Bach and Waack weren't around. I had to hold out.

How did they fasten on me? How did they pick me out? Do they know I know something about the American student movement? Do they just intend to pluck information out of me before they arrest me afterward? Or has a long-haired young American — they've read about our kind — come in and played a good game and fooled them? What about their jolly words, uttered amidst chuckles, about watching over me and keeping me prisoner? Did we both know perfectly well where we stood, and were we just acting on *both* sides? I hoped I was fooling them, and they hoped they were fooling me. They certainly weren't fooling me, but maybe I wasn't fooling them either. But it was too late to get out of things now. I had to keep acting and hope. Keep my fear under control, and think about another problem: how would I escape from their grip long enough to find out what the story is in this damn country? Isn't it bizarre what you have to go through just to be able to come in and stay some time in this place? What secrets they must have to hide. There was one little bit of consolation, though, as I went to sleep that restless night. One way or another, I'd have a book to write after all.

CHAPTER 4

THEY HAD A PROGRAM of activities ready for me by the next morning. That day I would visit Potsdam. Two days later Dr. Waack and I would travel to Schwedt, a "socialist new town" near the Polish border. For both trips we would be provided with official cars with chauffeurs, supposedly from the Academy of Sciences.

Potsdam was Prussia's Versailles, with royal grounds containing four castles. At a smaller castle outside the grounds the 1945 Potsdam Conference took place, and in another small palace is an East German war museum. Potsdam is in East German territory right outside West Berlin — you can see a section of the Wall from the park grounds around the Potsdam Conference grounds — and from East Berlin we had to drive around the circumference of the city so that the trip took about an hour by car.

Dr. Waack bought me a luxuriously printed book at the Potsdam Conference hall. It attacked American imperialists, first for wanting to dismember Germany economically to get rid of competition from German monopoly capital, and then for building up and saving said monopoly capital. Waack was curious about what we learned about the Potsdam Conference in our high schools. I told him we learned almost nothing, except that it took place. That surprised him.

"By the way, what is your opinion about the reasons for the

division of Germany after World War Two?" Waack prodded me.

"Well, I don't know too much about it. I haven't really studied the period. But I've always sort of thought that America and the Soviet Union both *said* they wanted German reunification, but actually neither of them really did. People in Europe were afraid of Germany after two world wars. So everyone prevented reunification." I really didn't know very much about the period, but hoped that I had answered acceptably.

"You say you don't know the facts. You should read the facts before you make a judgment. The facts show that the Soviet Union supported German reunification, and the West prevented it."

Were there no limits to what he could say with a straight face? I didn't know much about the events which led to the division of Germany, but I knew what was a bare-faced lie. But I just said I'd be interested to see his facts. Shit, they have lies for everything!

We wandered around the center of town looking for a place to eat lunch. The pattern was already familiar: the façades of the stores were grimy, the pavement was dirty. A family-owned bakery had chocolate eclairs with what looked like real whipped cream in the window, but they were closed for lunch. We didn't get enough food at the restaurant where we ate, but at least Waack kept quiet during lunch. I decided that when the chauffeur drove us home I would try to get a look at the identification papers he showed when we went over the control check between East Berlin and the rest of the D.D.R. Would it say Academy of Sciences or — Ministry of the Interior?

At least once for every castle we visited Waack mentioned how incredibly much money it cost to keep such things up. He appeared to feel the world should be grateful to the D.D.R.

for its unique contributions to the preservation of world culture. He also gave some enormous figure of how many miles of
pathways there were in the park. I was tired from walking
so much and often wanted to sit down on a bench, a tempta-
tion balanced only by my fear that this would increase the
chances for questioning proportionately.

A magnificent gold-framed painting of pilgrims in the Holy
Land glittered on the wall of the giant reception room in the
most striking of the palaces.

"Have you ever been to Israel?" Waack inquired casually.

"No," I lied.

"Do you think there will be a new war in the Mideast?"

Here we go again. "Well, I think that there have been some
good signs that Egypt is willing to accept Israel's right to
exist. That's positive. I think the Israelis should be willing to
withdraw from most of the occupied territories in exchange for
a peace treaty. But I sort of understand the Israeli position.
They don't know whether Sadat will continue in his willing-
ness to accept Israel's existence. On the other hand, if peace
is ever going to come there, the Israelis will have to believe
at some point that the Arabs are sincere."

"Steve, you underestimate the role of the Americans in keeping Israel obstinate. The Israelis would never stay in the occupied territories if they weren't supported by the Americans."

"That's not true." The words just flowed out. "The American
interest is for Israel to get out of those territories and conclude
peace. What interest does *America* have in Israel keeping
those territories? How does that help *America?*"

"The U.S. is gambling on the hope that Israel will conquer
the entire Mideast. In that way the position of the oil monopolies would be saved."

In many years of often crazy discussions on Israel and the

Arabs, I had rarely heard such a ridiculous statement — which is saying a great deal. *"Conquer the entire Mideast?* My God, if the Americans wanted to save their oil interests, wouldn't it have been easier to make friends with the Arabs, who have the oil?"

"But Israel was *created* by the imperialists as part of their global strategy."

"When the UN voted to create Israel, the Soviet Union voted yes and England abstained. The British imperialists opposed the creation of Israel."

He looked confused for a moment, for the first time since I had met Waack, confident Waack, the interrogating machine, actually halted, even stumbled. "Soviet Union — vote *for?* No, that's wrong. *England* voted for and the Soviet Union abstained."

Sorry, Waack, *wrong.* "Look, the American oil companies are anti-Israel. They lobby for the Arabs. Just last year some Rockefellers went to Nixon and told him that his pro-Israel policies were destroying their positions in the Mideast."

He fumbled again. He obviously hadn't read about it in *Neues Deutschland.* "All that — all that — all that is — is — just a question of trying to scare the Israelis, so they don't demand so much aid from the American government. It's shadow-boxing between imperialists." We had left the castles and were out in the park again. Waack stood up and tried to look relaxed. Since I'd met him he'd been wearing a fancy suede leather jacket, which must have made in the West and which he must have saved up to buy. Bach, in contrast, always had a scruffy worn sports jacket on, and a loose-fitting shirt whose collar never stood up right. Waack was a young man on the make.

But this time *I* was breathing down *his* neck. "In nineteen forty-eight the oil companies went to President Truman and told him that he should not allow the creation of Israel, because it would damage their good relations with the Arabs. If American oil interests in the Mideast are in danger, it is because we have been too friendly to Israel. We could have kept the oil otherwise."

"Look, you know the Jews." He stopped, to look for the right way to say it. "The Jews — they're good businessmen. In nineteen forty-eight the oil monopolies were afraid that if Israel was created, the Jews would take over the oil business from them. So they didn't want to let them get a foothold."

It was hard to control myself. "But you said the oil interests are *pro*-Israel? When did they change?"

He looked exasperated, almost angry. *"You're too interested in details, in facts!* You're a typical historian! The important thing is not the details, it is the political tendencies. Israel is supported by the imperialists. The Arabs are supported by the socialist lands."

"Look, why do you think the Arabs turned away from America toward the Soviet Union? Do you think it was political conviction? These leaders are complete opportunists; they'd ally with anyone who was anti-Israel. Israel is the only progressive country in the whole Middle East. The Communist Party is forbidden in every Mideast country except Israel! And the Arabs have all these old Nazis working for them. The man who translated *Mein Kampf* into Arabic is now active in the Egyptian Information Ministry. And there are a number of Nazi war criminals working for the Egyptian government. They'll ally with *anyone*."

"No!" he screamed. "That's a lie. There are no former Nazis working in Egypt." He began yelling; he had finally lost his cool. "You just read the capitalist press, the lies of the capitalist press! They never give the real motives. They only try to confuse people."

I tried to keep calm, and not raise my voice. It wasn't easy. "It so happens that this information on former Nazis in the Egyptian government comes from a distinguished American Communist who disagrees with the official stand of the American Communist Party on the Mideast."

He snapped back. "He is no Communist."

"Why not? Just because he has written about Nazis employed by the Egyptian government? He hasn't been expelled from the Party." Actually, I wasn't sure whether the man I was talking about, M. S. Arnoni, actually was a member of the Communist Party or not. But he had definitely followed a pro-Soviet line, even on issues like Hungary in 1956, except on the Mideast.

"He hasn't been expelled? He should have been!"

"Why? He is a distinguished progressive, who was once in a Nazi concentration camp. He has been an active Communist for many years."

"*Worthless scum.* Like Ernst Fischer, the Austrian. Look at his history as a Communist leader. Head of the Party for years! And then he goes over to the bourgeoisie." Fischer had criticized the invasion of Czechoslovakia and supported the reform policies of Dubcek.

"You just set aside any facts on the Mideast that don't go along with your views, even if they come from Communists."

"Facts, facts. Your facts don't change the political analysis. You must have your political analysis, then you can begin talking about facts."

I gritted my teeth. "Look, Doctor Waack. What facts that I might bring about on the Mideast could, *in principle,* change your mind? Are there any facts which I could tell you, at least in principle, that would cause you to question your own views?"

We kept walking, and I looked for an expression on his face. There was none. We were alone in the park. "Look, let's change the subject. Should we eat anything for dinner before the car comes to pick us up?"

On the trip home I leaned forward in the car for the first half-hour, hoping that when we passed the checkpoint, I might get a glimpse of the driver's identity papers. I didn't succeed.

I was about to get out of the car and go back to my room. "One more thing, Steve. The little ones, your two friends. I think it would be better if you don't see them anymore."

"Why?"

"It's Frau Koch. She has been very nice in offering you a place to stay. It is disturbing for her to have them come up all the time. Anyway, I don't think you can get very much out of talking with them. They're so young, and you can't really have a genuine political discussion with kids who are so young. They can't really have genuine opinions, just some stray feelings. All right?"

I felt the noose tightening.

*

I told Dr. Waack I planned to stay home that night, but in fact I went to a youth center near Alexanderplatz — in the same building which had the cafeteria Rudi and Karl had led me to — that ran a discotheque on Wednesday nights. I arrived about eight, and discovered that the discotheque would be lasting only until nine. One other boy was trying to get in when I arrived; the professional youth at the door, easily pushing thirty, told the kid he couldn't come in because he wasn't well enough shaved or dressed. "What about *him?*" the other boy said, pointing at me. "He's wearing dungarees also." I had on white dungarees and a striped red shirt with a collar. "His clothes are clean and his shirt is respectable." The kid went off sulkily; I went in.

In 1969 I had visited a place with pop music in East Berlin with an East German I had met. He was just visiting, and had heard that one F.D.J. club was holding a pop dance, but wasn't sure how to get there. After taking a long train ride, we got off and looked around. The kid went up to a policeman to ask directions. The policeman just shooed him off, but when the kid told him he was with an American tourist, the officer became much more friendly. "Are you an American?" the policeman asked me as I came up to him. "Let me see your passport." I took it out of my back pocket and he gave us directions and saluted smartly. When we arrived, they told us at the door that there were no tickets left. "I have an American with me," the kid said. "Let me see your passport," asked the girl at the door. They let us in for free. Meanwhile, my friend had gone into the bathroom to change from the blue jeans he had on into a pair of pants he had brought with him in a little vinyl bag. But I happened to have a torn pair of jeans on. As soon as I got upstairs, a guy came up to tell me that I couldn't come any further dressed like that. By then I knew the routine. "I'm an American," I said, and took out my passport. The kid invited me to sit at his table. In back of the bandstand was an enormous sign reading OUR FAITH, OUR LOVE, OUR SOCIALIST FATHERLAND. After a while, I asked him cautiously whether he didn't think the sign was perhaps a bit out of place. "Oh, don't pay any attention to it. That's just the old people who put it up."

There weren't many girls at the discotheque, and those who were there seemed taken. That was disappointing; at that F.D.J. club in 1969 the girl friend of the boy who invited me to his table had almost fallen at my feet. After looking over the scene for a few minutes — the locale resembled a high school gym lit up for a basketball game — I sat down at a table where two guys were sitting, and listened to the music. The disc jockey alternated between Anglo-American rock and East German pop music, invariably bubble-gum style.

"Do you come from Berlin?" I asked the one next to me.

"No."

"Do you have any place where kids can get together and dance like this where you live?"

"Yeah, sure."

I was surprised. "Enough?"

"Sure."

"Where do you live?"

"Hamburg."

I chuckled. "Oh, you mean you're just visiting East Germany?"

"Yeah. I have an aunt who lives here."

"How long have you been here?"

"Six days."

"How does your aunt like it here?"

"She hates it. She'd come to West Germany if she could."

"What's she do here?"

"She's a cleaning woman."

"Are you from the D.D.R.?" I asked his friend.

"Yes." He was proper-looking, with metal-rimmed glasses and a well-pressed pale green shirt. His mouth had a small twitch.

They were playing some ridiculous *D.D.R.–Schlager* — a bumpety-bump heart-thumping number called *"Wunderbar, Wunderbar!"* — and I beat my hands to the music on the formica table. *"Wunderbar, wunderbar,"* I chimed. *"Es lebe unsere D.D.R."* (Long live our D.D.R.) I laughed, and the East German smiled cautiously.

"Can you always tell the difference between a D.D.R. pop song and a West German one?" I asked.

"Yes, I can." He extended out his right hand. "My name is Wolfgang. I am pleased to meet you."

"Are you from Berlin?"

"No, Dresden."

"What do you do?"

"I study mechanical engineering."

"Could I ask you a question? I was in Dresden last weekend, and everywhere you go you see these signs about the Soviet Union. You know, the picture of Brezhnev in a shoe store on the Altmarkt, and a billboard about Soviet railroads right in front of the train station. And Honecker is saying every other minute about how the D.D.R. is bound to the Soviet Union. What does it do for your self-respect as a citizen of the D.D.R.? Do you feel you're a colony, or do you just not pay any attention to it?"

"No, I don't think we feel we're a colony of Russia. We don't pay any attention. You have to go on living your life. You can't pay attention to what they say."

The disc jockey announced the last song. We listened to the music for a moment; they were playing "Yesterday." Wolfgang looked toward me and started to speak, but he choked. He started up again. "*If they would only let us travel!* We would come back." He stared down at me intently. "We would. I promise, we would come back." He pleaded to me as if I were the Grand Inquisitor. "You can live all right here. *We would come back!*" He choked again. "But they are so afraid. They are afraid of the people. They won't let us go."

I was embarrassed. Why had he just burst out like that? We had hardly met, and he was almost shaking. The West German kid just sat there. I thought I had to do something.

"Look, Wolfgang, maybe we can all go out and get an ice cream somewhere. It's still early. All right?"

We invited the West German kid to come along. He had just graduated from tenth grade and was going to be looking for an apprenticeship in the fall but hadn't quite decided what yet. We went over to the same ice-cream bar where Dr. Waack had taken me the first day we met.

"You're a university student," I began. "I'm under the impression that the government is especially worried about university students — you know, with the student revolts in the West. Do they keep students under special watch?"

He thought about my question for a few moments. "They come around and check all the students' rooms sometimes, when we're not there. They check to see if our radios are tuned to Western radio stations. And they were very afraid at the time of Czechoslovakia. A student at our university was talking about what the Russians did. One of the students he was talking with reported him to the administration and the student was expelled."

"How can you live under such conditions?"

"You can't do anything, so you adapt. You can get used to anything." He spoke calmly this time.

The whipped cream of the ice cream was all air, and the West German started bitching. "Why can't you make anything decent in this country? Nothing tastes right here." He was angry at Wolfgang, it seemed. Wolfgang sat impassively and ate his ice cream. "And a discotheque that closes at nine! And where can you find a decent movie in town? It's all crap that they show. Who wants to see those films like *The Liberation*?" He was talking about a Russian World War II spectacular playing at the Kino International next to the ice-cream bar.

Wolfgang began to cower. "They send groups from factories and schools to go see those films. They are not very popular otherwise." He spoke at a snail's pace, like a pedantic professor. His eyes and face twitched.

"During working hours?" I asked.

"Yes. The whole factory will be taken to see the film. It is considered to be ideological education."

"But nobody would go otherwise! Right? Admit it, nobody would go otherwise. Right? *Right?*"

Wolfgang lowered his head and sighed. "Right."

"It's just a waste of money to make those films! They just waste money!" The West German kid sounded triumphant, but it was like a boxer punching away at an opponent who's already down. He went on relentlessly. "Admit it, *nobody* is happy in this place! Everyone you meet here is unhappy. All they want to do is escape to the West. Right? *Isn't that right?*" Wolfgang must have been ten years older than that pip-squeak teenager, but he was being beaten to death, punched hard in the solar plexus. I felt the punches in my own stomach. "In Hamburg, we never meet anyone who begs for *Eastern* money so they can go buy some chewing gum!"

Wolfgang began a pathetic crackle of laughter. Otherwise he kept silent. He had stopped eating.

"There's nobody in West Germany who tries to escape to the East! There's nobody in West Germany who watches Eastern TV." The kid was accusing. "But here, *everyone* watches Western TV. Right? Admit it!"

"Right."

"And your clothes! Everyone in the West has hip clothes, whatever they want to have. Here everything is the same. All you see is everybody wearing the same shirts, the same everything. Why can't you make any nice clothes?"

"Yes," Wolfgang drawled. "It is annoying to constantly see people on the street wearing the same things you have on." He pointed to a brown spring jacket he had on the back of his seat. "I see this jacket around all the time."

I couldn't believe what was happening to me; I felt the need to do something, to say something supporting East Germany, to stop the fight before Wolfgang collapsed. Stop that dumb kid from jabbing on against a listless body.

"Stop it! Look, *he's* not responsible for what the government does. Stop talking to him as if he's in charge of things here!"

*

Rudi and Karl showed up again early the next morning, bright and bouncing. They had of course no way of knowing about Waack's pressure against them. They wanted to go swimming. There was a large public swimming pool in Pankow, only ten minutes away by bus, they said. Herr Bach was coming over to take me out to lunch at one, but I thought it was O.K. to slip out until then.

At the entrance to the swimming pool was a sign saying it had been built entirely with thousands of hours of volunteer labor. It was hot and the pool was filled. My brother always makes fun of suntan lotion and says it's worthless, but here I saw endless waves of sunburned people, with only the occasional bronzed complexion. In East Germany they have no suntan lotion.

"Steve, we have to get some way for you to escape from Doctor Waack. He can't determine what friends you have and when you see them."

As if to contradict Karl's little bit of naiveté, I looked at my watch and said, "We've got to get going. Herr Bach is seeing me for lunch."

Bach was over a half-hour late. I was beginning to get their strategy: have at least one activity prepared for me each day, preferably in the middle of the day so as to break up my time into little bits and pieces. Announce one time and come much later, thus forcing me to be home even more and giving me less time on my own. Divide up my day so as to cut me off from the possibility of meeting normal people, off from anyone but themselves.

But I still didn't know what they were after, or whether I was fooling them. If it didn't involve me, this could be an interesting mystery to follow.

"I'm sorry for the long delay." Herr Bach waved as he entered. "I was tied up at the office and then there were all sorts of problems with the traffic lights on the way over. It's this damned heat, you know."

"Yes, it has been getting hot. You know, I hoped we could pick up some apple juice on the way back from lunch today. Frau Koch has run out."

Herr Bach kept silent for a second. "Yes, well, we can try. With this hot weather, you know, sometimes the stores run out of fruit juices. But they should have at least one flavor—maybe cherry."

Bach still had the office car. "Well." He beamed. "Did you spend the morning working on your report on the student movement?"

I hesitated, but then thought it best to tell the truth. "No, uh, I — I went to the pool with Karl and Rudi."

He glanced toward me in a fatherly way for an instant, and then looked back at the road. "Steve, I think it would be better if your friends didn't come over to Frau Koch's house anymore. Both of them are very nice, and Frau Koch likes them very much. But, the neighbors — her neighbors have been getting very suspicious. You know, they wonder why strange people are coming to visit her. They ask questions."

Instead of commenting about what Bach had just revealed about the type of society he lived in, I said only, "Sure. I understand."

"Well, when we're through with lunch, I'll drive you back home — and you can spend the rest of the day working on your report." Herr Bach's voice was boisterously friendly.

This time, at least, I'd better follow the advice and get some work done for them. Frau Koch was probably reporting on my comings and goings anyway.

*

Herr Bach had promised to come over the next morning around eleven to ask how my work was coming along. At twelve Waack was supposed to come, with a chauffeur, for our trip to Schwedt, the socialist new town.

"Any opinions?" I inquired, as Herr Bach looked over my three typed pages.

"We'll wait until it's all through." He smiled.

Waack was late, but Bach said he'd wait because he had something important to give him. While we were all sitting in the living room — I was reading the morning's *Berliner Zeitung* — Herr Bach asked if I would excuse him and Frau Koch for a moment. They went into the kitchen, closed the door, and spoke low enough so that I couldn't even hear them when I passed by the kitchen to go to the bathroom. It was surprising how Herr Bach didn't even *attempt* to explain why they should have something to discuss that I wasn't supposed to hear. A clue? Was this after all just a game where both of us were acting but *neither* was fooling the other?

After emerging from the kitchen, Bach tried to call Waack at his office. When nobody answered, he announced that he was going out to look for his colleague.

"But is that a good idea?" I asked, with genuine sincerity. "If he's not at his office, how can you know where to find him? He'll probably come here while you're gone, and then it will just create more delay. If you have to give him something,

isn't it best for you to stay put right here, and give it to him
when he shows up?"

He didn't even attempt to answer my point, but just repeated he was leaving.

We were alone again, and Frau Koch asked me to sit down
on the sofa. "Steve, I don't know if Herr Bach or Doctor Waack
has talked with you about this — and I hope you don't regard it
as a criticism of you or your friends — but there are problems
with Rudi and Karl coming here. They are very nice boys, maybe a little wild, but still nice. But the neighbors are very suspicious. The other day they were waiting outside the house for
you, while you were still sleeping, and one of the ladies downstairs asked them what they were doing here. Rudi said something about how they were visiting an American friend who
lived here, and wasn't he lucky he was an American and could
travel wherever he wanted to, and how they would like to live
in West Germany instead of the D.D.R."

"Oh, that's funny. That's strange they said that."

"So, you understand, Steve . . ."

She was part of the conspiracy. Too bad, she's a nice grand-
mother.

Shortly after one, Dr. Waack arrived. "Herr Bach left about
a half-hour ago looking for you." I sighed. "He had something
to give you. Now we'll have to wait for him."

"No we won't. I met Herr Bach and got the things from him."

Where did Herr Bach know to fetch Doctor Waack? He
wasn't at his office at the Academy of Sciences, so that meant
he had to be at his desk — where?

✻

Schwedt used to be a small agricultural village with a small
tobacco industry. During the sixties they developed it into a
petrochemical center using Russian oil piped in through Poland.

The construction of new housing there began around 1965. As a completely new town, it was a chance, Dr. Waack announced solemnly while we were driving there, to demonstrate socialist principles of city planning.

Schwedt was in the middle of nowhere, surrounded by farm-land and a narrow, winding road. Just outside the town were some small shacks. Dr. Waack said they were weekend homes of workers in Schwedt. Shortly after, apartment houses rose up from the golden-brown fields nearby. The area around the apartments themselves, however, was still muddy and bare, even though the houses looked old — more than five years old in fact. The center of town had a main street, with some white and red apartments that looked considerably newer and finer than the slummy areas on the road into the center. There was even a fountain to brighten things up. Did the white-collar workers and managers live there, the workers in the treeless wastelands, I wondered to myself. Across the street from the nice apartments was a half-completed Centrum Department Store, and a few other shops.

We got out of the car for about an hour to have lunch but didn't get a chance to see much. "I haven't been here for a long time. It's even nicer than I expected. Really quite an achieve-ment of socialist town planning. The next time you visit the D.D.R. it will be even better, I can assure you," Waack ex-plained.

"Nice, yes, *very* nice," I reeled off, but actually what I was thinking about was Waack's statement, "the next time you visit the D.D.R." In my search after clues, this was a positive one.

Maybe Schwedt impressed Waack simply because he had never seen so many newly built apartment houses in one place before. Otherwise, it was certainly hard to see what was par-ticularly socialist about it. I hadn't really seen enough to form an opinion. It would be great, I thought to myself, if somehow I could contact the guy from Schwedt I had met in 1969. I'd have to try to write him a letter from East Berlin. That would certainly get through, they can hardly check domestic mail.

One thing was curious: we were waiting in line to get some cherries outside a supermarket. A man came by whom Waack recognized immediately. "Hey, how are you doing? Haven't seen you for a long time."

"What are you doing in Schwedt?" the guy inquired.

"I have an American guest with me. I'm showing him the city."

At this point the man said good-bye with a smile and just went on, without continuing the discussion. He was, Waack said, a friend of his from Berlin. What was *he* doing in Schwedt, I wondered. And why did he stop the conversation so soon? Was he a friend from the secret police traveling around on an assignment in the provinces?

*

"Let's go in the water," I tentatively suggested as soon as we arrived at a lake on the way back to Berlin. We were to spend the rest of the afternoon there. "I have my bathing suit on right under my pants." There were maybe ten families scattered around the lakeside. One radio blared out rock from a West German station. I gave no sign of paying any attention to it.

"No, let's have a discussion first," Waack answered predictably. "We can sunbathe while we're talking, and then go swimming when we're nice and hot."

"O.K.," I answered bravely.

"I was interested in discussing with you whether you believe in the convergence theory."

That sounded obscure, or at best academic. I had no answer,

so I responded with a question. "You mean the sociological theory that socialist and capitalist societies are moving closer together as the level of economic development increases?"

"Yes."

Now, what would a Communist think about that, I asked myself. He would not particularly like it, I guessed — he wouldn't want to say that his society was becoming more like America or Western Europe. "Well, I don't think it's correct," I said, attempting authority.

"*Why?*" His staccato question came immediately, and sounded threatening.

"Why?" I hesitated for thinking space. "Because — because I don't think that — that the politically ruling groups in either society will encourage basic changes in their systems. And I think that both America and the Soviet Union are relatively stable countries politically."

I frankly wasn't very satisfied with the orthodoxy of my reply, but it was the best I could come up with on short notice. I looked at Waack for his reaction. He didn't appear to have one, in fact he didn't appear to have been listening. Instead, as soon as I was through, he bounced back. "So, in other words you support the action of the socialist community in Czechoslovakia in nineteen sixty-eight."

That Czechoslovakia would come up eventually in some "discussion" I had accepted as inevitable, and I had even thought through my approach to the subject. But Waack's incredible jump took me utterly by surprise. For once, I reacted impulsively. "*What?* I don't understand your point. What's the connection?"

"The convergence theory is the part of the imperialist global strategy designed to fight socialism in the already socialist part of the world. It tries to mislead people in the socialist countries that they should take a step forward to bourgeois democracy and Western freedoms. The imperialists tried to apply this strategy in Czechoslovakia, but they were defeated. Or — or do you have a different version of the events?" He almost leered. What he had said of course bore no relationship to the convergence theory, which was an academic theory in the early sixties associated mainly with those who tried to argue that the Russians weren't so bad after all, because gradually they'd become more democratic. But, ignoring that, I began instead speaking from memory my prepared reply on Czechoslovakia.

"I feel that the action of the Soviet Union in Czechoslovakia was necessary from the viewpoint of the security of the socialist camp. It would have posed a great military threat to the socialist camp if, for example, West Germany gained a foothold in Czechoslovakia. But from the internal point of view of Czechoslovakia, I think the Czech people under normal circumstances should have had the right to make whatever political changes they wanted to make. Except that in this case that right unfortunately had to give way to the security needs of the socialist bloc. So the Czechs had to make a sacrifice. You see my point?"

Waack picked up the long stem of a weed and started playing with it. "There is no contradiction between the interests of the Czech people and those of the socialist camp. We acted in the Czech people's interests. What the socialist community did was to prevent the Czechs from taking a step backward. *That* they are not allowed to do — they can't turn back the clock of history."

"But certainly there is overwhelming evidence that Dubcek had the support of most Czechs in doing what he was doing."

"They were misled."

"*You* may believe they were misled. Even *I* may believe they were misled. But under normal circumstances, the people have the right to make the political decisions they want to. As I said, larger considerations came in here, and therefore I support the actions of the Soviet Union, but it was too bad for the Czechs."

He looked at me like an elementary schoolteacher who has begun to get annoyed at a pupil who is particularly slow at learning his multiplication tables. "Steve, I have already told you that you are much too concerned with what the people happen to think. It doesn't matter the slightest what the people of Czechoslovakia happened to think at the moment. They cannot be permitted to take a step backward."

"But what do you think the basis of legitimacy of a government is then? How many mistakes is a government allowed to make before the people have a right to replace it if they want? What if ninety-five percent of the people are for a change?"

"Certainly the Czech government made mistakes. And these should be corrected. But the people cannot be allowed to turn against socialism just because a government makes mistakes. It is this that the Czech people were misled to do."

"Misled? Misled by whom? All the press and mass media were controlled by the government, they always told about how good the government was. If people turned against the government, it must have been because of their own life experiences."

He stared at me. "It's those *radio stations* — Radio Free Europe, RIAS, the whole filthy lot." His expression became suddenly wild and fiery. "The ones whose business it is to incite people against socialism. Those rabble-rousing stations got everyone to listen to their lies."

"But why did people listen to them?"

He raised his head toward the sun shining down bright on us. He didn't raise his voice, but he spoke with steel in it. "First they attract them with the wild music. That makes them listen, because our radio stations don't play such music. And then — and then they also listen — they also listen because we tell them not to. We tell them they shouldn't listen, so our people become curious. It's just natural curiosity, nothing more." Waack had clearly stopped thinking about Czechoslovakia and was reflecting now about his fellow East Germans.

The natural response was too good to avoid. "But if you know that telling people not to listen to these stations just makes them listen, why don't you just stop telling people not to listen?"

I got the annoyed-teacher look again. "But these stations are telling *lies*. We *must* warn our people against them."

"But why are you so worried about them if they're lying? People won't pay much attention to them for long if they're lying."

He wrenched his head away from the sun and looked me in the eye. "My friend, that is our great problem. These stations have unfortunately convinced many of our people that *they* are telling the truth, and that *we* are lying."

There was no reply I dared give, so I suggested that the time had come to go into the water. We could continue the discussion afterward.

"You know, Doctor Waack," I began after drying myself off in the sun after bathing, "a lot of the things you've been saying bring us back to a question I raised that day we went to the Soviet war memorial. You know — about decision-making in the socialist countries, the so-called dictatorship of the proletariat. This is the biggest question I have about practices in the socialist lands. Let's take the SST plane. In America many people said it was a waste of money, and that we should spend the money on hospitals or houses instead. What about the Soviet Union? Wasn't there anyone who thought it would be better to spend the money they're spending on the SST on houses instead? We all know the Soviet Union has a big housing shortage."

"The decision was unanimous."

"Unanimous? I can't believe that. You mean *nobody* opposed the SST?"

"Well, maybe at first. But in all decisions the procedure is for the representatives of the people to discuss a decision until they all come to a common position. The final decision is then unanimous."

"But what about the discussion before the final decision? Could the public take part in it?"

"No, what would be the good of that?"

"What would be the good? Well, so the people could say what policy they wanted the government to follow."

"Are you serious? Why do the people elect representatives if not to make decisions for them? Your idea would be the *death* of socialism. This is your famous American democracy — your so-called 'public opinion.' This is America, 'the freest land in the world.' Not for the socialist countries! For the socialist countries, this is pure *poison*."

"Why would it be the death of socialism to have a discussion?"

"Steve, you are so naive! With the capitalists always looking for any opportunity to stir up dissension in the socialist countries. You don't realize how *long* it takes to convince people of socialism, what a difficult task that is. You think things were bad in Czechoslovakia! They've had socialism for *fifty years* in the Soviet Union, and *still* forty percent of the people are not convinced, I'm telling you. Them, and all the waverers. How long do you think a government could hold power if they allowed the kind of discussion you talk about? Our discussions must be top secret. That's the only way to survive."

On the trip home my rage welled up inside at Waack's hatefulness. For them everything is a one-way process. It's all right — indeed, it's required — for Communists in the West to exploit for their own ends all possible discontents, injustices, and grievances. *But* — once they get power, the show is over! There's no possibility to change your mind, regret your decision, turn the clock back. The same — or worse, much worse — grievances cannot provide the occasion for shifting rulers. I wanted to ask the bastard: if "your famous American democracy" can survive all that open discussion, why can't the places *you* lord over?

Instead of staying home that night, as Dr. Waack thought I would, I went into town to the new Bowling Zentrum off Alexanderplatz. I told Frau Koch I was going bowling, which was clearly better than saying I wanted to meet people while bowling.

I got a look at the Bowling Zentrum, but the place was filled up and the lady behind the cash register told me there were no free places the entire evening. An old man in a railroad conductor's hat standing at the door checked to make certain people were dressed right, and inside were maybe fifteen lanes with AMF equipment.

"On a Friday night like this you have to make a reservation a week or so in advance. Remember, this is the only bowling alley in the D.D.R." On my way out I had stopped a young, smartly dressed couple who were also on their way out, and asked them whether it was always hard to get an alley. When they found out I was American, the guy said, in English, that he was studying English, and invited me to join them for a drink at the bar of the Interhotel at Alexanderplatz.

"This is East Berlin at night," the boy said grandiloquently, returning to German and sweeping his arms to encompass Alex.

"Not much compared to New York, heh? But it's an improvement on what we had before. And wait — in five years there'll be even more."

"What did you have before?"

"Nothing," the girl retorted.

She wasn't exactly good-looking, but she had a certain class — her hair was done up, but not too ostentatiously, and she was made-up, but not too gaudily. We sat down at a tiny table in the small bar, and she planted her legs so they pressed mine. A stereo system in the background played Tom Jones.

"I notice they have Western music here. Isn't that usually disapproved of?"

He answered. "They want to get Western tourists to this bar. Anything for foreign currency, you know." He rubbed his fingers together expressively.

"But you think things are getting better here than the way they were before?"

"Yes, definitely."

"How?"

"Well, like the Bowling Zentrum. We're still way behind, but at least they provide *some* things for people now."

"What do you think?" I asked the girl.

"The problem is that everything is so inefficient. Everything has to be according to the plan, you have to have a quota for everything. I work at the D.D.R. Travel Bureau, and we have a plan for how many tours we must sell. And each worker is supposed to meet his quota for selling tours."

"What happens if you don't meet your quota? Do they take it off your wages?"

"Well, usually the problem is just the opposite. The number of tours we can sell is regulated by treaties between us and other socialist countries. We sign an agreement to offer them so-and-so many tours for their people to the D.D.R. in exchange for them offering us so-and-so many tours to their country. But it's never enough. We always run out of tours, especially for a country like Hungary, which is popular. So sometimes we'll just have weeks and weeks where people will come in and we have no tours to offer them. We just sit there at work and do nothing."

"But can't people visit these countries alone?"

"Well, some of them they can visit, but it's much harder. They have trouble getting hotel reservations as individuals, so they have to camp out or stay with people they know. And sometimes it can be a problem getting a visa. For Russia, if you want to travel on your own you need an invitation from a Russian, and they make sure it's a rich Russian before they let you go, so you'll get a good impression, because most Russians are very poor. Actually, they prefer people to travel in a group. But another problem is that a lot of time we'll have a group reservation with another country, and then they will cancel it at the last moment because they've gotten a Western tourist group in that hotel space instead. They want to get the Western currency so much that they just cancel our reservations and pay us damages. But then we have nothing to offer the people who made the reservations except their money back."

"Let me ask you both another question. If there were a completely free election, and people could vote for or against the government, what do you think would happen?"

"I would love to know the answer to that," the guy mused, sipping his gin. "But you can't know. Berlin is very reactionary, you know, because of West Berlin nearby and all that. But if you go out into the villages, I bet that there they believe everything that's fed them."

"Lars, I think you're exaggerating," the girl said, turning her face to him. "The only ones who are convinced are those who get paid off by the system."

"Well, it depends what you mean by convinced. I think that a lot of younger people believe in socialism, but they criticize the way it is practiced here."

"How does that compare with the older people?" I asked.

"The older people take more extreme positions. A few people absolutely *love* it, and many absolutely *hate* it. I think young people are more pragmatic. We don't have any great hopes. We just adapt to the system. You can get used to anything, you know."

"You can get used to anything — I've heard that before."

"That's what you have to do. You have to adapt. It's the only way."

"Lars, I think that *our* children will be convinced by the system. They get to them so early — our Jan is getting Lenin in his day nursery already."

"Look," I asked, "when you say you have to adapt, what is it that's hardest to adapt to? What is it that bothers you most?"

"It's the sham of everything. You're not allowed to have your own opinion," she exclaimed. "You have to put on a false face all the time. You know, last week we had a meeting in our office about the new Five-Year Plan. Everyone had to come. The workers came because their section leader said they had to. The section leader called the meeting because his boss said *he* had to. *His* boss was told by a higher boss. Nobody believed in it. They all just did it. They told me I had to give a report for the meeting. So I just copied something out of the newspaper and read it right out. My boss didn't care that it was just copied. Nobody was listening, half the girls were dozing. My boss didn't care about that either. Just as long as they go through the motions, so they can say they had their meeting."

"You know," I said, "that's something I've been giving a lot of thought to since I came here. Who actually *believes* in the system here? Is it all a huge game, or are there at least some people who *genuinely* believe in it? If everybody is acting, who are they acting *for?*"

"All those meetings are making somebody up there very happy, but who knows how high up you have to get before people start actually believing in them."

*

Saturday and Sunday I was supposed to work on finishing my little exercise, interrupted by a Saturday dinner with Waack and a Sunday visit to the season's final performance of Bertolt Brecht's old Berliner Ensemble. Since my arrival I had been talking about my admiration for Brecht, and humming Brecht songs, only to note a somewhat dampened tone about him from Bach and Waack — "Yes, Brecht is fine, but not only Brecht." Maybe they were less than enthusiastic because Brecht's disillusionment with the East German regime in the years before his death in 1955 was even greater than the West knew. At any rate I had been promised tickets for *The Threepenny Opera*, and, even after it turned out that tickets were sold out at the public ticket bureau, Bach told me he could probably arrange something.

When Waack came over for dinner on Saturday — I had actually stayed home working all day, listening on the side to the American Forces Radio from West Berlin on Frau Koch's radio in my little room — he gleefully took a ticket out of his wallet and thrust it before me. A fourth row seat — I was happy enough even to forget for a minute how I felt about him.

"May I see what you're planning to wear tomorrow, Steve?"

"Oh, don't worry, Doctor Waack, I plan to dress up. I'll have a jacket and tie."

"Let me ask you something. Remember you said when you

came back from Dresden how dirty you felt after not shaving for a few days, how you couldn't understand how people wear beards?"

"What about it?"

"How can you wear *such long hair?* It's so unkempt, so sloppy. I can understand why youth in the capitalist countries want to wear long hair and dirty clothes as a protest against their societies, but you're in a socialist country now. Here we expect that our citizens keep themselves presentable."

"I like my hair long. I'm not wearing it that way as a protest — you sound like my mother! And I can't change hair styles just because I come to another country."

"Steve, may I ask you to get your hair cut?" It hadn't been cut since March in Hong Kong, but I didn't want to cut it again yet.

"Look, I'll be wearing a very nice jacket and tie tomorrow. You'll see, I'll look very nice." I offered to go to my room and put on the outfit for him.

It was a dark green jacket, yellow shirt, and wide tie which I had gotten custom-made in Hong Kong. When I emerged from my room, Waack longingly looked at me, and finally came up and felt the material on the jacket and the tie. "Well," he sighed, "people will certainly know tomorrow night that you don't come from the D.D.R."

For the first time, I came upon an electrifying thought: Maybe even Waack is not *really* convinced!

*

Monday I was to go to the SAS office in East Berlin about a ticket for Stockholm for August 9, finish up my student movement paper, and pack for the trip to Leipzig the next day. The

SAS office, on Unter den Linten, told me they could not sell tickets and that I'd have to go to the East German airline Interflug offices on Karl Marx Allee — and also that they had no Swedish newspapers because they couldn't be brought into the D.D.R. That gave me a free hour or so before Dr. Waack was supposed to telephone to ask how I was doing. I walked the little distance along Friedrichstrasse, past the Hotel Unter den Linten, where a large crowd of people were standing gaping at an American car parked in the entranceway, toward a canteen selling soft drinks right near the Friedrichstrasse border crossing. I was hot, hot enough even to buy an East German Club Cola after they were sold out of lemon soda at the little stand.

"What are all those people waiting in line for over there?" I asked a middle-aged lady with me at one of the small metal café tables, with a sun umbrella over it, next to the canteen. On the other side of the street a fruit-and-vegetable stand had a good fifty people waiting in a double line. My question was mock-naive; I assumed they were queuing for peaches or bananas. Every day on the trip from Binzstrasse I had seen an enormous line outside of one particular stand, while other similar stores, which had no fresh produce, were empty.

"They're waiting for tomatoes," the lady answered in a bored tone.

That did genuinely surprise me. "Tomatoes? They make a line like that for tomatoes too? I thought tomatoes were pretty easy to find in the summer."

"Nothing decent is easy to find. You a foreigner?"

"American."

"Let me tell you. In your country, the stores fight with each other for customers. The customer is king. Here, the customers fight with each other for things to buy, and the stores couldn't care less."

"But let me ask you something. Aren't things getting better than they were before?"

"Getting better? Who told you that?" She guffawed, looking toward her husband sitting next to her sipping a soda. "Things just get worse. They're worse now than in nineteen fifty-seven. You know, before that you could get fresh vegetables. Ever since the Wall, they know they have us caught here."

"But what about things like the new buildings at Alexanderplatz?"

"What's the use of having new buildings at Alexanderplatz, when still none of them sell any bananas?"

"Another question. You know, I read about 'socialist competition,' and 'fighting for the state title Collective of Socialist Labor.' What does all that mean?"

"It means they try to get workers to work harder and faster for the same pay. They work them so fast in the factories that the quality is horrible. And we get all the worst junk. If a refrigerator or a TV set that they're going to send to Hungary doesn't pass the test, they sell it to us. They don't care if it breaks down and it takes months to get it repaired."

The husband was a balding gray man with a mustache and a worker's cap. I asked him where he worked.

"I'm a waiter in a restaurant."

"How many tables do you work?"

"It used to be six, but now it's eight. I should be retired already, but who can live on the pension they give us, so I keep on working."

"The only decent things around are in the Intershops," interrupted the wife, scowling. "But of course we can't go there."

"Don't you have any West German relatives who can send you money?"

"No, we don't."

"It's discrimination, that's what it is," I declared. "Imagine having stores in your own country where *you* can't go but foreigners can. It's like when the British in India kept the Indians out of places."

The lady gave a vindicated look. "See what the boy says, Willy! It's discrimination. That's what it is. *Discrimination.*"

"It must be pretty hard to put up with, ma'm."

"And I'll tell you another thing! The shoes they make — they're horrible. My legs ache after walking around in them a little while, they're so hard. And I wanted to get some leather boots, plain boots — the kind every woman in your country has. *Six months* I had to wait before they got any in stock. Six months!"

*

I was curious to see whether they would search the baggage I was leaving in Frau Koch's apartment while I was gone, so I prepared six small tests to be able to check on returning. There was a penny hidden in a pair of shorts sprawled over the top of the suitcase. Even the slightest movement of the shorts would cause the penny to move from its position inside one of the legs, which position I indicated with a pen mark. The end of the string along a Japanese fan was made to coincide exactly with the edge of a handkerchief. Two airline baggage-claim checks among many in an envelope — souvenirs from the Asia trip — were placed exactly back to back against each other.

I was, however, worried (as opposed to just curious) about my notes. I didn't dare take my notebook with me because I assumed that Waack and I would either be sharing a room, or that he would search my things. I put the book in the vest pocket of one of my three sports jackets hanging on a hanger on the door of my room. The top button of the jacket I closed. I stuck the left pocket flap inside the pocket. That might give me an indication of whether they had been checking around. I put some sheets of loose paper into the back pocket of the blue jeans I was planning to wear to Leipzig. It was a deep pocket, and I could write my notes while going to the bathroom at night.

Having answered Dr. Waack's phone call for the day — it came almost two hours late — and packed my things, I went to Alex for dinner. The grill bar has, I noticed, a peculiar arrangement by which the main course and dessert are served in two separate, but adjacent, establishments, so that if you want a dessert you have to get up, go over into the milk bar, and wait again. I got myself both courses, and waited twice.

It was a dark, cool evening with a navy blue sky, and the fountain at Alex was lit up. A drunk was splashing himself in the water, and yelling out incomprehensible things. Then he started climbing onto the metal discs from which the waters spouted. First people chuckled and cheered him on, but then, when he got up to the top, singing and hovering, they realized that the man might fall and crack his body to pieces. Soon the man tumbled down into the shallow water and started crying. When he fell, two policemen who had been standing around got him from the water and took him away.

As they were leaving, a tall, blond boy next to me turned around and whispered, "You want to sell your watch?"

"No."

"What about money exchange?"

"What about just sitting down and having a friendly conversation?" I said.

"O.K. Where is your watch from?"

"Japan. You know, it's funny. Japan is in terms of income poorer than the D.D.R. But think of all the things they make that people want to buy. Does the D.D.R. have anything you can sell to places outside the Communist bloc?"

That had been a rhetorical statement, but the kid answered anyway. "We have beef and pork that the West Germans want. The West Germans come to our collective farms and just put their stamp on all our best meat. We get what's left, if anything."

"How do you know that?"

"I'm an apprentice cook in a restaurant. I can tell you a lot about how our so-called socialist economy functions. It's not like what they teach us in school."

"What do you mean?"

"They teach us that in a socialist economy all the workers work for the good of the collective. That's a lie. Every worker works for himself and only himself. He couldn't care less about helping other workers. And the conditions! In our kitchen it's over one hundred degrees most of the time. You can almost die. That's why I try to skip work as often as I can. Once I believed in this system, but you learn different as soon as you get out and work."

"Let me ask you. The schoolbooks also say that the Communist Party is the party of the working class. Do the workers where you work regard it that way?"

"No, why should they?"

"How many are Party members?"

He thought for a moment. "None, I think. The only Party member is the boss of the restaurant."

"The *only* one?" I was honestly taken aback.

"You know what S.E.D. stands for?" an old, weatherbeaten guy with gray whiskers and two missing teeth, sitting next to the kid, asked me.

"Yeah, *Sozialistische Einheitspartei Deutschlands*," I replied, Socialist Unity Party of Germany.

"Wrong. It means *So endet Deutschland*." So ends Germany. The blond kid laughed.

"Let me ask you — those houses over there — who lives in them? Is it just bosses and Party members, or are there any workers there?"

"The Saxons," punctuated the old guy. The kid laughed again.

"The Saxons? I don't understand."

"Ulbricht is from Saxony, Leipzig. He brought up his cronies to Berlin to help him run things."

"Son, let me say something to you," the old man began. "I'm a Communist. I mean, I *was* a Communist before the war. But this is no Communism the way Ernst Thälmann preached it. This is just the Saxons getting rich and the Russians stealing half of what we make. You know what, son? The big shots, the Saxons, they get paid part of their wage in Western money, so they can shop at the Intershop in there." He pointed to the Interhotel.

"Is *that* true? I didn't know that," the kid gasped.

"I know someone who works in a bank where they come in and collect their Western money. They have little slips which entitle them. They call it 'for special services to the state' or something like that. But let *us* try to get a little money on the black market so we can go in there, and we're criminals."

"Another question. You work at a factory, sir?"

"Yeah. Lathe operator."

"What about strikes? Would the workers want to strike if they could?"

"De wo'kers can't strike against dose who own de means o' production, becoz de'd be strikin' 'ginst demselves." He imitated Ulbricht's heavy Saxon accent.

"Well, what about it? Do people believe that?"

"The only thing people believe is that if you put a lot of meat and a little water together in a pot and cook it, you'll get some broth. But who can do anything? They would come in with the army if any workers lifted a finger to strike. And the Russians would come in if we just rose up. You know what happened in Czechoslovakia."

Suddenly a camera flashed twice in quick succession, dramatically breaking the night's darkness. "Plainclothesmen!" the man spat out. "It's the damn plainclothesmen again, harassing people." That got me scared — that *I* might be in their picture. I said I'd have to be getting home because I was leaving for Leipzig early the next morning. But maybe we could all meet again after I came back. I got the kid's address and promised to write him during my trip away from Berlin. And next time we all met, I'd bring along a jar of coffee.

"Sir, let me just ask you one final question. What about diplomatic recognition of the D.D.R. Should the West do it?"

"No, no, never. It would just give the Saxons legitimacy. They would use it to crush people's will to resist. And let me tell you something else. You shouldn't get out of Vietnam either. America must be strong, or else the Communists will take over the world."

So, Leipzig is where Ulbricht is from. Well, while I was there, I'd somehow have to find out what the Saxons thought of him.

CHAPTER 5

FOR THREE DAYS in Leipzig Waack never let his eyes off me. We were to have a busy schedule: museums by day, films by night. At least we got separate rooms, next to each other, in a hotel opposite Central Station. The first night Waack took me to see an East German World War II resistance film, about an underground group with a spy in the army staff. He warned me in advance that the theater would probably be empty, the picture having come out "last spring already." It was, although there actually were other people there besides ourselves.

The movie characters spoke like editorials in *Neues Deutschland.* "When Hitler attacked England, France, and Norway," a member of the resistance group told an exile, with Alpine skiers in the background, "he was not attacking them to change their social system. But the attack against the Soviet Union is an attempt to turn back the clock of history!" Or, a man by his hearth: "We must think of a new order after Hitler, which eliminates the system which uses fascism as a way to save itself."

Leipzig, site of a 900-year-old trade fair which businessmen from the whole world still attend, was the first city to be rebuilt, as a semishowplace, after the war. In front of Central Station are a modern department store called Konsument and a few new apartment houses. When we got an overview of the entire city from atop the victory monument against Napoleon (erected after 1814), I could see that the city's only other rows of new apartments were built adjacent to the fair grounds. An enormous Leipzig Information Center near the station provides information for foreign visitors. It was air-conditioned and virtually empty. A hundred yards away is the D.D.R. Travel Bureau, for the natives. It is a fourth the size of the Information Center, but had ten or twenty times as many people in it.

Leipzig is filled with *Gendenkstätten der deutschen Arbeiterbewegung* (memorials of the German Labor Movement). Lenin lived there for a time and put out his newspaper *Iskra*. Karl Liebknecht, co-founder of German Communism, grew up there. Hitler's Reichstag Fire show trial took place there. We visited all the *Gedenkstätten* in detail. "One of the best films our film industry ever made was about the life of Karl Liebknecht," Waack told me. "But then the actor who played Liebknecht defected to West Germany, so now we don't show it anymore."

Waack was a demanding restaurant customer, always complaining about the service. The morning after we arrived he told the waitress that the coffee was cold and the bread hard, and demanded she take them back. Whenever we had to wait at a restaurant, he would go up to people and tell them to hurry out. There was a fish restaurant near the hotel which was quite good, and where we went three times in three days, despite the waits. The second time he made a move to rush up and grab two seats which were being vacated. "No, Doctor Waack, let that couple take them," I said, pointing to a man and wife at the other side of the restaurant. "They were here before us."

"What are you talking about? When there are no seats like this, you have to just watch out for yourself."

I restrained Waack with my arm, and the couple got their seats.

Waack generally ordered us both a beer as soon as we came in, and then we got another one, or sometimes a glass of juice, during the meal. He would often get a third beer, but I rarely did. "I'm underweight, you know, Doctor Waack. So I drink beers partly to keep my weight up. But I shouldn't drink too many, because I hold alcohol very poorly. I just get sick and throw up if I drink too much."

Waack smiled the first human smile I had ever seen from him. "Steve, you won't believe it, but one night I had *twenty-six* beers with some school buddies. We all just kept drinking the whole night, till five in the morning. And with that, I had two whole bottles of wine! Wow, what a time we had — but I didn't get sick, I didn't get a hangover, you know, I didn't even feel that drunk."

I had seen Waack's human side.

As we left the hotel the second day, he asked me where I was keeping my money. In a drawer in the desk, I told him. "Hide it. Hide it in one of those magazines, and stuff it into your duffel bag. It could get stolen otherwise."

"But— "

"Look, Steve, remember this: men are still bad, even under socialism."

We waited for a tram after breakfast in front of the station. Some men were taking down some big D.D.R. and Red flags flying from a huge flagpole on the other side of the street. It was drizzling, but flags were left lying on the ground for several minutes until all of them had been taken down and could be put in the truck.

"Doctor Waack, isn't it considered disrepectful in the D.D.R. to let the national flag touch the ground? It is in America."

Waack glanced at the flags and looked straight at me. "No, it's not disrespectful. If it were, the police would be here — quicker than you think."

After our Czechoslovakia discussion he had promised to lend me his personal copy of a recent book, *Ernst Fischer: Ein Moderner Marxist?*, which dealt with the former Austrian Communist leader who had, as Waack put it, "many of the misconceptions you have." He presented it to me on the train to Leipzig, and told me he hoped I could read it soon so we could discuss it together.

"I hope, Steve, that in general you'll ask me more *questions* than you've been asking up to now. That's what I'm here for, to answer your questions."

"O.K., I will."

Waack hesitated the slightest moment, as if for dramatic effect. "Just one thing. No provocative questions — like that one in Treptower Park about why we don't produce more blue jeans."

My God, how did he remember *that?* Again I felt scared. Was he taking notes on what I was saying, just as I was taking notes on him? For what?

Our last day in Leipzig, I had indicated, I wanted to spend some time walking around on my own, just seeing "what the city is like." Waack had listened to my request without reaction at first, and the only thing we had planned for the day was the visit to that victory-over-Napoleon monument. Maybe I'd get the afternoon free.

As we were walking back to the bus stop from the monument, I proudly told Dr. Waack that I had started the Fischer book. "Doctor Waack, I was interested in knowing whether Fischer is given a chance to defend himself. It's good that there is an attack on him, but can you read Fischer's books also?"

"*Fischer's* books? Certainly, if you are a legitimate research scholar who needs them for academic purposes, there is the possibility of getting hold of them."

"No, but let's just say the normal university student."

Waack chuckled. "No, no, of course not. That is *your* system — if you have a book *against* Fischer, you must also have a book *for* Fischer. That is not the dictatorship of the proletariat. Our students can read a summary of what Fischer says in books like the one you're reading. It's a question of trust. Our students must trust our scholars to make accurate summaries."

"Well, I think it's a *strong* point of the system in America, not a weak point, that different views can be presented. What do you have against that?"

"What I have against it is that our people are not mature enough. They — "

"Just a second, Doctor Waack," I interrupted, pointing back fifty feet. "Isn't the bus stop over there? Haven't we passed it?"

"No, the bus stop back to town is in a different place. We'll be there soon."

"O.K., go ahead with your point."

"Yes. Our people are unfortunately not in a position to be able to distinguish error from truth."

"But don't you think your scholars make good enough arguments against what people like Fischer say?"

"Unfortunately, people like Fischer use certain attractive words, like *freedom* and *liberalization,* to mislead people. They cover up their intentions with these nice-sounding phrases."

"But Fischer calls himself a socialist. He just has a somewhat different interpretation of what a socialist society should be. Maybe his interpretation is wrong. But I don't understand why he can't be allowed to defend himself if he is attacked."

"In the D.D.R. there is only one interpretation. Don't you see, Steve? Your famous free competition of ideas just *confuses* people. You have the truth competing with lies, and some people believe one thing and others another thing. Don't you realize — that's how the bourgeoisie intends it. They *encourage* all these different ideas, so that people will be less likely to understand the truth. That's the whole purpose of your famous freedom of speech. In the D.D.R. we're lucky enough to have scholars who know the truth. Why should we permit a return to the old confusion?"

One thing I did realize by this time. We were way past our bus stop — indeed, past several bus stops — and Waack's intention was obviously that we would walk the whole two miles back to the center of town. The bastard wanted to waste time and tire me out, so that I would have as little free time as possible in the afternoon.

We walked along silently for a few minutes. I was thinking, and holding back my rage.

Finally, I opened my mouth again. "Doctor Waack, there's just one thing I don't see. Look, my opinion is that socialism is clearly superior to capitalism, you know, it's much better for the people. And I think people are intelligent enough to see the advantages of socialism and choose it if they're presented with the alternatives."

"That's your big mistake," replied Waack with gusto. "You think that people are intelligent. *People are stupid.* They won't see."

"That is hardly a socialist view of man, that he is stupid."

"When I was at university, I was like you. I believed we should have socialism by *convincing* people — the whole shit. I remember, we had a group of students who tried to set up a political club outside the F.D.J. They wanted to agitate for liberalization. It was around the time of Hungary. Of course, the university officials wanted to throw them out immediately, but we in the F.D.J. leadership took a soft line. We said we should try to *persuade* them and *convince* them. The administration listened to us, but we turned out to be completely wrong. Those students were hopeless — they were counterrevolutionaries. After we had pleaded for them before the administration they turned around and handed out *leaflets!* Steve, that taught me a lot about my illusions of bringing about socialism by convincing people. *We must also know how to punish!* Sure we try to educate and convince, but that is so difficult. Our people complain they are bored with too much politics in everything. They ask why there always has to be politics in movies and television and the newspapers. The answer is that there has to be because the people are so hard to convince. So we can't only get along by convincing. When necessary, we have to use the club. If people don't see the truth, we must club it in to them." He chuckled.

I gasped a deep sigh inside for the poor people of the German Democratic Republic. And thought about how much Waack had changed since that first day when he caught me for saying that everyone in the D.D.R. only "seemed" to be happy.

*

He gave me no free time that afternoon. I obviously couldn't just tell him to get lost when he asked to come along to see the Konsument Department Store with me. So in we went together. On the first floor I wanted to buy some razor blades, just to try them and see what the quality was like, so I told Waack I had left my blades back in Berlin by mistake.

He squirmed. "Uh, Steve, I wouldn't buy those blades if I were you. Our razor blades aren't very good. I use Gillette myself."

Then we saw the radio-TV section. If you bought a transistor radio, you had to purchase the slipcover separately from the radio itself, and a girl was complaining that all the slipcovers were too small, and didn't fit on any radios. A brownish goo leaked out of the batteries displayed by the checkout counter.

I said I wanted to look at the bookstore selling Soviet books which was located centrally in a modern store near the old City Hall. I had remembered from 1969 that it was practically empty, and wanted to check on it again. Waack left me there while he mosied over to the Polish Cultural Center to look for some modern music records he said he couldn't get in Berlin. In almost an hour and a half, three East Germans, plus perhaps ten Russian tourists, came into the store. The only purchase was a tourist map of Kiev. The stores had six sales people. I thought about the East German labor shortage.

Was the bastard going to succeed? Was I going to stay in Leipzig for three days without meeting *anyone?* I gnashed my teeth in desperation waiting in the Soviet bookstore. *That night* — that night I'd have to sneak out of my room and go somewhere, meet at least *somebody* in this damn place. Waack had no movies planned; I was to dutifully continue reading the attack on Ernst Fischer.

I had the feeling he suspected something. We had a late dinner, which he dragged out further by ordering things we had never had before, like a cup of coffee. Than we went back to the hotel, and said good-night. It was a little after eight, but I had resolved not to sneak out until 9:30, thinking that he might come in to check on me.

A little after nine, he knocked on the door. He was breathing down my neck, but I had outsmarted him. I sat in bed, smiling, reading my little Fischer book. A half-hour later I sneaked out. If he came in again, I could tell him the next morning I had gone out to get something to eat.

When I left, I took with me the letter I had written to the cook's apprentice in East Berlin, suggesting that we meet at 7:30 in front of the Bowling Zentrum the day after I returned.

I had hoped people would still be sitting on benches in the new square near the hotel, but it was too late for that. A nice

Konditorei on the other side of the street was closed and an open ice-cream bar next door was so crowded I would have had to wait forever for a seat. I cursed Waack; maybe it was too late to meet anybody. I kept walking toward City Hall Square, peeking for an open place. Finally my ears pricked up — I heard music. It was a bar, with no dancing but with a live combo, playing soft background stuff. There were two empty seats at a sort of booth where a girl and a guy were sitting.

"Uh, excuse — excuse me. Do you mind if I sit here?"

"No, go ahead," answered the girl. She had a cute nose and flowing brown hair.

"Uh, excuse me," I started again, five minutes later, after my first beer had arrived. The two weren't saying anything to each other, just holding hands across the table. "May I ask you a question? I'm visiting in Leipzig, and I wonder whether the government is more popular here than in other parts of the D.D.R?"

"No, why should it be?" the girl sitting next to me replied.

"Well, you know, before the war the Communist Party had a lot of support in Leipzig. And Ulbricht comes from here of course."

"No, it's pretty much the same."

"Pretty much the same?"

"Yeah. Everyone would leave if they could," she declared nonchalantly.

"Where are you from?" asked the boy. "Mecklenburg?" That's the northern part of East Germany. I felt glad to have been mistaken for a German, an East German at that.

"No, no," I answered. "I'm from America."

"America? Why did you want to come *here*?"

"Oh, to visit friends. It's also interesting to look around. A different way of life."

"Yeah," said the girl. "You go to the stores to get ten things, and you find only five. That's our way of life."

"Were you serious about what you said before about everybody leaving? I mean, if the Wall opened, would *you* leave?"

"Sure, why not?" said the boy. I looked at his hands. They were calloused.

"You mean, you would just leave your own country? All your friends and everything?"

"Of course." He swigged down some beer. "I'd be able to meet most of my friends over there. They'd go too."

"Why?"

"There are just so many things you're *forced* to do here," said the girl. "They force you to join the F.D.J. when you go to school, even though nobody really wants to."

"How can they *force* you?"

"Oh, if you don't, they always ask you questions. So finally everybody gives in and joins."

"What happens in high school? I mean, do kids ever question the things in their textbooks, or do they just go along with what the teachers say even if they don't believe it?"

"Sometimes a kid will say something," the girl answered. "You know, just a little thing, nothing very important. But they'll take him to the principal's office and the principal will talk to him until he repents."

"I don't know why I did it, I guess I just got angry one day," the guy broke in. "But one day in our school I called the class F.D.J. secretary a political slut. It was when I was in ninth grade. They almost threw me out of school."

"What about the teachers?" I went on. "Do *they* really believe in what they say, you know, in citizenship ed classes? Or are they just mouthing words also?"

"Most of them don't really believe it either," the girl said.

"That's what I don't understand about this place! It seems to be just a huge act. The newspapers write about all the achievements in socialist construction and building a new socialist man, and everyone knows it's a lie. School kids lie to their teachers, and they know that neither they nor the teachers believe in what they're saying. But they say it anyway. How long can you go on like that?"

"Who knows?" The boy shrugged.

"Look, let me ask you something. When Honecker says that the purpose of socialism is to do everything for the good of the people, is *he* just lying? I mean, is he sincere and has it just not worked out that way, or is he just lying also?"

"We don't know." The guy shrugged again. "We wish we did."

"You know," the girl said, looking at her boy friend, "you shouldn't get the impression that *everything* is bad here. We get free education. That's good. Right?"

"Look, let's stop talking about *politics!* We have a meeting at the construction site tomorrow afternoon, and that'll be dull enough. Can we all just get a beer?"

*

As soon as we had arrived in Dresden and checked in to our Interhotel rooms right on Prager Strasse, I told Dr. Waack I'd want to take the tram over to Radebeul to inform Manfred I had arrived. Waack was hesitant, but I insisted it would be impolite not to do otherwise, since he was expecting me.

I took the tram over to Hans and Käte's.

"Steve, did you hear Nixon's going to visit China?" Hans cried out as soon as he saw me.

"No, *what?*"

"Nixon's going to visit China. I heard it on RIAS this morning."

My immediate reaction was to wonder how *Neues Deutschland* would handle the story. Hans had a different immediate concern. "Do you think there's a good chance the Americans will line up with the Chinese against the Russians?"

"I don't know."

"I hope so."

I had to tell Hans about Waack. "Look, I have to be very careful while I'm in Dresden now, because I have this sort of 'companion' from the government who's following me around wherever I go."

"They'll do anything, won't they?" Käte sighed.

"Who is this guy?" Hans asked.

"He claims to be from the Academy of Sciences, that they are interested in academic contacts with American students. But I bet he's from the secret police."

"Oh-h-h, it would be fantastic to meet the scum." Hans sighed.

"Yeah, well the problem is that I don't want him to know I have any East German friends. Their idea is that I should only talk to them, not with any normal people. I told this guy I was going to visit a friend whom I had already met in nineteen sixty-nine when I was here. But he's actually in Bulgaria now."

"Hey," popped up Hans, after a pause. "What's your friend's name?"

"Manfred."

"How about if I came with you and said *I* was Manfred?"

"Hey, not a bad idea."

"Käte, we can tell you about what happens later."

"Hans, just one thing. Be *very* careful what you say to this guy. Remember, he might be from the secret police."

"Don't worry, I know the type perfectly."

We went to the hotel restaurant for dinner.

"Would you like a cigarette, Doctor Waack?" Hans began politely, as soon as we sat down. I was relieved how cultivated he was acting. He was a careful guy, I guess.

"Not *that* poison!" snapped Waack.

"Poison?" I asked.

"This cheap brand. It's unsmokeable. I have my own cigarettes, thank you."

Hans and I glanced at each other. I, at any rate, was stunned.

"What do you have planned for Steve while you're in Dresden?"

"Well, we'll of course visit the Zwinger and the other art museums."

"You should get there early, especially tomorrow. Saturday it's always very crowded. People like the old works of art, you know. It's the same thing with the theater: it's very hard to get tickets for classical plays, but whenever there's a modern play the theater is empty."

"Why do you think that is?" Waack asked in an even-tempered voice.

"Well, it's that the modern plays aren't anything different from what you see on TV every day. If people go to the theater, they want a bit of a change."

"Yes, but the purpose of the modern plays is to build up socialist consciousness. They teach us that we must not work for ourselves, but for the future."

"But that will *never* happen. People will always work for themselves."

I looked a bit startled at Hans. "What do you mean by that, Manfred?"

"I have a friend who's visited the Soviet Union. He told me

that even there, after fifty years of socialism, everybody still works for himself. Just like here."

"That is not socialism, if people work for themselves instead of the collective."

Hans' lips tightened. "Why *should* they work for the collective? All the leaders of the factories are worried about is fulfilling the plan. They don't care about the workers. Why should the workers care about the collective?"

My stomach started turning, and I wanted desperately to yell stop. *What was happening?* Was Hans losing control of himself? Didn't he know what he was saying, whom he was talking to? I felt sick and hot.

"What are you saying, Manfred? The workers have a large degree of influence in the factories. They determine what those plan targets are going to be."

"You know very well the workers have no influence," he jabbed back. I swallowed. "They make the plan from the top. Everyone knows that."

"The workers can make suggestions."

"Yeah, I've seen people try to make suggestions. The manager just tells them they're idiots."

Waack seemed to be keeping calm, but who could tell what was going on inside him. I tried to keep on eating calmly.

"The problem, Manfred, is the ideological influence of West Germany. The last thing the West Germans want is that our people develop a socialist consciousness. So they attempt to sabotage us by their diversions and tricks — egoism, consumer society, sex, drugs. The whole filthy mess. And sometimes their ideological diversion can even affect managers in our socialist factories." He gulped his beer self-consciously. "It can even affect you, Manfred. Right?"

"Don't blame everything on West Germany. There is nothing

wrong with West German music, or clothes, or things like that. There's no reason why we can't have more of them in the D.D.R. There are some areas where we even have things to learn from West Germany. That's my opinion."

"Wrong," barked Waack. "We need *nothing* from the capitalist lands. Nothing."

"Nothing? Not even any technology?"

"Yes, technology we can take, but we will use it in our way, in a *socialist* way, my friend. But *none* of the ideological poison, not one drop. There's too much of it in our country already, and it is destroying socialism! That's what they said in Czechoslovakia, Manfred. 'Let's just take a little more from the West here and there, it won't harm the socialist system.' Well, look what broke loose there. And Hungary in nineteen fifty-six or Poland in nineteen seventy. The evidence is clear what happens."

"Well, *obviously* you can't let the situation get out of hand," parried Hans, with a knowing flourish of his cigarette. I almost laughed in my relief. Thank God, just in time he had controlled himself. I looked down thankfully at my empty plate, and sighed inside.

"Yes, of course, Manfred. *You* don't want it to get out of hand. But there are many forces which exploit the situation as soon as you open the door for them. That is why we must maintain the dictatorship of the proletariat." Suddenly he was looking kindly at Hans. "Manfred, the only reason I'm discussing with you is because I think you're honest. I'm trying to show you the way."

"What do you mean by that? There are many different ways."

"That's where you're wrong, Manfred. There is only one way."

Hans said he was to meet some friends at 9:30 at a café in the Altmarkt, and asked whether I could come along. It was clear Waack didn't want me to, but I assured him I'd be back within an hour.

"All right," droned Waack. "I'll see you back in the room then."

As soon as we got outside, Hans stomped his foot to the ground, and grit his teeth, slamming the brick hotel façade with the side of his fist.

"O-o-o-o!" he wailed. "I could give that man a punch in the teeth!"

"I told you he was bad. But what happened to *you?*"

"Steve, you can't possibly know how bad he is, because you don't have to *live* here," he said in a crescendo. "He is *typical* of them, he is unbelievable, the damn cop! I'm sorry I got carried away, I'm usually very calm, but he made me lose my temper. Did you see what he was *wearing?* Everything he had on came from the West. The suede jacket, that beautiful blue shirt. That was a West German brand. I recognized it. And his eau de cologne — oh, so finely groomed I could *bust!* He, *he* of all people — *he* says we have nothing to take from the West. Of course, *we* can't take anything. But *he* can take whatever he wants, because *he* has socialist consciousness."

"You know, Hans, I've always hated him, but you're right — I never thought about him just that way. Once I asked him about his suede jacket. He told me it was East German. But I never noticed anything else."

In the café we sat with a blonde girl and her Mediterranean-looking Bulgarian boy friend, who was studying in Dresden. "Steve, Birgitte is one of the girls who is in our group that passes around West German magazines."

"West German magazines?"

"Yes, every once in a while we get hold of some. Someone we know from West Germany smuggles one in, or we pool together to buy some on the black market. Of course, we keep the sex magazines from her!"

"When I was in Bulgaria last summer — that's when I met Georgi — a West German gave me a copy of *Der Spiegel* he had finished reading, and I got it back in."

"So you pass these magazines around?"

"Only to fully reliable people, of course," Hans said. "Birgitte, tell Steve about some of the things you saw in Bulgaria."

"Oh, it was just incredible how East Germans were treated with complete contempt. One of the tourist groups had moved into their hotel, and then after two days they got thrown out because a West German group had arrived suddenly. It was for the Western money, you know, but it was so embarrassing! And then they wonder why we're not proud of the D.D.R. Also, I saw this bathing suit that was made here. I recognized it because I had been thinking of buying it. Here it costs one hundred marks, there it was thirty-two."

"Steve, the way they play around with things is just incredible. They sell that bathing suit in Bulgaria at that price to increase our 'fraternal ties'! And here, they send goods where they will impress visitors most. You can always get bananas in Leipzig during the trade fair. And now, they're really turning Berlin into the showcase of the Republic. I've seen things there you *never* see in Dresden. It's all political."

The Bulgarian guy hadn't said a word the whole time. Now he told Hans that perhaps he should keep quiet; this was a public place and the people at the next table looked suspicious. Hans agreed and called for the bill. He insisted on paying for my sundae. "Steve, I have nothing else to spend my money on."

Even though I returned before an hour had passed, I was

scared shitless to face Waack again. Timidly, I knocked on his door.

"You know, Doctor Waack," I began, like a son talking with his father, "I was really depressed by the discussion between you and Manfred tonight."

"Why?"

"Because I *know* Manfred. I know he is of good will. He is no enemy of socialism. And if even *he* raises all these complaints —"

"Steve, my friend," Waak purred, his mustache standing out and almost enveloping his face, "it just shows how hard it is to bring about socialism by convincing people the way you talk about."

"Yeah, but it's sad."

His tone suddenly became harder. "Steve, I have to say something to you. Here in the D.D.R., you are a guest of the Academy of Sciences. We have made your trip here possible, and we are spending a good deal of time and money to make your trip enjoyable. I've given up my vacation to come along and show you around. I'm not your keeper, and I can understand you have a friend like Manfred whom you want to visit. But *wasn't seeing him last week enough?* What am *I* supposed to do while you are out with him? I had thought we could go to a movie tonight, but here I am instead in my room bored. Isn't that asking too much of me?"

"I'm sorry."

"Steve, you said something at dinner about a party Manfred was planning for tomorrow." That had in fact been an excuse to go see Hans again. "Well, you know, I had made plans too. While you were at Manfred's, I went over to the Dresden Tourist Information Office to check on getting tickets for the

Laterna Magica from Prague. There was a cute girl working there, so I invited her on a date for tomorrow night."

"A date? You two are going out?"

"No, all three of us. I expect you to come."

"O.K., Doctor Waack, sure, I'll come. Sounds like fun." I said good-night and went into my room next door.

The bastard had used some pretty thin excuses during the weeks I had known him, but *this* was indubitably the most meager yet. If he'd invited a girl out on a date — "a cute girl" no less — why the hell would he want *me* there with him? You'd think he'd be glad to get rid of me. I pounded my fist against the pillow in bed as I lay thinking those thoughts, and fell asleep only after a long struggle.

✱

For a long time I had planned to ask Waack if I could take his picture. If he let me, I thought, it would mean he was less likely to be from the secret police. Saturday morning provided the perfect opportunity: we were going sightseeing, and the weather was sunny. The fountains and modern buildings of Prager Strasse, right outside the hotel, were the perfect backdrop.

"A picture of *me?*" Waack chuckled. "No, no-o. I'm not photogenic."

I didn't press the point — I didn't want him to get suspicious — and just took pictures of Prager Strasse.

As we walked along, Waack picked a youngish guy out of the crowd, and yelled hello. Just like in Schwedt, he quickly said he had an American friend with him. He introduced me, everybody smiled, and we left without further discussion.

The weather was too nice to get worried.

We had a whole day of museum visits before us — the classic Zwinger gallery filled with Titians and Dürers and such, the crown jewels and royal treasure of the Saxon throne, and an exhibition of German art in the twentieth century. The museums all lie near the river Elbe. Some of the area had still not been rebuilt after the hard bombings during the war, and was overgrown with weeds. Dresden is said to have been one of Europe's most beautiful cities before the war.

The Zwinger opened up with a room giving a "political" history of the museum since the war. When the Russians occupied Dresden, they took with them virtually the Zwinger's entire artistic content, and it was several years later, after Western pressure, that they gave in and returned the art. Needless to say, however, this was not the version of the events the East Germans presented. First they spoke about the threat to the paintings from the Anglo-American "terror bombing attack" against Dresden in 1945 — no mention that Stalin had encouraged the Allies to bomb so as to ease the way for the Russian armies. But the "proletarian internationalist training" of the Soviet soldiers enabled them to save the art, which was brought to the Soviet Union for "safekeeping." Everything was eventually returned to the German people, while the Americans stole many art treasures they never returned.

After the propaganda came the Titians and the Dürers and the rest.

We ate lunch nearby, in the restaurant in the cellar of that huge cafeteria complex where I had eaten the previous week. The service was no slower than usual at such places, but Waack heaved a demonstrative "it's about time" when the food finally came. Then he plunged his fork onto his plate in disgust when he saw that the mushroom omelette he had ordered contained only three tiny mushrooms. He called over the waiter, who told him to go in and see the chef. Five minutes later he returned with a ladleful of extra mushrooms.

At the Royal Treasury after lunch, I remarked that I liked

some of the simpler art objects better than the bright and gaudy jewels: "But see, Steve, nobody is looking at them. The big crowd's around the diamonds." He was right. "You know why? Deep inside, they all dream that they themselves one day might own their own diamond. People are so bourgeois, Steve."

At the twentieth-century art museum we were surrounded by dreadful D.D.R. art: "As you see, Steve, our post–1945 art puts men in the foreground — optimistic and conscious men."

For our big date that evening, Waack had gotten me into jacket and tie. We were supposed to meet our date at six in front of the new city theater on Thälmannstrasse. We came early, but she was late.

"I make it a policy never to wait more than fifteen minutes for a woman. They have to be taught to be on time." Waack positioned his leg up on a bench as if he were posing for a fashion ad and held his head up so it was looking straight out toward the horizon. He was, as usual, wearing his damn suede jacket.

At almost 6:30 she finally arrived, wearing a black fur-trimmed coat and wide, round, mod sunglasses with light blue lenses. Her name was Christine. I wondered what she was: plant, prostitute, or genuine working girl?

"Joachim," she purred, "I got those two tickets for the *Laterna Magica* for you. Since your friend is an American, it went all right." That was the first time I had ever heard Waack's first name.

"Well, Christine, where shall we eat?"

"What kind of place were you thinking in terms of?"

"Something nice — you know, a little less crowded, a little more exclusive."

She puzzled for a moment. "There's a very nice Hungarian restaurant right down the street."

It was only a short walk away. "Gee, that's too bad — no luck," I said, disappointed, as we got to the door. "The sign says TEMPORARILY CLOSED BECAUSE OF OVERCROWDING."

Christine put her hand on my shoulder suggestively. "Don't you worry, my little Steve, I know the people here, and they should be able to find a place for us." And then, to Waack, "I deal with these people on the job, when we have visitors to conventions and so forth."

When we came in, Christine headed straight behind a closed door. There was a lobby near the entry with a coat check and two sofas. The restaurant was up a flight of spiral stairs.

"The manager says he should have a table ready for us in fifteen minutes."

Waack smiled benevolently and gallantly took her coat. "I don't mind waiting. And I see they also have some decent cigarettes here." As he checked in Christine's coat, he bought a package of Winstons for $1.75. "I've been trying to get decent cigarettes ever since we got to Dresden, but all they have anywhere is that Bulgarian weed."

"Well, the problem," Christine answered knowingly, "is that they promised to buy up Bulgarian cigarettes as part of our trade agreement, but they can't sell any. So they've just taken all the other brands off the market until they get rid of them."

"Doctor Waack," I said, "you know, in America the trade unions boycott Winston cigarettes, because it's a nonunion shop. You should have gotten some other brand."

Waack kept silent. Instead, he looked over the cigarette displays: "Christine, look at this! They're selling these *Chinese* cigarettes for as much as the American ones. I wonder what idiot made the decision to put *that* price on them. What poor soul is going to pay as much for Chinese cigarettes?"

As we walked up the stairway, I felt somewhat as if we were

arriving at a palace ball. Everything was padded with nice blue carpeting. Everyone was seated at a table; nobody stood up waiting. Two fiddlers played Hungarian gypsy music; the waiters wore tuxedos. In New York it would be considered a pleasant, unpretentious place — here it was a palace.

"Steve," Christine began, wide-eyed, as we sat down, "tell me something about New York! We all long to go there so much. All they ever show on our television is the dirt and slums. But tell me about the exciting things!"

"But, Christine, I don't think our television is inaccurate," Waack said. "I think they probably give a good picture of conditions there. Right, Steve?"

The bastard had turned an eventual answer into a political test, and I had to grit my teeth before opening my mouth. "We-l-l, of course there is a lot of poverty and dirt in New York. Many people say the city is falling apart. But you can't deny that the entertainment is very exciting. There are loads of fantastic restaurants and movies and discotheques. It's lively."

Christine started talking about how limited her vacation possibilities were. Waack said his favorite vacationland was Bulgaria, because of friendly people and good food. Christine said something — I didn't quite get it; sometimes I have problems understanding German if two people are talking with each other and I'm not involved in the conversation — about the D.D.R. secret police being worried about D.D.R. tourists in Bulgaria escaping to West Germany from there. Perhaps she meant that the Balkan border control was not equally efficient. I wasn't sure.

"Does our secret police have men in Bulgaria to watch things?" Waack asked.

"Sh-h-h!" she whispered. "Don't talk so loud about them.

They're all around here." She took a sip of wine and giggled. "I'm in charge of getting hotel space for delegates to conferences in Dresden, you know. We know exactly how many of them are present at every conference. A lot of people don't know it, but Konsum is always there."

Konsum, I wondered — those are the cooperative stores in East Germany. It must be a popular nickname for the secret police, Lord knows why.

"You can always tell a man from Konsum. You know how? They have free passes to travel on the buses."

I had the quite definite feeling that the time had come for me to play dumb. Christine was saying things I shouldn't have been hearing. "Konsum?" I asked. "The workers at Konsum? Why do they get special bus passes?"

Waack looked knowingly at Christine for a second. "So they can get to work on time."

"Oh." I nodded and returned to my chicken paprika and Hungarian red wine.

I had drunk three glasses of wine before we left. Waack and Christine had also had a shot of whiskey. The bill was quite reasonable, not much more than at a hole like the cellar of the restaurant down the street where we had eaten lunch.

"Where are we going now?" I inquired.

"That's for Christine to decide."

"Steve, do you have any suggestions?" Christine asked, kittenish.

"Does Dresden have any discotheque?"

She giggled. "There is one. But — but — but nice people don't go there."

"Let's go anyway," I said.

"Yes, maybe Christine isn't a nice girl." Waack laughed.

Christine halted in her tracks and made believe she was pouting. She puckered her lips sourly and began swaying her head demonstratively back and forth.

"Steve, Joachim has insulted me."

"Christine, I'm sorry," Waack emoted melodramatically.

"Steve, what should he do to show he's sorry?" she said, puckering up her lips again, this time in an inviting way.

"I don't know. What should he do?"

"What should a man do to pay back a woman he has insulted?"

This whole game was starting to disgust me. "I don't know. What should he do?"

"Steve, *how* old are you?" She giggled.

"Twenty-three."

"Twenty-three, you're as old as I am, and you still don't know about kissing!" Whereupon, she slapped a kiss on my lips.

My major reaction to the whole absurdity was that I could hardly believe she was only twenty-three. I had assumed she was pushing thirty, which would have made our "triple date" all the more ridiculous.

We were promenading over the newly completed Elbe Bridge, which went off from Thälmannstrasse right where the big yellow building with the neon sign SOCIALISM IS WINNING stood, after going through a new underground passageway to get across the intersection. Unlike similar passageways you see in West Germany and Austria, this one was completely bare — without shops or stands or anything like that — except for a few pictures of the construction site manager with a Party button and some exemplary workers.

"Joachim, did you know that this passageway had to be opened without getting any safety inspection first? It's supposed to be a big secret, but I found out."

I pretended not to listen.

"How come?" asked Waack.

"You know how they are. The first thing they built here was this big yellow building. But it got built twenty meters too long by mistake, so it just jutted out into the street. So they had to redo the plans for the whole area — the underground passage, the bridge, and the road. Some of what they had started had to be torn up, and by the time they were ready to continue, they couldn't get the building materials. So it got to be further delays, and when they finally started they had to put workers on night shift. Originally, everything was supposed to be ready a few years ago, but when they saw they could get it done this year, they rushed things up again so they could be ready for the Eighth Party Congress. You know how they like to dedicate things together with big events." She laughed, and so did Waack.

From a tram stop on the other side of the bridge we took a fifteen-minute ride through a part of Dresden I had never seen, and got off right in front of an old hotel. "They have rock music here on Saturday nights," Christine announced. There was a line at the entrance. "It's a very wild element which comes here, you know," she uttered throatily while we waited. "Here there are girls who have three men in one night." She ran her hands through my long hair. Waack seemed to be holding the entire phenomenon at arm's length.

The dance floor was large, smoky, and even darkened, with small wooden tables. Lots of people were standing up, but we succeeded in getting a seat in a corner, far from where they were playing the records. Waack ordered a bottle of champagne. "Tonight," he proclaimed to Christine, "we are going all out."

At our table sat three long-haired boys, one man with gray hair, and a strikingly beautiful (in a teeny-bopperish sort of way) girl with a twiglike figure and long blond hair. I couldn't keep my eyes off her, and Waack seemed to be staring too.

He was. "Steve," he said, cupping his palm around my ear, "look at that girl next to you. She looks as if she is bewitched by the music. Look at her eyes! She's hypnotized, like the people in that pop music film we saw in Berlin." And then, out loud, semidirected at the others at the table, "If I had my way in this damned country, I'd blow all these places up in the air!" They must have thought him drunk, and maybe he was. "Blow them up, the whole kit and kaboodle. You hear me?"

I didn't say anything.

We had gotten lucky seats, it turned out. The group at our table was the live band, and they were setting up on a bandstand right next to us. Soon they began: they could only croon onomatopoetic approximations of the song texts, sounds rather than words. I felt so sorry for them; I felt like crying.

"We hear the songs on Western radio, and we can figure out the guitar chords. But we can only guess at the words, because we can't buy sheet music."

"Tell me what songs you play," I said. "If I know any, I can write down the words for you."

The kid named a few songs which I had never heard of. But then he came to "Proud Mary" by Creedence Clearwater Revival, and this time I could oblige him with the text. "Do you have a pen?" I asked.

Nobody did. Then Waack, who had been listening to our conversation, drew a pen out of his suede jacket. It was a Parker T-Ball Jotter. Momentarily, the musician's wonderment moved away from me and toward Waack's pen. "The best pen in the world," Waack declared knowingly.

"I have a pen from the West too!" blurted out Christine. "A West German tourist gave it to me as a present." She took out a plastic ball point with the emblem of *Hör Zu,* the West German equivalent of *TV Guide,* owned by the conservative Springer publishing empire, which is the constant target of official East German anger.

Waack didn't say anything.

"My friend," one of the young musicians said, moving himself closer to me across the table, "would you like to exchange any money? I can give you a good rate."

Without even eying Waack, I came back lightning fast. "No, thanks."

"So, my friend," the graying, flannel-shirted musician came in, his voice raspy like a cracker-barrel philosopher, "how do you like this prison?"

My stomach clumped together, and my heart thumped. I had already heard so much that was inconvenient that evening. Now this. Christine had asked her question about New York before, I was torn between the desire not to give her a D.D.R. propaganda answer, and the necessity not to offend Waack. I despaired, but this time the man's statement was too challenging to duck.

"*Prison?* You mean this discotheque? Well, I'll admit it's not as nice as some of those we have in America, but it's pretty good. And you musicians play very well."

"No, I don't mean the *discotheque.* I mean this damn *country!*"

"The D.D.R.? Oh, well I'm enjoying my stay here very much. The people are very friendly, everyone's been giving me a great welcome. For example, my friend Doctor Waack from the Academy of Sciences, he has been really helpful. He's even agreed to sacrifice his vacation to show me around the D.D.R. and take me everywhere."

Waack bowed his head a bit and gave a sort of "it's nothing" gesture.

The old guy seemed to get the hint. At any rate, he proceeded no further, and soon the band's break was over and they got up to play again.

"You know," Waack began to Christine, "it's useful to have things like this pen. It's a great way to meet girls, for instance — show it to them. Or, of course, a cigarette lighter. You offer to light a girl's cigarette, and they expect you to come out with a match. But then they see you have a cigarette lighter. If they come from outside Berlin, maybe they've never even seen one before. They go wild for you right off the bat."

"I have a few Western things, but not that many," she replied. "This pen. And these sunglasses I'm wearing. I got them at Exquisit. You know how much they cost?"

"How much?" Waack asked playfully, squeezing the hand she had taken up from her lap to put on the glasses.

"A hundred marks." Twenty-five dollars. "But it was worth it."

"They make you look even more beautiful."

"And also I have an empty bottle of Cinzano at home."

"You know what the best thing I have for meeting girls with is? I have one of those British umbrellas, the fantastic slim kind, you know, with a button that you just have to press and then the umbrella goes up. Wow! One time I was waiting at an S-Bahn station in Berlin, and there was a cute girl next to me. So I just pressed the button of the umbrella — and did *she* stare! Gave me her phone number right on the spot. We were together for almost six months."

What a slimy creature he was. The new class incarnate. A one-man revolution betrayed. Hans' observation had opened up a whole new dimension to Dr. Joachim Waack's loathsomeness. By now I was hard-pressed to decide which was worse, his ideology or his deportment. No doubt it was the mixture, the utter hypocrisy. Interesting to learn, among other details, that he has a telephone. He and Frau Koch — and not many other East Germans. He has no decency, no shame. Was he now just too drunk to care what picture of himself he was painting for me? Maybe he wasn't from the secret police, maybe he was merely pitiful — *they* couldn't be so incompetent. I thought to myself: twenty-three days left in the D.D.R.

"Steve, come with Joachim and me to the bar downstairs," said Christine with a drunken verve. "There we can get some *hard* liquor."

Down there the atmosphere was wild: guys sousing beer and slapping each other on the back, couples seated in Munich beer-hall style wooden booths embracing, and lots of people standing around and lots of noise.

"Down here is where the really wild ones come," began Christine. "See that boy over there." She pointed to a guy who was deeply embracing a girl he had pinned against the wall. "*Er ist bi.*"

He is — what? I didn't understand the last word, which came out sounding like "bee." "*Bi.* What does that mean?"

"Oh, my poor innocent little Steve! *Bi,* that means he loves both women and men."

Waack boomed out, "Christine, order a whole bottle of brandy!"

"Are we going to drink a whole bottle of brandy?" I asked. "Not me, I can't stand brandy."

"Oh, we don't have to drink it at all, don't you worry. Whatever we don't drink, we can pour down some girl's blouse. Steve, you know, I'm not just a political man."

He wasn't joking. As soon as the bottle of brandy came, he opened it and started pouring it down the back of a girl's sweater. Christine stopped him. "Joachim, Joachim, we must save it for drinking!"

"It's just as good for pouring!" he thundered. "Why, this crap is even *better* for pouring!"

Christine started slurping kisses on both of us, and then took us both in her plentiful arms. "You two men are *wonderful!* I love you both."

"We love you too," I burbled, in a somewhat lower voice.

Actually, I didn't love anybody. Maybe it was the liquor, but I felt sad and empty. We went back upstairs, and Waack went out to the dance floor with Christine. When the song was through, I sneaked up to the middle-aged man playing drums and whispered, "Sir, I understood what you said before about this place being a prison. I just had to say what I did because that man is guarding me."

"Don't worry, son. I could tell." He smiled in a fatherly, kindly way and patted me gently on the shoulder. I felt as depressed as I could be that I would have to leave this man behind in the prison. I put my head down on the table, but even the blaring music didn't relieve my loneliness and sorrow. The band played the song "Reach Out, I'll Be There" — which they onomatopoetized as "Rich-ard" — and I thought of my family back home in New York.

*

I got up after noon on Sunday, having gone to sleep at four the morning before. The discotheque closed at midnight, but instead of going home we went to a small nightclub on a little street in a nice residential neighborhood ten minutes' walk from the discotheque. There it was forty-year-olds foxtrotting in a *nouveau riche* atmosphere. Who even knew such places existed in the D.D.R.? Waack got himself a Melde brand East German whiskey, after complaining loudly to the waiter when he was informed they were out of Johnny Walker. He did, however, get the pack of "decent cigarettes" he asked for. I had never seen him go through anywhere near a pack of cigarettes in a night the way he had done. We took a taxi home in the dawn, and agreed to meet Christine for lunch at 1:30 the next day at our hotel restaurant. Afterward, we would visit a medieval palace.

I sat reading *Neues Deutschland* in my room before Waack got up. The whole week the paper had been filled with glowing accounts of something called Baltic Sea Week, a propaganda festival in Rostock where they invited Scandinavian delegates, plus Poles and Russians. This morning there was an article on the "Youth and Student Meeting" of the Baltic Sea Week, which adopted some incredible resolution supporting the Moscow position on every foreign policy issue, even the status of West Berlin. How could these Swedes — they weren't all Communists, those who were invited — go along with this crap? Did they just get them drunk, or was it just all lies? It was probably the latter: the article contained a quotation from Dag Klackenberg, head of the Swedish National Union of Students, expressing full support for the document. That had to be a lie; I knew who Klackenberg was; he's a conservative. He couldn't have said that, no matter how drunk he was. Angry feelings of powerlessness stormed through me.

Christine knew the personnel in the hotel restaurant also. So Waack asked her to ask the waitress why the orange juice they had ordered was completely tasteless.

"Well, you know, we have a good brand of orange juice too. It's just that we had to buy some of these two other bad brands because the government got them in a foreign trade agreement. So it's just luck which one you happen to get. I'm sorry."

"Look, when you are paying two marks for a tiny glass of

orange juice, you should at least be able to drink it," Waack
spat out.

"I'm sorry, sir, but there's nothing we can do about it."

✦

Monday I had to go to visit the Schwers in Grosspostwitz to
pick up the transistor radio that I had by genuine mistake left
there. It was declared on my customs declaration when I
entered the D.D.R., and I would get into trouble if I didn't take
it out. Despite his reluctance to let me go, even Waack had to
accept the legitimacy of my excuse. He told me to try to be
back by dinner.

The previous night, however, Hans had come to visit me in
my room a little after ten. I told him I'd be escaping Waack's
grip the next morning, and that perhaps we could meet at night.
He suggested the bar at the big Interhotel on the other side of
Prager Strasse, and promised to bring along an old friend from
high school. I had to leave to make the train that would con-
nect to Grosspostwitz early in the morning, so I used the simple
expedient of leaving a note for Waack in his box at the front
desk saying Manfred had invited me to meet a friend of his,
and that I'd be home late.

Hans and his friend arrived in the bar wearing jackets and
ties about five minutes after I did. I just had a regular shirt.

"Jürgen is an old school friend, a real regular guy. We've
been friends for I don't know how long. Except that he was
luckier than I was, at first."

"How?"

"Well, I wanted to go to university, but I didn't get to go because I was in Czechoslovakia in nineteen sixty-eight before the
Russian invasion. That made them consider me 'politically un-
reliable' right off the bat, even though I had just gone as a

tourist. The D.D.R. sent plainclothes policemen to Prague to observe East Germans, you know. All those petitions the Czechs put out, for freedom and for standing up to the Russians — half the foreigners signing them were from the D.D.R."

"So people followed the events in Czechoslovakia closely?"

"*Closely?* Very closely."

"So how was Jürgen luckier than you?"

"He got to go to university, at first at least. But then they threw him out."

"Why?"

"I failed Marxism-Leninism one year."

"And if you fail *one* course, you're thrown out of university?"

"Not for the other courses. Only for Marxism-Leninism. That's the only subject they care about. They say that 'political maturity' is a prerequisite for being trained in your field. Usually we have written exams, and they sit students very close to each other — it's like they were *encouraging* cheating. But for Marxism-Leninism, the professor himself gives you an *oral* exam."

"Why oral?"

"So they can see the expression on your face. It's easier for them to judge your sincerity than if you just write down words."

"And you weren't sincere enough?"

"I guess not."

"So you were flunked out."

"Right."

"Jürgen, how do course requirements work at a university here? Marxism-Leninism is a required course, I understand. What are the other requirements?"

"Everyone takes Marxism-Leninism no matter what they study. Otherwise, you have your field of study, and that determines your other courses."

"What about courses outside your field of study?"

"What do you mean?"

"Well, let's say you study engineering but want to take some art courses."

"That's impossible."

"*Impossible?*"

"You have no courses left. All your courses are according to the study plan of your field of study. They are all already decided."

"You mean you can't even choose any courses *inside* your field of study?"

"No."

"Jürgen," said Hans, "tell Steve your Marxist analysis of the system here." And then, to me: "They taught him all this Marxism stuff at school. He's good at it."

"Steve, as a foreigner you can't realize what it's really like, just how bad it is. The whole purpose of the system is to split the workers and keep them divided."

"How?" I asked.

"The workers aren't allowed to have unions to protect their interests. Every factory has workers who are paid to spy on the other workers, just like they have student spies at the universities. They pay the workers by piecework so they will compete against each other. And the workers have no way to complain. Let me give you an example. Last year, when they flunked me out of university, I got a job in a plastic factory. Well, you know, my sight has always been bad, but the particular job I had made it much worse. I wanted to get a transfer into another division, and I got a note from a doctor confirming that the job had hurt my vision. Well, the factory manager just laughed when I showed it to him. In West Germany, a worker could take his case to the union and they would defend him. But here that's useless — it's just going from one Party big shot to another. Six months ago they raised our production norms without raising wages. The excuse was that the 'Innovator's Campaign' had brought new suggestions which could increase every worker's production. What it really meant was that wages went down. But instead of defending us, the union just tells us to produce more. The workers are split, and the Party bosses can stay on top."

"Do you think the people at the top actually believe their own propaganda? Do *they* think they're bringing about socialism?"

"They are so hypocritical, I don't think they believe anything. You know, the head of the Marxism-Leninism department at the university drives around in a *Ford Mustang*. That car isn't even *for sale* to the public, but he obviously doesn't care that he is showing contempt for everything he's supposedly teaching. Steve, they're just doing the whole thing for the Russians, to make them happy. The Russians keep them in power, and in turn we have to bow before 'our Soviet big brother.' "

The contrast was eerie between the semichic surroundings of the bar in the Dresden luxury hotel and the depressing stories of ruined eyes and production norms and factory spies. They played soft Andy Williams music in the background, as we sipped gin and tonic.

"Steve," said Hans, holding his head up, "for me the worst thing is the lack of personal freedom. Bananas I can live without. But always having to look left and right over your shoulder, living with the fear that one day you will get too angry and go too far — always having to bottle yourself up. That's the worst."

"You couldn't believe it would be this bad?" Jürgen said

softly. "You couldn't believe they completely prevent us from *breathing,* could you?"

The music played on, then it died.

❋

There was no room key in my box when I returned, and that got me scared nearly out of my mind. I had left the key there in the morning, and there was absolutely no reason for it not to have been there. I expected to go upstairs and find my room open with Waack sitting there waiting. Instead, though, the door was locked and the inside dark. I went down again and asked for a master key. They asked me if I had my check-in card; no, Waack did. They asked me my name. I was not checked in, it turned out. Both rooms were in Waack's name. It was almost one in the morning, and I offered to give a description of what toilet articles I had in the bathroom, and the contents of my suitcase. They finally let me in; my stomach knotted in anticipation of morning.

❋

"I am very disappointed, Steve, that I wasn't invited to last night's discussion. Was there any reason I couldn't come?"

His voice sounded relatively unperturbed, but I had to think lightning fast. I should have known that question was coming: it was a dumb mistake not to have thought out an answer before. Was I slipping, getting tired of the game and thus playing below capacity? "Doctor Waack, I think Manfred is overwhelmed by you a little bit. You know, he is just a working-class kid who's never been to university, and I think he's afraid of all your degrees. But don't worry, I can tell you what points were raised on the train ride back to Berlin. It was a very interesting discussion."

He let the point drop, and claimed to know nothing of the missing key.

I got a seat on the train this time, because Waack had reserved places — in the first-class car.

"Manfred's friend had studied in the university. His description was generally very interesting, but there was one thing that disturbed me. He said that students couldn't take any subjects outside their field of study. I mean, it was impossible for a mathematician to study some European history just on the side, for fun."

Waack looked at me in a dumb, surprised way. "Now, Steve, how in the world do you expect us to get the money for an idea like *that?* Where in the world can a student take courses outside his field of study? That's completely utopian."

"Sure, but wouldn't it be a good idea?" I replied, carefully ignoring his question about where such a utopian idea might be practiced.

"It would be an excellent idea. But it would cost so much money. We have to train people in their skills. We don't have any money to just throw around."

"Well, but I mean, when do you think it might be possible? When might you get enough money?"

"Never, Steve, never." He halted, and corrected himself. "Wel-l-l, maybe when we reach the final stage of Communism — in a hundred years, maybe two hundred."

The train shrugged on; we both took a little nap.

"Steve, I'm looking forward to hearing Herr Bach's reaction to your paper on the student movement — and to reading it myself. From what I know of the American student movement, its main problem seems to be that it is split into so many different groups. A movement can only become strong if it is unified."

"I agree with you, Doctor Waack. But the problem is that

each one of the factions thinks *it* is right, and they don't want to unite on any but their own terms."

"Of course each one *thinks* it is right. But only one *is* right, only one *can* be right — the Communist Party. That you can be sure of — because only they operate on the basis of scientific principles."

"Well, I think the Communist Party has certainly played a very good role in the student movement. But the problem for me, as a student trying to decide which group to join, is that the Communist Party has so little strength."

"Yes, but Steve! *Why* do they have so little strength? Think of all they have to work against. The most powerful bourgeoisie in the world, the entire mass media working day in and day out against them."

"Well, quite honestly I think the bourgeoisie regards the various Maoist and terrorist and black revolutionary groups as a greater danger. The FBI has said that the Communist Party is no longer the greatest danger to 'internal security,' that the Maoists and the Black Panthers are instead."

"Those groups! The FBI just promotes these Maoist sects — they give them publicity so as to split the revolutionary movement."

"No, but before they called the Communist Party the greatest threat. They were afraid of them. Now they've stopped doing that."

"The only reason they stopped calling the Communist Party the greatest threat was because when they did, it just increased the interest of the masses for the Communists."

❖

I was relieved to see when I got back to Frau Koch's that my luggage had been undisturbed.

CHAPTER 6

"HERR BACH LEFT A NOTE before leaving for Bulgaria saying that everyone thought your survey of the American student movement was excellent, truly excellent. So, Steve, congratulations!" Dr. Waack had come on time, more or less, to greet me the next morning at Frau Koch's. "So now he has another project for you to work on, if you're agreed. He is interested in Harvard. We know that Harvard is the outstanding university in the United States, and he has a series of questions that are of academic interest to our research group."

"What are they?"

Waack asked me to sit down, gave me a pen and a pad of paper, and suggested that I take notes.

"Number one: The significance of Harvard for the education of the American intelligentsia in the past and the present. Here Herr Bach wants you to include names of American and foreign political, diplomatic, and business leaders who have graduated from Harvard, and also information about Harvard's ties with foreign universities.

"Number two: The administration of the university. Herr Bach wants all the important positions and administrative organs, with a summary of their theoretical and actual influence. We also want the names of those who hold these positions.

"Number three: The structure of the university. We are thinking here of the different schools and departments, together with their relative importance and the number of students attending each one.

"Number four: How the university is financed. Here particularly we are interested in the use of government funds.

"Number five: The admissions process. What are the criteria for admission, and what is the process like? Here you should give examples from your own personal case as illustration. What steps did you go through, and on what basis was the decision made?

"Number six: The course of study. What courses are available to students? How much freedom do they have in choosing their area of study? And so forth.

"Number seven: Scholarships. What are the requirements for getting a scholarship, and on what basis are they given out?

"Number eight: The career choices of students after graduation. What influences direct a student's choice of career? Do private firms or government agencies influence this process? Also, we are interested in knowing the process by which one becomes a professor at an American university.

"Number nine: International student and professorial exchange. How many foreign students are at Harvard and how are they selected? We are very interested in knowing the attitude of Harvard students toward foreign students. Also, we want specific examples of Harvard professors who have taught abroad and of foreign scholars at Harvard.

"Finally: Student life. What kinds of student clubs are there and what is the content of the meetings they hold? What kinds of discussions or speeches take place on campus? What kinds of activities does the university arrange for the students during summer vacations?

"Is that all clear?"

"Yes," I answered cheerfully. It was all *too* clear: this stuff was on the verge of *spying*. I felt overwhelmed by the sensation that I was into this whole thing way over my head. Maybe *that's* what they have in mind for me here, to recruit me as a spy? Oh, my God. Right now there was nothing I could do except attempt to tell myself that no information I would give them in answering these questions was secret and that a good deal of it could be obtained by writing Harvard. But I didn't persuade even myself.

"Now, we're going to be leaving for Rostock Sunday morning, so that only gives you four days to get all these questions answered. That'll keep you pretty busy, so we won't have time for many activities. However, on Thursday I have arranged for an official car to take us to the site of the last illegal meeting of the Central Committee of the German Communist Party in March nineteen thirty-three. Tomorrow I thought we could go to the Museum of German History and the Pergamon Art Museum. And tonight we can go to the movies. That will leave you this afternoon free to work."

That night, however, I was supposed to meet that apprentice cook I had written from Leipzig. Once again, I was forced to think fast to decide what I was to say to Waack. Oh, was I tired of having to make snap decisions, of weighing the alternatives of telling the truth or lying with computerlike speed, and then inventing a quick and believable lie if that was my course. This time, I took the plunge and told the truth.

"Uh — well, uh, going to the movies tonight will be impossible. I'm meeting someone I met here in Berlin while eating lunch once."

"Who?"

"He's an apprentice cook. A very nice guy."

Now Waack had to do some quick thinking, his part of the dramatic farce. "I don't see what you can possibly gain out of meeting such — such youngsters."

"This guy isn't a youngster."

"Steve, if he's an apprentice he certainly can't be older than twenty."

Actually, he was nineteen. "Well, look, I'm only twenty-three."

"Steve, we have invited you here as our guest, and the academy feels we have the obligation as your hosts to keep you entertained. So you ought to come to the movies."

"But I can't just not show up after we've agreed to meet. It would be impolite."

"All right. I'll meet you tomorrow morning at ten by the big clock at Alex. We can go to the Museum of German History from there."

I was supposed to meet the kid at 7:30 in front of the Bowling Zentrum, and went to the grill bar at six for dinner. There was, I had discovered, a certain strategy involved in waiting for a seat at the grill bar. The basic problem was that no internal understanding had ever grown up among the customers to let people take seats in order of arrival. Impolite people, who just rushed to take a seat as soon as one became vacant, even if five other people had been there earlier, invariably proved that bad manners definitely did pay. Thus, while it was more pleasant to wait for a seat sitting on the Formica area along the window, it also assured much lengthier waits. You had to stay standing the entire time, watching over your territory and poised to prevent interlopers from snatching a stool ahead of you.

The ideal strategy was to see how far advanced the people at the counter were with their meals, and then to stand directly over the shoulder of the one who was closest to being finished. There were usually several others doing the same thing, so even with this strategy you always had to wait twenty minutes. Sometimes I preferred waiting thirty-five minutes sitting down to twenty standing up, sometimes I felt too sorry for the people trying to eat with others breathing down their necks; but when

I was starving, or when I was angry with people stealing seats who had come in long after me, I did it too.

That night a girl was being particularly aggressive in her application of this method with the lady seated next to me. She was telling her to hurry up and ask for her check, and then calling over the waiter to have him take her bill. I looked over from my pepper steak to see her: she had a tearfully beautiful, thin, sad-sack face, with big pink lips and dark eyebrows and straight dirty blond hair flowing down from all over her face. Her tight polo shirt was the kind that had a cowhide string running down the middle. Hers was untied and loose; from the side I could see part of her left breast.

Damn, though, she was being impatient. Probably one of those one-day visitors from West Germany, I thought. Unused to the way things operate here. "Hey, you," I said, putting a broad smile on. "Be patient! This isn't West Germany here."

"I'm not a West German," she answered immediately. "I come from here."

"So what are you being so impatient for? You know things always take this long."

"You have to say something once in a while, or else you go under completely."

"Oh," I muttered, taken aback. "I see what you mean."

"Look at all these tourists who come to Alexanderplatz! Finally, the Party has gotten its monument, something to put on postage stamps and show tourists so they can take nice pictures. Except that they don't want their monument disturbed by people. They'd prefer it if they could close the area off. Then it would be better for photos."

"You a student?" I asked.

"I used to be. But I got kicked out, for 'social democratism.'"

My heart skipped a beat. "'Social democratism'? I'm a social democrat also — Comrade!" But then I looked at my watch, and saw it was almost 7:30. I couldn't talk anymore, damn it. "Hey, I'm really sorry, but I have to leave right now to meet someone. But I'd sure like to meet you again. Where do you live?"

"Just come to the fountain here at Alex anytime. I'm usually there. Otherwise, ask any of the young people hanging around the fountain where Suzanne is."

As I got up, she pressed her warm palms against my ears and kissed my forehead.

The apprentice cook didn't come. I waited an hour, and he still hadn't come. So I went back to Alex to look for Suzanne. But she wasn't there.

*

During my stay, one of the major barriers between me and a nervous breakdown had been the American Forces Network out of West Berlin. I couldn't hear it in Dresden or Leipzig, but in East Berlin it came in clear and sharp. It was like an American pop station, with teen-lingo DJs and top-forty music. They had news on the hour and even baseball scores, so I could follow how the Dodgers were doing. Since receiving a letter addressed in care of Manfred in Dresden at the beginning of July, I hadn't heard a word from my parents — they didn't know where to reach me as yet since my letter informing them of my address at Frau Koch's didn't go out until ten days before. That made me even more dependent on AFN. Having been away in Dresden and Leipzig, I had not heard a genuine news broadcast in a week — I knew nothing about Nixon's China visit except *Neues Deutschland*'s minute notice, which I never even would have seen had I not been looking for it because Hans had told me — and on my first day back in Berlin I wanted to hear the long news broadcast AFN ran at ten A.M., the time

I was to meet Waack. So I took my transistor, freshly recovered from the Schwers, with me when I went to meet Dr. Waack. I checked the radio in at the entrance of the Museum of German History. "That's a beautiful radio," said the lady with curly hair and a blue uniform behind the coat counter. "May I listen?"

I pressed the on button. She listened lovingly for a minute or so, and then turned it off and stroked it. "It makes a beautiful sound," she uttered respectfully. "Does it have four bands?"

"Yes."

"How much did you pay for it?"

"One hundred forty marks."

"Oh," she sighed, closing her eyes.

✱

Thursday was to be a work day, but in the middle of the sunny afternoon I told Frau Koch I was going to see the city's panorama from atop the new television tower off Alexanderplatz — for which I knew there was a four-hour wait. Again, I wanted to find Suzanne at the fountain, but she wasn't there, so I went to do some checking at food markets around Alex for what wares they had and what quality they were. When I came back, Suzanne was sunning herself near someone's transistor radio.

"Suzanne, what do you do now that you've been thrown out of university?"

"I have my vacation now, so most of my time I'm with the people here at the fountain."

"And then?"

"I'm a salesgirl here at the Centrum Department Store."

"How old are you?"

"Twenty-two."

"Suzanne, what do you mean by the people at the fountain? Are there special people who come here?"

"There are about fifty of us who sort of live here."

"Did you know each other before?"

"No, we just started coming together after they opened the fountain last fall. Not because of the fountain itself — it's pretty *kitschish*, isn't it? — but because there was a place to sit, and lots of foreigners came here. Now we all know each other."

"Who are the kids?"

"It's a pretty mixed group. Some of them are just lazy and want to get money by black marketeering. Lots of Western tourists who come, they don't know what their money is really worth, so they'll exchange money with these kids one for one." One West mark for one East mark, the official rate. "And then these kids can sell Western money for three to one. Kids like that don't have very many political opinions, except that they hate the D.D.R. But a few of the people are very politically conscious."

"Don't these tourists know they have to get bank receipts for all the Western currency they exchange, or they can get into trouble when they leave?"

"No, they're very naive. They think things are free like in their own countries."

"It's really funny how every day the papers write about the Western monetary crisis and how it shows the crisis of capitalism and all that. Once I went to exchange some money, and I said, 'You don't want my crisis currency, do you?' 'Oh, yes, yes, please!' they answered, of course."

"Oh, that's just all complete hypocrisy, what they write about that in the newspapers. Typical. I never even bother to read any newspapers or magazines. The only thing I ever read is books. They know very well what Western currency is worth. If you're an East German you have to wait eight years to get a

Wartburg car, and it costs eighteen thousand marks. If you're a West German and order one for a relative here, you pay only six thousand West marks, and you get the car immediately — no wait, whatever color you want."

"Why do you come here to the fountain?"

"Here I can be freer, a little freer. I can talk with people from the West, and get a glimpse of what it's like to *live*."

"What is it you get a glimpse of, Suzanne?"

"A place where there is some *joy* in living, where it is more than just gloominess. Here everything is more or less slowly falling apart, because nobody *cares* enough to take the trouble to keep our lives in shape. You get a pair of pants or a dress, and it falls apart after three weeks. You have to wait five months for a repairman or a plumber or a carpenter, so things just stay broken forever. It makes everything so sad. And people are just indifferent to everything. In high school and at the university, ninety percent are against the F.D.J. — I know, because I was once an F.D.J. leader in my high school — but they wear their blue shirts anyway whenever they're told to. All the noise and junk and propaganda from the government goes in one ear and out the other, but people go through the whole blah-blah-blah like trained animals. In public, everybody is for the system!"

I hadn't asked her anything about what she had said about being thrown out of university — I didn't want to rush into it, and sensed that she too felt we would be getting to know each other better, so there would still be time — but now she had whetted my appetite further by just dropping the fact that she had been an F.D.J. leader once. Who *was* this girl with the bewitching sad-sack face?

"Suzanne, you were a leader of the F.D.J. once? How did that happen?"

"Steve, I can't tell you now. I promised to meet a boy I know at the Bowling Bar at five. Anyway, it's better to talk in private. Can you come to my apartment Friday night at eight?"

I said yes, and, as yesterday, she kissed me on the forehead.

✻

I made a slip again on my outing with Waack on Thursday, and felt a gnawing anxiety all day over it. We had driven out to a restaurant on the lakes outside East Berlin where the illegal Communist Party meeting had taken place. In addition to us, there was a group of twenty or so Young Pioneers, maybe five or six years old, crammed into the little room, which had a table, chairs, and pictures of the members of the Central Committee on the wall.

What made me gape was how these tots were being shamelessly indoctrinated. The deification of Ernst Thälmann I could almost accept — we learn about George Washington as the father of our country, even if not in the same way. But the kids were then told that Thälmann's brave visions had been realized in today's D.D.R., where the working class holds power through its Party, whose brilliant policies have created a brighter future for the people of the D.D.R. The only saving grace in the Pioneer leader's talk was that its fancy political words went undoubtedly way over the tots' heads. But I kept thinking about what that young lady had said that night at the Interhotel bar about the next generation getting Lenin from the cradle.

"What's wrong, Steve? You looked disturbed." Waack aroused me from my reflective revery. Damn it, I had given myself away again.

I woke up with a start. "Uh, no, no, not disturbed. I was just thinking — I mean, is it really right to bring up politics with such young children? Is it fair to tell them all these things at such an early age?"

"We feel we must entrust even our youngest citizens with political information," Waack replied in his best ceremonial style. "Remember, we have so much to fight against — reactionary homes, West German television. If we don't indoctrinate the children in one way, they will just get Western indoctrination."

We were walking after lunch through a clearing in the lakeside woods near the restaurant. "Steve, I had been meaning to ask you after our visit to that discotheque in Dresden how you can listen to that horrible pop music. Now, I'm not old-fashioned. Some of this new music is all right. I like a song like 'Yesterday.' Or the American protest songs, Joan Baez. But the loud stuff, the noise — how can you listen to it?"

"Well, some of the really loud stuff I don't like either."

"It's not a question of like or dislike. As a politically active person trying to change your society, can't you see the political effect of this music?"

"Political effect? I don't think it really has much of a political effect. It's mostly entertainment. If anything, a lot of pop music contains social criticism."

"No, Steve, don't you see? Pop music is promoted in order to make young people stupid, to pacify them. They listen to it, they become entranced, and that's it! And then, of course, the West also uses pop music as part of its attempt to sabotage socialism in the socialist countries. It is clear that the West Germans launch a group like the Rolling Stones mainly for use in psychological warfare against us."

"Doctor Waack, the Rolling Stones aren't a West German group. They're English."

"Oh, are they?" He seemed just a whit taken aback. "You see my point anyway."

"I can understand your point to a certain degree. Perhaps rock attracts a different type of person in the D.D.R. than in the West. In America just about every young person — including those who are politically active — listens to rock. Maybe here it's more an antisocial element. I mean, I must admit I was disgusted by that kid who wanted me to exchange black-market money. It was shocking to see someone openly defying the law like that."

Waack's tone modified suddenly. "Why was it so shocking?"

"Well, just that he was willing to break the law . . ."

"Sure, but he probably didn't have any specially evil intentions." I wondered what he was trying to get at. "He probably needed Western money to buy some sort of amplifying equipment or something for his music that we don't make in the D.D.R."

"Well, I don't think that justifies breaking the law. But why can't you manufacture such things in the D.D.R., if people want to buy them?"

"Because such things are not necessary. We only make things that are necessary."

"Necessary. Necessary for whom?"

"Necessary for the state, of course."

The quiet forest path was sublime. There was a touch of mist on the ground, and deep green moss everywhere. The crowd of people from the steamship that made the rounds of the Berlin lakes was in a festive mood as they descended the gangplank to get themselves some beer during the half-hour the boat was docked. We embarked with the other passengers when the rest pause was over. It was no time for a political discussion, and I sincerely hoped we could avoid one.

"Steve, you've finished the book I gave you on Ernst Fischer by now, haven't you? Maybe it's time we had a discussion about it."

"O.K.," I whined, attempting hard to avoid a drone.

"Well, give me your impressions."

"Generally, I thought it was a good book." Actually, it was a piece of drivel that tried to "meet" Fischer's arguments mainly by showing where they contradicted Lenin's views, convincing only to someone who accepted Lenin's views as divine. "It took up just the areas where I have questions, like the necessity of the dictatorship of the proletariat."

Waack smiled warm-heartedly. "I know. That's why I gave you the book."

"Well, I understand the author's argument that, given the strength of the West, the socialist lands cannot allow the luxury of so-called bourgeois freedoms. But I think the author fails to deal with the question of *desirability* of greater freedom, at least in principle, if this diversionary activity from the West did not exist."

"What is desirable about greater freedom?"

The water splashed off the side of the boat below us, making an enchanting sound. I was holding my head up toward the sun to try to get some more of a tan, and I thought for a moment so as to phrase my reply correctly. "Let me give you an example. In any society, there are some who would prefer to work very long hours, and get paid correspondingly, and others who prefer more leisure to the extra money. In capitalism, hours of work are usually the same in all factories of a type. But I think that in socialism, it should be possible to set up some firms which have long hours and where the workers earn correspondingly more, and others where the hours are a little shorter and where the vacation is, say, five or six weeks long."

"I don't see your point," he answered indifferently. "What would be the advantage of that?"

"Well, people have different *preferences*, as I said. Socialism should increase people's possibility to *choose* according to their preferences, and make decisions themselves. Then they feel happier."

"*Feel!* What is feel? I have already told you, *feel* has nothing to do with socialism. We can't go around letting workers in some factories have shorter hours or more vacations, because we must produce more and more so as to increase the economic and military strength of the state, and of the entire socialist camp. We can't let 'feelings' interfere with that, my friend. That's just what the capitalists want us to do! Think of the struggle for influence in the world, Steve! Imagine we have an important export shipment to Egypt, which will increase the standing of the D.D.R. in the Arab world, and then suddenly the workers in that factory decide they want more *vacations.* Are you crazy? Are you insane? If our workers had more vacations, how could we build up our basic industries? How could we build more cars? Steve, this is the mistake your beloved Yugoslavia made." Who ever knew my brief mention of Yugoslavia would one distant day be transformed into the golden thread of Waack's ravings? "They talked about vacations, about consumer goods, instead of building up their basic industries. And where are they today? Steve, I can assure you, the imperialists are not stupid: they know where to prey, they go to the weakest link. Now that they've failed in Czechoslovakia, they've chosen Yugoslavia as their next target."

"Doctor Waack, but even in the capitalist countries workers can try to get more vacations, either through their unions or through legislation."

"We will give our workers precisely as much vacation as they need to rest their bodies so they can return to full productive working strength, not a second more. Some vacation they need, otherwise they can't work efficiently. That our experts will determine. And if any bum in a factory starts crying out about more vacations, we will hit him over the head, and hit him so hard that nobody else gets any ideas. We can't let things get out of control. First they ask for more vacations, and the next thing you know they're asking for more *wages* — and then everything just falls apart." Waack had by now worked himself into one of his glassy-eyed frenzies again, when he spoke not so much to me as to the world. "Steve, can you imagine what would happen if we just gave people a little more money? They'd become completely corrupted, all they would care about was their little car and their TV set. My friend, you are so young! People are more evil than you think." He turned his head to look right at me. "*Du bildest Dir ein, dass der Sozialismus ein menschenfreundlisches System ist. Das ist es in Prinzip, aber in den Einzelheiten nicht.*" You are under the illusion that socialism is a system friendly to human beings. It is that, in principle, but not in the details.

Even after all Waack had said before, all the horrors and the hypocrisy, I was not psychologically prepared for this tirade. I listened dumbfounded. I had been in the D.D.R. for twenty-eight days and had heard of so much evil from those who were on the whipped end of Waack's lash. I prided myself on self-control because I knew how vital it was for me personally. It was relatively easy to listen to Waack's earlier propaganda about the D.D.R. as a kingdom of bliss on earth, for that was simply lies. But the truth, Waack's naked admission, left me dumbfounded. Waack's "argument" for what he calls socialism, when you come down to it, is probably simply that it is historically inevitable, according to "Marxist science." Certainly nothing he had said about it indicated it was *better!* Maybe his little bit about creating people who were uncorrupted by cars and consumer goods. But he knew what a lie *that* was — from his own English umbrella and suede jacket. People are far more consumer-oriented and materialistic in the D.D.R. than in any Western industrial society, simply because *getting* consumer goods is so hard. And the lack of consumer goods just creates a new form of class society — in the D.D.R., privilege is to be able to buy a bar of Lux soap in an Intershop, just as in China privilege is having mastered the thoughts of Chairman Mao best. People can see other things beyond consumer goods only when they have the consumer goods — the Socialist new man can only be a product of abundance, as Marx predicted, not of the moral preachments of a totalitarian state.

"Doctor Waack!" I screamed desperately. "SO IF YOU THINK THAT'S WHAT SOCIALISM IS, WHY SHOULD ANYONE CHOOSE IT?"

Some people on the boat turned around toward me, and Waack's eyes, suddenly perked up from the fantasy trance in which he had conjured his chimera, darted around the ship. Just as quickly, his expression turned as steel-hard as it had been intoxicated moments before. "Steve, let me warn you! If a citizen of the D.D.R. spoke the way you have been speaking, he'd have his head kicked into this lake here." His voice softened, just a drop. "This is a dictatorship of the proletariat, and a hard one at that. You know what it is to go around talking with people about Yugoslavian socialism or about more vacations, you know what that is?"

"No, what is it?"

"It is enemy propaganda. And let me tell you this, my friend; we are not soft. We punish hard, and our rule can only be that if you're not with us you're against us."

"But, but — you told me to — to — to *discuss* things with you, to raise questions I have." My voice was small, meek, pleading. "You know that even when I raise questions, I am still above all a friend of the Soviet Union. You know that, don't you?"

"The discussion is over." Immediately, the threats and the anger vanished. He simply fell silent and began looking at the fancy summer cottages we were passing in the little islands along the lake. But what had been the purpose of all that? I thought up and down and went through all the permutations of possibilities one more time, all the evidence so far. Again, I asked myself the big question: Am I a guest or am I a future prisoner?

We ate dinner at the restaurant in the municipal hall in the Köpenick district of Berlin, a famous working-class quarter. My goulash had not a single trace of meat in it — it was only sauce and fat. Following Waack's earlier examples, I asked him whether I should complain. He was back in his normal mood, as if nothing had happened on the boat, and said I should. The waiter absolutely refused to listen to our complaints, whereupon we huffed out of the restaurant without paying my portion of the bill. "You know why there was no meat on that goulash, Steve? Because the cook and the waiter stole the meat the restaurant was given and kept it for themselves."

"You mean they stole *state property*?" I said wide-eyed, with an air of outraged innocence.

"Of course, what do you think? It happens all the time. My friend, if I teach you one lesson during your stay it will be this: men are evil, and under socialism they continue to be evil."

*

I worked on my Harvard questions most of the next day, but left in time to arrive, my heart beating fast, at Suzanne's before eight. She lived alone, in a tiny garret of an apartment on a street which was neither small nor large. It was up three long flights — no elevator — with high steps that you couldn't skip two at a time. There were no lights in the hallways. Her room was nice. She had on blue jeans.

"I have twenty-six tape bands of Western rock. What would you like to hear?"

"What do you have?"

"Some of it's by groups and some is just hit lists. It's whatever I could tape off RIAS. But I haven't taped anything for a year now."

She put on, according to my conventional request, some Beatles.

"You know, my 'companion,' Doctor Waack — the guy I told you about — he thought the Rolling Stones were a West German group."

Suzanne had that lost, blasé, almost freaked-out look in her round, brown eyes. "Of course he would." She gave a laughing grimace. "The Rolling Stones gave them problems two years ago, when people thought they were going to give a concert near the Wall. A lot of students got thrown out of schools then."

"Because they participated in the riots?"

"There were no riots. Kids were just milling around and the police came in. A lot of students came because they were curious."

The Beatles were beautiful; I hadn't heard them for a long time. "Do you understand the words, Suzanne?"

"Oh, some words here and there. But what's the use of learning English? I can't go anywhere where I can use it."

She had an antique-looking typewriter with a high black back sitting on her desk. A sheet of half-typed paper was in it, and several typed sheets at the side.

"What are you working on here?"

"It's just for myself. I am writing an essay on the similarities between the Third Reich and the D.D.R."

I looked at her, and blood rushed to my head. I wanted to hug her right there, not only because she was beautiful, but because of the beauty of what she had discovered — on her own, from inside the prison, the insights of free social scientists.

"So far, I've written about things like the destruction of parties and trade unions, the use of political indoctrination in schools, the glorification of the leader, and the use of scapegoats — the Jews in the Third Reich and West Germany in the D.D.R. But there's a lot more."

"Where do you get your information from, Suzanne?"

"On the Third Reich, from any book in the D.D.R. On the D.D.R., from my life."

"Suzanne, you have to explain to me about your life. How could you one time have been a class secretary for the F.D.J., and now have been thrown out of university? Did you believe in the System once?"

"Steve, wait. I'll tell you later — it's such a long story. Let's go out for a walk first. It's too hot in here, and I want to show you our quarter."

It was a warm night as we walked along the cobblestone sidewalks. "See how everything is running down," she began. "All the small shops are closing down, you see boarded-up windows everywhere. Just a few years ago we had five neighborhood restaurants — you know, the type of places where workers got together for a beer after work. Now there's one. There were five bakeries, now they're all closed. The cakes you get at the stores are all stale — you can see they've started to crack right there on the shelves." Suzanne dragged her hand lazily across the building façades. "Look at how the plaster is crumbling."

"Why have the stores closed down?"

"The old people who owned them die off, and they don't give out new licenses."

When we got back to her apartment, I asked her to sit down and, once and for all, tell me her story.

"My father settled voluntarily on the Eastern side of Berlin after the war. He was a socialist, sort of, and he thought things would be better here. Oh, did he become disillusioned — but he always gets angry at me anyway, says I should just get used to things and not protest, because it's no use."

"What does he do?"

"He works at a savings bank."

"What about you? Did he teach you to believe in socialism?"

"Well, I don't know whether he taught me, but I believe in socialism, even though I always saw all the faults of the system here. But first I thought that the best way to change it was to get into things, and play along, until you got a high-up post in the government, where you had some power and could do something. Of course that's not so easy for a woman. But I wanted to try."

"So that's why you became active in the F.D.J.?"

"Well, it was partly that and partly to collect points so I could study philosophy at the university. I thought that if I really mastered Marxism, I would get a better understanding of the faults of the D.D.R. and how to change them. Here, let me show you something I wrote then, when I made my application to be an F.D.J. leader."

Out of her desk drawer she took a brown folder with many papers in it bound together by paper clips and opened to one of the pages. "I am respectfully making this application for a position of trust within the Free German Youth in order to fulfill my class responsibility for the education of our D.D.R. youth in the spirit of socialism," it read. "The West German class enemy spares no efforts to mislead youth as part of its revanchist plans to turn back the clock of history and topple the socialist order in the German Democratic Republic. The ideological education of D.D.R. youth, which dedicated leaders in the Free German Youth are in the best position to give, is the best safeguard against their efforts and for the defense of our Republic."

I was taken aback that this girl with long stringy hair and rundown blue jeans could ever have written such lines. Immediately I thought of those old high school graduation pictures that Jerry Rubin always shows of himself. "Suzanne, did you *believe* this stuff when you wrote it? How could you?" I asked.

She sighed. "The incredible thing is that I don't know whether I believed it or not. It's hard to separate what you believe and what you don't believe, even in your own mind, because you know that that's the form you have to write it in." She paused. "I don't know, I guess I believed that there were reactionary forces in West Germany who were trying to misuse kids here for their own ends."

"Do you still believe that?"

She paused again. "Well, the C.D.U. in West Germany. I don't like them, they are still an enemy as far as I'm concerned." That's Adenauer's old conservative party.

"So what was it like to be an F.D.J. leader?"

"It was sickening. I couldn't hold out. Almost every other person who was active was in it just as a careerist. Maybe ten percent of the kids who were active did it out of conviction. And I saw how ridiculous it was to have everyone in high school and college members of the F.D.J. How can you have a serious organization when most of the people in it don't want to be in it? You know, Steve, there's a story about how 'voluntary' all these 'voluntary' things are. They want to get a cat to eat mustard, but want it to eat the mustard voluntarily. So they put some mustard on the cat's mouth, but the cat spits it out. They try again, but the cat spits it out again. So finally they put the mustard on the cat's ass. It stings the cat like hell, so the cat licks the mustard off his ass to stop the pain. They're happy, because they've gotten him to eat mustard voluntarily. But the top leadership just wants to show their little statistics — ninety-nine point nine percent of all young people are F.D.J. members, so they can have something to write in the newspapers. It's typical of them: they had this discussion about why young workers all left the F.D.J. as soon as they left school and went to work. It was embarrassing because membership is supposed to be voluntary in school. But all they really wanted to do was keep the membership figures up, so what they did was let people remain members of the F.D.J. until the're fifty, so Party hacks can fill up the rolls!" Her voice again assumed that distant, reportorial quality.

"So all this got you disillusioned."

"Well, I couldn't hold out as an F.D.J. leader, so I stopped being active after I graduated from high school and went to work. But I still had my dream about trying to make it up in the Party, and I still wanted more than anything to study philosophy."

"Where did you go to work?"

"At a cosmetic factory. And there I decided to make an application to be a candidate member of the Party. I went to all these Party meetings, and donated a day's pay every month to Vietnam. After I worked there for a little more than a year, I got permission to enroll at the university to study philosophy. But by that time I was depressed and confused about what to do — I was so sick of them that I wanted to withdraw my application for candidate membership in the Party. I hated them too much."

"Why?"

"You just can't believe how closed their minds are. Oh, how many discussions I had with Party members where they just repeated the same blah-blah, the defense of our socialist fatherland, the West German class enemy. They were completely afraid of *anything* new, afraid that it would overwhelm them like a huge tidal wave. The worst came after Czechoslovakia. Since I was a candidate member, I got this thing they passed around inside the Party." She took out a yellowing booklet from her drawer, and gave it to me. The title was "On the Events in the Czechoslovakia Socialist Republic: The Standpoint of the German Democratic Republic," and was dated September 1968. The first line read, "The citizens of our Republic have welcomed the Moscow Communiqué (after the meeting of Czech and Soviet leaders) as a document which serves the cause of the socialist community and the securing of peace." I looked up at her.

"Read this, if you want to see how low it is possible for human beings to sink in defending the indefensible. See the words they use against the socialists in Czechoslovakia who wanted to bring freedom there! Keep it; take it home and read it." Her voice became raspy and emotion-filled.

"So what happened to your candidate membership?"

"I knew I couldn't withdraw it before I got to the university, that would have been the end of my chances. The whole thing was eating me up inside, I couldn't make a decision: when I made my application, it was because I really wanted to work for socialism in the D.D.R., but now I was staying in like so many others just to get advantages. I felt disgusting. And then, it was so hard to decide whether to make that final decision to give up on changing the Party from within."

"What happened when you got to the university?"

"It was the same thing again. I went to a few F.D.J. meetings. My God, the crap they took up. They had on the agenda discussions of some students whom they thought had too long hair. Trying to talk with the professors there was like trying to talk to a stone wall."

"Are all the professors Party members?"

"Of course. You have to be to teach at the university."

"What did you try to bring up?"

"Well, I asked them why we couldn't study the works of Stalin. Twenty years ago he was considered our great socialist father, and now his works aren't even available. But look." She pointed to her bookshelf. "I got his *Selected Works* from an old man my father knows."

"Why did you want to study *Stalin?*"

"He was a mass murderer, wasn't he? Don't you think it's important to study his theories to see how they could lead to such crimes?"

"So what did your teacher say?"

"They just got angry at me. And I just became more depressed. Then one day I got a letter from the university administration calling me in. The dean told me that I was expelled from the university for 'social democratism.' I asked him if he could be more specific, and he said no. I asked him for a written confirmation of my charges, and he said that nothing could be written down."

"I assume there was nowhere you could go to protest."

"No. That was it, I was out. A few days later I got a letter saying I was no longer considered an applicant for candidate membership in the Party. You know what my problem the whole time was, Steve?"

"No, what was it?"

"I thought too much of theory, I didn't look enough at the reality, the things around me. No, I mean I looked at them, I saw them, but I kept that separate from the theory. I kept telling myself: well, at least we have the socialist *base* in the D.D.R. But finally I realized: what good is the base? How does it help anyone? How does it make anyone's life better? You know, that's what the Party people have to do, the ones who are convinced by the system. They have to look at the theory instead of at what happens in their daily lives."

I got up to look at her bookshelves. Three volumes of Marx's *Das Kapital*. Then a whole section of West German books: two by Wilhelm Reich, one book on the Summerhill method of child rearing, Solzhenitsyn's *The First Circle*, Rosa Luxemburg's critique of the Russian Revolution. Rosa Luxemburg, the radical German socialist from the First World War, is of course an official D.D.R. goddess, but this pamphlet of hers criticizing Lenin is banned in the D.D.R. I flipped through Suzanne's edition, which was profusely underlined. She had put stars and double underlining around Luxemburg's passage about freedom never meaning freedom just for supporters of one party or one ideology alone, about how freedom meant something only if it included freedom for those who think differently. It was fantastic how she had come upon ideas and insights that the entire scholarly community in the West has fastened on: that passage from Rosa Luxemburg has always been viewed as the most famous one in the pamphlet.

"Freedom," I said to her, "is the freedom to say two plus two equals four. You know who said that?"

"No, who?"

"George Orwell, the British writer."

"Who is he?"

"A famous writer, a great socialist and democrat. He wrote a book called *1984* about a totalitarian society of the future, modeled on Stalin's Russia. The main character breaks out and discovers the meaning of the word *freedom*. In the world of *1984*, the ideal is to say two plus two equals five if Big Brother says it's true. Freedom, says the hero of the book, is the freedom to say two plus two equals four."

CHAPTER 7

SUZANNE TOLD ME shortly afterward I ought to leave, for her boy friend would be coming home soon. I'm not certain what I'd been expecting when she invited me over for the evening; I knew I'd have to get back to Frau Koch's sometime before the night was done. But nevertheless I was disappointed: she was an uncommon girl. She told me to look for her at the fountain when I returned. We weren't saying good-bye to each other forever. But it felt that way when she first said I'd better go.

I had decided in advance to be a good boy in Rostock. Already I had gathered enough material for the *New Yorker* article. At the same time I was still tense from Waack's outburst on the steamboat. In Rostock I would make no attempts to escape him. Instead, I would relax at the seashore and show Waack I could be dutiful.

That decision made, I was able to enjoy five genuinely pleasant days. Rostock was the nicest place I had seen in the D.D.R. We saw on a bus tour a few almost *gemütlich* apartment areas built in the mid-fifties, with trees along the streets. The harbor, right near the Interhotel Warnow, where we stayed, blew a fresh wind onto the downtown streets. The satellite towns around Lütten Klein — built to accommodate the population expansion from the development of Rostock into the D.D.R.'s major port and shipbuilding center and lying right along the highway for tourist transit traffic from Scandinavia — were less impressive. There were rows of identical apartment buildings, in parallel lines, with almost no lawns and few playgrounds for children. Also, except for food stores and one restaurant, there appeared to be almost no other services for the tens of thousands of residents. Waack, however, limited his commentary largely to the observation that the name Lütten Klein involved a pleonasm, as *lütten*, the name for the old settlement near the present development, was the word in the local Plattdeutsch dialect for "small," while, of course, *klein* meant the same thing in regular German.

Most of the time went by in the same relaxed spirit. We spent two full days on the beach at Warnemünde, which unfortunately failed to improve noticeably my pitiful tan; and I read, largely undisturbed by the interruption of discussion. First I made my way through an English-language paperback printed in the Soviet Union, *The Foundations of Historical and Dialectical Materialism*, which Waack said would provide me the "building blocks of Marxist science," which he thought I lacked. That he thought an American college graduate would be so ignorant of Marxism as to need the elementary-school-level explanation this book imparted was revealing, and I told him, in the friendly terms that marked our time in Rostock, that very little of the book's content was new to me. Afterward I began to plow through Volume Six of *The History of the German Labor Movement*, a thick hardcover sold at the subsidized price of three dollars a volume in East Berlin. Volume Six covered the period 1945–1949.

Right along the beach at Warnemünde was a just completed hotel, the Neptun, built by a Swedish construction firm but owned — unlike similar foreign-built hotels in Yugoslavia, Hungary, and now even Czechoslovakia — by the East German government. We went inside to look around. Waack got to see the Westinghouse elevators, where the electric-eye doors opened up again if you touched them while they were closing. At the Interhotel Warnow I almost got my arm strangled when I put it in the elevator door to try to stop it from closing. One or another of the elevators at the Interhotel was broken the entire time. "It's a problem in these new high-rises, like at Lütten Klein," Waack told me, "because we have a shortage of repairmen and it often takes several months for them to get to an apartment building when the elevators break."

Friday night we visited the bar downstairs in the Interhotel, with the inappropriate name Boutique. Waack kept the drinks coming — gin and tonic I always got — and also paid for two girls who had sat down next to us. "What was it like during the Baltic Sea Week recently? Was it fun?" I asked one of them, bespectacled and plain-looking, without even one memorable feature.

"Well, the people in Rostock are so busy working for the foreign guests that week that it's not much fun for us. Just tiring."

"Rostock is a port town," I went on. "Port towns are usually pretty wild, with all the sailors around. Do you have a lot of night life here?"

"Well, there's this bar. And — and then there's the discotheque at the Hotel Neptun."

"That's it?"

"Well," she answered shyly, "we're grateful we have that much."

"How's the discotheque?"

"I don't know. We've never been there — it's too expensive. Ten marks."

The other girl, who had her hair done up in one of those

hornet's nests that were fashionable in the fifties, took out a cigarette and some matches, at which point Waack saw the chance for his cigarette-lighter trick.

She was suitably impressed. "It's much better than with these matches we have. All you can get in the stores now are *Vietnamese* matches, and two or three of them always break before you can get one to light."

"Where do you girls work?" I asked.

"We work together in the clothes purchasing department for Rostock HO." HO stands for *Handelsorganisation,* the state corporation that runs most stores and restaurants.

I thought for a while before going on. "May I ask you a question about your work, or would you prefer not to talk about it on a weekend?"

"No, go ahead," the girl with the hornet's-nest hair answered.

"I've been reading in the newspapers about the problem of getting some clothing factories to produce clothes that customers want to buy. The papers say the stores purchase the clothing, and then it just lies on the shelves. But, I mean, do the stores have any way to put pressure on a factory that produces things the customers don't want? Can't you just stop buying clothes from them?"

"Well, there's a contract with the factory —"

"No, but I mean after the contract runs out."

"Yes, well, most of the contracts are for two years. After that, in principle we can stop buying from the bad factories. But in practice it's impossible because we have a plan target for how much clothing we have to buy from the clothing factories, and it's hard to get a hold of all the clothing we need to fill the quota. So we have to be thankful for whatever we can get."

"Oh."

"How is it in America?" the other girl asked tentatively.

"Well, if some type of clothing doesn't sell, the store just stops buying it."

"*Really?*" the first girl cried for joy. "What a wonderful idea." She sounded as if it was new to hear. "But," she went on, "what about the store's plan target?"

"They don't have any plan target."

"Yes," Waack said blithely, puffing at his cigarette, "this is the famous flexible adaptability of the free market system."

My eyes twinkled, and I glanced quickly at Waack, who was looking suave and at ease: the bastard, *he* didn't believe in the system either!

*

Even the problems and the discoveries in Rostock took on a different character, a chess game for fun and not for keeps. One morning at breakfast we heard the cackle of New York accents at the other corner of the hotel dining room. I had heard the same group the night before at the fish restaurant where we had eaten dinner. As the group passed by our table to leave, I raised my voice and greeted them with a hello. They were three married couples, and the second they flocked around the table and I saw two of the ladies wearing FREE ANGELA DAVIS buttons, I understood what a blunder I had made. Holy shit, I realized, they're obviously New York Communists, and they might the hell know my name. Damn it, what a way to be exposed!

"Where are you from?" came the inevitable question from one of the matrons.

"Great Neck, New York."

"Oh, Great Neck! We have all sorts of *friends* in Great Neck." I could imagine.

"Great Neck," a balding guy gurgled. "So your pappy made

so much money that now he can afford to send you off to visit the socialist countries."

"Well, actually, I'm a guest of the Academy of Sciences. This is my host, Doctor Waack."

Waack nodded his head in recognition.

"So tell me, what's your name?" a yenta came in.

My mind went blank for a second. Then, I gave the name of one of Great Neck's better-known pro-Communists. Lucky Waack doesn't speak English, I thought to myself.

"Yeah, yeah. I think I know the name," one of the Angela-Davis ladies said haltingly and reflectively. "Uh, what's your mother's first name?"

Now I went completely blank. Shit, I couldn't think of this woman's first name, even though I knew it. "Sylvia," I blurted out, giving *my* mother's name.

The yenta repeated the entire name I had given her, both first and last, and pondered for a moment. "Yes, yes — I think we know them. I think we do. Say hello to your mother from Shirley Lagercrantz, will you?"

"And enjoy your stay in the German Democratic Republic!" the man burst out.

"You too," I came back, as they all left. And then, to Waack: "Very nice people. Quite progressive, I think. Yes, very progressive."

The presence of the Americans prompted me to bring up something else with Waack. "You know, Doctor Waack, these grapefruits we've been eating at breakfast — they're American, Sunkist brand. But, you know what? The American capitalists are cheating the D.D.R. These grapefruits are of very low quality." They were extremely sour, and about the size of oranges. Normally, I thought, they'd probably be thrown out.

"My friend, you can be sure that our foreign trade experts are not being cheated. Those grapefruits are all we can afford to buy." Even for an Interhotel.

*

This time Waack and I shared the same room, under the ludicrous pretense that we had gotten the last room the hotel had. Obviously, after my performance in Dresden Bach and Waack wanted to keep closer watch on me. But in Rostock I didn't let that bother me. Instead, I hit on a plan to do a little spying of my own. I had noticed that Waack's shaving brush, which he left on the wash basin in the bathroom, read MADE IN GERMANY, that is, West Germany, as East German products say MADE IN THE GERMAN DEMOCRATIC REPUBLIC. I became determined to inspect Waack's toilet case, which he kept in a nice brown leather traveling kit on a shelf in the clothes closet in our room.

Before we went to sleep one night I left open the door to that closet, which was right across from the toilet in the hall. About an hour after we had turned out the lights, I got up out of bed, and opened the bathroom door so that it hid the hall from the rest of the room. Behind this cover, I grabbed the toilet case without disrupting my stride to the bathroom. I sat down at the toilet seat, the darkness broken only by the streetlights shining in the window, and slowly and noiselessly opened the zipper. For those moments, I had no feeling for the absurd in what I was doing: I saw myself only as a minor James Bond.

A minor James Bond — who found what he was searching after. What loot inside the leather bag: Colgate toothpaste, Brylcreem hair cream, Lux soap, Nivea skin cream, Prell shampoo. The materialistic son of a bitch! I flushed the toilet, washed my hands, and returned to the room and went to sleep.

That wasn't the only revelation. As he was taking some change out of his wallet one morning to get us bus tickets — normally it was my duty to come up with small change for the buses, but that time I was short — I got a glimpse of some curious inhabitants of his change purse. Namely: one West German mark and one American nickel. I breathed a deep, wide smile of contentment inside — it was contentment I felt, not abhorrence as I should have. I thought back to what the old guy at Alex said about certain officials getting part of their salary in Western money. Dr. Joachim Waack is obviously not the type who keeps Western small change around as a souvenir picked up from tourists as a token of admiration for the West. Nor does he have, I had asked him about that previously, any relatives in West Germany who might send him money. Unless he was a black marketeer, one could only draw the conclusion that — elementary, my dear Watson, right?

All this was sickening, certainly. But it tickled me inside to learn — better, to discover, by tricks and logic — new details about Joachim Waack. More and more he seemed like a Marquis de Sade of the betrayed revolution, someone who tingles in the sublime knowledge that hypocrisy need have no limits, corruption no regrets.

*

But the sun turned into clouds the very last night of the trip. After dinner, Waack told me to go up to our room, he had a brief errand to do and would be up shortly. I was sleepy and lay down in bed, taking the opportunity to tune in the Voice of America on shortwave. About a half-hour later, just after the nine-o'clock news, the ringing of the room telephone awoke me from a half-slumber. It would be Waack, I assumed, with some excuse about why he had taken so long.

"Hello, this is Roland," said the voice on the other end. I recognized it immediately. It was Bach.

I was still half-asleep, and the whole thing came so fast that I wasn't ready for a thought-out reaction. "Do you want to speak to Doctor Waack?" I babbled.

"Who is this?"

"This is a friend of Doctor Waack's. Doctor Waack is not here now."

Without another word, the party on the other end disappeared. "Hello, hello?" I repeated into the phone, jiggling the receiver. Nothing.

As I hung up, I thought through what had just happened. It was definitely Bach's voice. Obviously, Waack's little errand had been to reach Bach in Berlin. The long-distance call took some time to place, and when Bach came back the hotel switchboard made the mistake of connecting the call to Waack's room instead of to the telephone booth from where Waack was calling. But Bach had given his first name as Günter. Roland was Bach's *cover name* — and a romantic one at that, not clumsy German but rather filled with *une mystique française*. But what did Waack have to tell him?

Ten minutes later the phone rang again. This time it was Waack. "Where are you?" he said demandingly. "I've been waiting for you down here in the bar for a half-hour."

"But you said you'd come up to the room when you were through. You didn't say anything about the bar."

"Of course I did. Hurry up, come on down."

When I met him downstairs, he asked me, in his best matter-of-fact tone, if anything had happened while I was upstairs.

"Well, there was a phone call."

"Who called?"

"Oh, I don't know. I think it was a mistake, they got the wrong room."

"The wrong room? What a scandal! You should protest at the desk that they bothered you that way."

"Oh, it was nothing."

"Nothing? No, Steve, I would complain. The switchboard

caused you to be bothered by ringing our room when the call was not for us."

Twice within the next hour Waack came back to the phone call, each time with an emphasis in some way on the call as a mistake, one that he hoped hadn't disturbed me too much. He did protest too much.

At the bar, I had hoped to get my normal gin and tonic, but when Waack returned he told me that they had no gin, so he got us each a vodka with Club Cola. I protested good-naturedly. "Doctor Waack, vodka and orange juice is O.K., but I must say I don't particularly like vodka and cola. And this Club Cola is, I have to say it, especially bad. Here, *you* take the drink. I don't want it."

"Drink up, Steve, you'll get used to it."

"No, I don't think I will. I really can't stand the stuff."

Waack looked at me through his glass, which was still clear because he hadn't poured the cola in it yet. His face looked like that of a blustering fish staring through an aquarium tank, his mustache heaving mightily back and forth like fish gills sucking in air from the water. "Steve, man is a very adaptable creature. Man can live in the Arctic and man can live in the tropics. No other animal can do that. *Der Mensch kann sich an alles gewöhnen.*" People can get used to anything.

Waack paused for dramatic effect, and broke out in the tiniest of smiles. "And this *freedom* you speak about, Steve. *Wir glauben, dass wir unsere Menschen allmählich davon abgewöhnen können.*" We think we can gradually get our people to get used to living without it.

My stomach sank in revulsion, and I reverted to that mood of mixed disgust and dread which had set its indelible mark on my entire journey in the D.D.R.

❋

On the train trip back to Berlin, we mainly listened to my transistor radio. As we were switching around the knob, we heard a loud, piercing, shrill tone. "Stop turning the dial," Waack burst out. "Steve, you know what that is?"

"No."

"That's our jamming of RIAS on AM wave lengths." He sounded ever so proud to report this to me, despite what among other things was the huge waste of electricity the jamming brought about in a country with such an electricity shortage. "Unfortunately, we can't jam it on FM because it is technically infeasible. The same thing with West German television. It's too bad."

No fewer than two telegrams awaited me at Frau Koch's on my return. The first from my parents:

> WHY DON'T YOU COME HOME FOR A MONTH AFTER DDR
> BEFORE RETURNING TO SWEDEN

That was a brilliant idea which I would never have thought of on my own, and it made me happy and excited. With the youth fare the cost would be minimal, and there would be nothing I could use more than a return home after the D.D.R. I would check at the Interhotel at Alex to see if I could order a ticket to America from East Berlin.

The other telegram came, like a shot out of the dark, from my 1969 friend Mattias from Schwedt.

> ARRIVE BERLIN SUNDAY   MEET YOU AT 2 PM IN FRONT OF
> MILK BAR AT ALEXANDERPLATZ

He had gotten the letter I sent from East Berlin after all, and still was at his old address. The only problem was that it was already after two. I showed Frau Koch the telegram and said I'd have to leave immediately for Alex.

There was nobody waiting in front of the milk bar, as I feared. But Suzanne was at the fountain with another girl and a boy lying on the girl's lap. I ran up to her.

"Suzanne! Hi, I just got back from Rostock."

"Oh, Rostock," she said, with her far-off voice. "I got thrown out of Rostock a few weeks ago."

"Thrown out? How?"

"I took a train up there, wanted to go to the beach for a few days. I was going to stay with a friend. There were police all over the train station. I was checking my pack into a locker when a policeman came up to me and just told me to take it out and catch the next train back to Berlin. It was Baltic Sea Week, he said, and they didn't want any people like me making a bad impression on the foreign guests."

"How did he know you'd make a 'bad impression'?"

"Blue jeans and a polo shirt. A proper girl should have a dress and a blouse."

"Rostock is a nice city," said the boy. "A lot of foreigners, good young people."

"I liked it," I said.

"Steve, did you hear what happened here yesterday?" There was a bit of hesitation in Suzanne's normally reportorial monotone and she chewed nervously on some strands of her long hair.

"No, what happened?"

Stefan stood up and spoke. "The police let loose."

"How?" I asked.

"A boy from Munich with a guitar started singing at the fountain, and kids gathered around to listen. After about ten minutes two truckloads of policemen came to the fountain and this big guy got out and told us to leave. Our pal Martin asked the cop what we were doing wrong. He said we needed written permission from the police to have a public assembly. Martin said it was just some kids singing. The policeman answered they had to stop."

"The West German kid said he couldn't believe it," Suzanne broke in. "And a lot of the kids said they were going to keep singing anyway."

"Yeah, well then the policeman gave a signal to some of the guys in the trucks, and three of them came out and just took Martin." Stefan looked at me, shrugging his shoulders. "Then another guy, Willy, asked why they had done that — he said Martin hadn't done anything. He told the cop maybe they could talk things over, like why it shouldn't be all right for some people just to sing. The cop said, look, he didn't want any trouble, couldn't we just understand his position. He was sorry, but he couldn't let us sing. After that, I thought we should just lay off, 'cause I didn't think the cop was doing what he was do-ing because he hated us. But some of the other kids kept argu-ing and they got arrested too. Finally, the rest of us just got lost. They must have brought thirty policemen. Shit. I was scared, and people were mad."

"Steve, the police are getting harder and harder. They're afraid of young people," Suzanne said. "Last June, they took me to the police station one afternoon because I wouldn't take my feet out of the water at the fountain. Afterward, I wrote a letter to the Ministry of the Interior with a picture from the *Berliner Zeitung* we had seen that showed people with their toes in the fountain pool. Was it all right for old ladies but not for us? Didn't they know they couldn't just build Alexander-platz up like this and then say that only old-age pensioners could come?"

"You didn't get any answer to the letter, did you?"

"Yeah, in fact I did. They wrote me that the policeman had shown bad judgment, and that there was nothing illegal in what I did. But now, this last week, the policemen patrolling around Alex have again started harassing kids who have their feet in the water. They tell us it's creating a bad impression for the foreigners."

"You should tell them that it would create a good impression for foreigners to see people being allowed a little freedom."

Suzanne let out her tinny, self-mocking laugh. "Yeah, we should."

✻

The service desk at the Interhotel told me I could get plane tickets to America only from West Berlin, so as soon as I welcomed him back from his Bulgarian vacation the next morning, I showed Bach my telegram from home and asked if I could go to West Berlin the next day. Bach was a smiling cherub that morning, with rosy cheeks and a suntan, and he was agreeable. Unconsciously, I realized, I now regarded Bach as a jovial father figure with whom I could be relatively at ease after nerve-racking sessions with Waack.

"Steve, before we go to lunch, I have something to talk with Frau Koch about."

They closed the living room door, and I went into my room and turned on AFN. Ten minutes later Bach knocked on my door and came in. "Steve, Frau Koch has told me that unfortunately she has to leave Berlin tomorrow for the next few days. Her daughter and son-in-law are out of town, and she has to go out to Oranienburg to watch their child. That means we'll have to find a new place for you to stay."

I sat there dumbfounded. Was one permitted to ask why I had heard nothing about Frau Koch's supposed plans before

Bach said *he* had something to talk to *her* about? Once more I sat staggered at their assumptions about how naive I was.

"We will try to find a hotel, but I'm afraid the hotel situation is pretty tight now. We may have to put you into a private house somewhere."

Everything clicked. They had found out from Frau Koch that I had been sneaking out between the times they watched over me. Under the pretext of being unable to find any hotel space, they would now move me someplace far away from the center of town so they could keep track of me better. I placed a bet with myself that that's what would happen. At the same time, I was filled anew with anxiety.

"And one more thing, Steve. I'm going to be busy during much of the rest of the week — it's always busy the first days after vacation, you know. Doctor Waack and I will of course take time out to eat with you, but we may not get to the larger discussions I wanted to have."

"How was the work I did for you on Harvard?"

"Excellent, exactly as we wanted." He smiled. "At any rate, we would be most grateful if you could extend your stay in the D.D.R. by two days, from the tenth to the twelfth. Then I could talk with you on Tuesday and Wednesday next week."

"Leaving the twelfth, you mean?"

"Yes, you could leave the morning of the twelfth and fly home the next afternoon from West Berlin."

"But my visa is valid only until the tenth."

"We can extend it without any problems. I will take care of that."

I raised no objections and we went off for lunch.

Bach had with him an office car. His own Moskvitch, which he had left for repair after our visit to Dresden at the end of June, was still — on the second of August — at the workshop.

"I'm sorry I'm leaving tomorrow, Frau Koch. You have really been wonderful to me here," I said to her with some sincerity after Bach had brought me back from lunch. "Have you been to West Berlin since the Wall?"

"I have a sister there, and I visited her once when I became old enough. It is nice, but I had a bad feeling while I was there. You know, Steve, you've asked me a lot of questions while you've been here about World War Two, and what life was like under Hitler. Well, we have the feeling that the people who were responsible for all that suffering are still in power over there."

"Oh, I see what you mean."

"And, then there's another thing. You mention the Wall. We should have talked about this earlier. I don't know what you've heard in the West, but it was absolutely necessary for us to build that Wall. You can't believe how it was before. All the illegal currency exchange — they said our mark was only worth one fourth of their mark, so West Berliners could exchange one of theirs for four of ours, and come over here and buy up all our products from us, because they were so cheap."

I didn't want to explain to the nice old lady that if that had been the main irritant the D.D.R. could simply have accepted the free market rate, devalued their mark by 400 percent, and raised all prices and wages by 400 percent, and then West Berliners would no longer gain from buying East German bread or sugar. The economics would have been too complicated. Frau Koch sat and darned some of my socks, and I told her I was going into town to see the view from the top of the television tower at night.

"Shit, Suzanne, am I excited!" I greeted her, hugging, near the grill bar. "I'm going to West Berlin tomorrow to get my tickets home to America."

Suzanne just nodded her head up and down, seemingly half-indifferent. "Oh, so you'll be getting out of this place for a while."

"Suzanne, don't look so sad-faced. Tell you what — let me treat you to dinner at the grill bar. O.K.?"

"O.K. Today a boy I know is working there. He'll be able to get us a seat fast." We went inside, and she winked at the guy, indicating there were two of us. As soon as two people left, he put a small sign saying RESERVED on the two seats and we sat down.

"Steve, could you do me one favor while you're in West Berlin?"

"What?"

"Get me a package of a candy called Haribo Lakritze. They're the most delicious things I've ever tasted."

Lakritz is the German word for "licorice." "Can't you get licorice in the D.D.R.?"

"What, are you crazy?"

"You mean not at *any* store, even one?"

"Whatever one store doesn't have the other stores won't have either. There's no such thing here as one store going out to try to get something that another place doesn't have. Why should they bother?"

I told her I'd get her some Haribo Lakritze.

"Suzanne, you know it still feels horrible for me to go to the border crossing at Friedrichstrasse. Every once in a while I get the urge to make a run over the Wall — you know, even though I can leave legally anytime I want. Suzanne, I want to think that I can understand how it feels to be walled in this country. I want to try to know."

"You get used even to the Wall, even to the most sickening thing on earth, a government which has built a wall around its people."

"Every time Waack and I are on the S-Bahn and pass by a stretch that goes near the Wall, I try to make believe I don't notice it's there. But *he* always stares right at it. Fuck, Suzanne, he almost seems to be *proud* of it! Once he told me some solemn words about how that Wall marks the boundaries between two completely different social systems. All I can think of is what it looks like right outside the crossing point at Friedrichstrasse, with the crying people seeing off their West German relatives. Suzanne, don't you ever feel like one day, real late at night, when no policemen are there, just writing on the side of a building somewhere 'The Wall Must Come Down'?"

"What would be the use, for *one* person to write it? If one night *everybody* wrote it, so that people woke up in the morning and saw 'The Wall Must Come Down' everywhere they went, *everywhere*, then I would write it, I would write it all night and forever." She looked tall and wild and free, like a thoroughbred horse.

✽

It was sublime to be in West Berlin. I took a deep breath as I got out the S-Bahn Station Zoologische Garten, and took in the colors around me. I had decided to call up my parents and tell them what my situation was. But they told me at the post office that they could not be at all sure that phone calls from West Berlin were not tapped by the East Germans. So I called, but didn't get to say much. However, just being able to hear my mother's voice — she was the only one home — was indescribable.

That and drinking a cold Coca-Cola with a slice of pizza on the Kurfürstendamm were the two high points of my day. You don't know how much you miss something like Coca-Cola until you can't get it. Unfortunately, having to buy the ticket home, and being expected back in East Berlin at five, I hardly had time to look around. I was rushed, sweaty, dead-tired, but incredibly happy the whole few hours. I wrote a quick letter to my parents explaining briefly what had happened to me, and saying that if I didn't call them the morning of August 12 they should immediately begin contacting all the people we had agreed on to help me if I got in trouble. I quickly looked around a department store to check prices and quality — and was joyfully blinded by the colors and shades and variety. In the stand-up bar at the department store I guzzled down a *Berliner Weisse mit Schuss*. The syrup in it was fresh green, the taste was snowy and wild in that blazing sun. I went into a little grocery and bought two cans of Pepsi-Cola and two bags of Haribo Lakritze. Last, I stopped in the Berlin Information Office nearby and picked up a little picture booklet, with beautiful photos, on West Berlin. I also tore out an article from the day's *International Herald Tribune* on a Gallup poll of American voters' presidential preferences, crushed it up, and shoved it into my left pocket. The map I folded up into my back pocket.

I got both of them back into East Berlin without any trouble.

"Steve, unfortunately we were not able to find any hotel rooms for you." Bach was trudging along, the swinging back and forth of his shabby briefcase marking time with his strides. His hair stood up in the late afternoon wind. "Believe me, we tried, but there isn't a single free hotel room in the city." That sounded, to say the least, unlikely. "So you'll be staying with a lady whose name we got from the Berlin Tourist Information Center. I haven't met her yet." Bach had already gotten me into his car and was merrily playing confidence man. "But it's in Eichwalde, which is unfortunately rather far out." Unfortunately. Kelman, I said to myself, you're pretty good at predictions.

I was dead-tired, and kept my eyes closed trying to sleep for most of the trip. But, God, was it way out — a half-hour drive, mostly on bumpy roads, with our final destination a semirural area of single-family houses.

When we arrived, I first asked to put my two Pepsis in the refrigerator. I was hoping to have one that evening. "Oh," Bach said longingly. "You got some Pepsi-Colas while you were in West Berlin." He hesitated in uncertainty. "Steve, do you think you could perhaps — perhaps invite me to a Pepsi sometime?" I felt sorry for the poor man.

Bach stayed in the kitchen to talk for a while with Frau Luger, while I was left to inspect my quarters in the living room. Frau Luger, it developed, was a widow who only occasionally took in guests. Looking around the living room showed in what kind of typical East German home I had been placed. There was a framed photograph of her husband on the wall, with some artificial flowers under it. He was wearing a Party button. The bookshelves contained two volumes of the *Collected Speeches of Wilhelm Pieck,* East Germany's first president, several novels by Mikhail Sholokhov, and a picture book on Moscow. With a symbolism almost too obvious to be real, there was a volume by Joseph Stalin tucked, only barely visible, behind several volumes stacked horizontally on the shelves.

"Steve," Bach began as he got out, running his hands through his hair, making them wet with sweat, "Frau Luger is being very kind in taking you in as her guest. Try not to bother her with any guests here, or messages, or telegrams, or anything like that."

"O.K."

"And another thing. This is unfortunately rather far out. So you won't be able to visit town as often. When we have an appointment to get together, you'd better stay around the house until I come. You have books to read, right? And also, try not to stay out late at night. It would be hard on Frau Luger."

"What do you mean by late?" I asked.

"Try not to be out after nine or nine thirty. For Frau Luger's sake." He oozed.

"Herr Bach, do you have my new visa for the two-day extension?"

"Yes, of course. Here it is." He took my passport out of his bag, like a small-time magician doing the rabbit-in-the-hat trick. "Remember to carry it with you at all times. Eichwalde is outside the Berlin city limits, and that means a policeman can ask to see your visa whenever you take the S-Bahn here from inside Berlin."

I nonchalantly opened the passport to see the new visa — like the first two they got me, it was a piece of paper that I put into my passport with a paper clip rather than the normal stamped visa you get from the D.D.R. Suddenly, I swallowed in horror.

"But — but — but Herr Bach, this visa says on it that the last day is August *thirteenth*. You said I was going to leave the morning of the *twelfth*."

"Oh, don't worry," he answered calmly. "I had that put there just in case."

I was more than worried. Not just because I had told my parents to assume I had been arrested if I didn't call them the twelfth. No, even more because of that date the thirteenth. Already, signs had come up everywhere over East Berlin telling people to get ready for the festive celebration. August thirteenth was the tenth anniversary of the Berlin Wall.

CHAPTER 8

FRAU LUGER WAS a tiny lady with gold-rimmed glasses and a hoarse voice. Her first question was how I had been enjoying my stay in the D.D.R. I was having a wonderful time, I said. Yes, she replied, the D.D.R. standard of living was quite high, wasn't it? Before I went to sleep she asked me what I wanted for breakfast the next morning.

"A roll, a very hard-boiled egg, and some juice if you have any."

"What about some coffee?"

"No thank you, ma'm. I'm not a big coffee drinker, and I know it's expensive here."

"Expensive?" she looked at me wide-eyed. "For *us* it is not expensive." No, you old lying bitch, it only costs ten bucks a pound.

Frau Luger said that her deceased husband had been the district's mayor for many years. She had a brother in West Berlin, she went on, but had no desire to visit him. "We have everything we need here." Where, I wanted to ask her, did she get the Nivea cream lying next to the shower in the bathroom? And, could one consider going to see one's brother even if one didn't want to get anything from him?

✿

I was to meet Waack in town the next day at two to go see the film *Oliver*. I went into town early, telling Frau Luger I was going to have lunch first. The trip to Alex took fifty minutes by S-Bahn.

"Suzanne, I've been resettled," I cried out to her, attempting to imitate her blasé voice. "They moved me out of Pankow to Eichwalde."

"Eichwalde? That's outside of Berlin."

"And you wouldn't believe the lady I'm staying with — books by Pieck and Stalin on her shelves, and she told me coffee wasn't expensive in the D.D.R.!"

"Hmpf, not expensive." She snorted. "It's just like the Nazi times, when they put foreign visitors up with 'pure German families.'"

"They said there wasn't a single free hotel room in the whole city, and that's why they had to move me to Eichwalde. Let's go over and check in the Interhotel and see how many free rooms they have."

"Ma'm," I asked the girl at the desk of the big skyscraper, "we have a bet. Could you decide it by telling us how many free rooms you have at the hotel now?"

"Free rooms?" she answered, looking a bit startled. "Not many."

"How many?" Suzanne asked.

"Oh, maybe fifty or a hundred."

Suzanne and I smiled quietly at each other and left. "They lied to you," she said. "But I guess that's no surprise."

I took the two packages of Haribo Lakritze out of my little bag, plus the map of West Berlin and the Gallup poll of voters' presidential choices. She opened up the big Berlin map and took in the swarm of bright pictures. "When I think of cities in the West, it just makes me want to cry with longing." A little life had come into her voice. "The beautiful advertising, the bright lights. *There* they have a life."

"Suzanne, look at this article from an American newspaper. They have asked the American people which candidates the two parties should nominate. That's even *before* the election — the people have a say not only in who is finally elected, but also in which candidates the parties nominate."

She looked through it. "What about the Communist Party? Where are their candidates in the poll?"

The question surprised me, to say the least. I knew the East German media presented the Communists as a major force in America — one afternoon East Berlin's afternoon tabloid paper had plastered the banner headline GUS HALL SAYS: US COMMITS WAR CRIMES IN VIETNAM over the entire front page. But it was strange that someone like Suzanne would have that impression. "Suzanne," I said softly, "the Communist Party is an insignificant force. They have almost no support."

"Oh," she said, looking almost disappointed. She stopped and ruminated. "But are the American people opposed to the *idea* of socialism, or just to the fact that the Communist Party is tied to the system we have here?"

"Unfortunately, I don't think they make any distinction. They see what things are like in places like the D.D.R., and they just know they don't want any part of that. What do the people around the fountain think of America?" I asked.

"It represents the ideal of everything they dream about — freedom, music, travel, everything." I thought that's what she would say, and at the same time thought how curious it was — frantically pro-American hippies.

"Steve," she said, suddenly lowering her voice, "do you know anything about helping people escape to the West? You know, false passports or anything?"

That came suddenly. Maybe she thought that since I had been asking so many questions, I was some sort of Western agent. "No, Suzanne, why should I?"

"I don't know, you've met so many people here, you've been here so long . . ."

"Well, I've wanted to see what life is like here."

"Steve, what you have to do when you get back to America is write about what you've seen here. Tell people how it really is."

I smiled inside, but didn't say anything. "Suzanne, you know it's crazy to try to escape. You know that better than I do."

"There is this person I know who has spent years trying to get out. He's a secret member of the West German Christian Democratic Party. You know, some West German brought him a membership application to the D.D.R. One time he tried to swim the river Spree into West Berlin, but they shot him and then he was in jail for a few years. As soon as he got out, he tried the Wall. That time they almost killed him. He is lucky to be alive. The only people who try the Wall now are adventurers, because there's no chance to get over, not with all the electronic things and soldiers. The only practical chance is over the green frontier. You know, the forest between Saxony and Bavaria."

"But it's all crazy. You'll just get shot or killed."

"Steve, I promise you this: within ten years, we will meet in the West."

*

Dr. Waack was getting pretty desperate taking me to see *Oliver* — but I told Suzanne that after dinner I'd get on the S-Bahn to Eichwalde, and then get off and change lines to get to her apartment. I arrived around ten, and her boy friend was there.

"Steve," Suzanne began, "this is Peter. We've been going together for a year and a half now. He used to live in this apartment, but now he lives in Dresden and comes to Berlin on weekends."

"But now I have my vacation," Peter said with a heavy Dresden accent. He was Abe Lincoln, tall and spindly, with hair down to his shoulders and heavy eyebrows.

"Steve, you got a telegram from your friend Mattias in Schwedt." I had sent him a telegram after we failed to make contact the day I got back from Rostock, suggesting I come visit him in Schwedt on Monday the ninth. Since Bach had already informed me that I would be leaving Frau Koch's, I had told Mattias to send his answer to Suzanne. He said the ninth was fine with him, and that I should telegraph him about my time of arrival.

"Peter, let me ask you something. You're from Dresden, right? I was there a few weeks ago, and I had been there in nineteen sixty-nine. Don't you think things have improved somewhat since then?"

"Improved? How should they have improved?"

"Well, the new Prager Strasse for example."

He lowered his voice and looked at me sort of bitterly. "The new Prager Strasse, you say?" He sort of imitated me. "You know that was supposed to be finished *two years* ago? Where is the movie theater, where is the department store? They stopped work on them last fall, and *nothing* since then. Just empty building sites."

"Why?"

"No money, no building materials. They've decided that they finally have to build some more houses for people and everything is going into that. So they just stopped work on what they had already started."

"But most of Prager Strasse is finished."

"Look, you're a tourist. Hasn't Suzanne spoken with you

about things? I mean, don't believe what *they* tell you. Don't believe what's in the newspapers — they don't say anything. They didn't even mention that work had stopped on Prager Strasse, not to speak of why. And what about the new postage rates? They shot them up on July first. Not a word in the papers. But if they raise the price of butter in West Germany by one pfennig, then you'll see a big story."

"So you don't think things have improved since nineteen sixty-nine?"

"If anything, they've gotten worse."

"How?"

"Less things in the stores, more annoyances in trying to find what they've run out of. And we know that every year we move further and further behind West Germany. I mean, that's what we make the comparison with. Don't believe what those liars say about the Zone. It's still just as bad." *Die Zone* — "the zone," the Soviet Occupation Zone — my God, that was the expression commonly used for the D.D.R. around ten years ago in West Germany. Today it's considered hopelessly reactionary, out of step with the new reality of accepting the D.D.R. I couldn't believe I had just heard an East German using the expression about his own country. "And let me tell you one other thing. If we didn't have West Germany nearby, we'd be much worse off. West Germany is the only thing that makes them do *anything* for us."

"You sound pretty cynical."

"You're right. I should just learn to be indifferent and get used to it, but I still can't help getting angry sometimes."

"Angry at what?"

"At the way they treat people. They keep such close track on you. I mean, they already were out against me because I had missed some army drills in high school."

"In high school? Do you have army drills in high school?"

"Yeah, to prepare for your time in the army. Everyone has it. I thought it was a waste of time. So I skipped it a few times. That got them against me." While Peter was talking, Suzanne got up and made some tea. "Anyway, when I graduated from high school I came to Berlin to work at the State Trading Corporation using computers."

"Computers?"

"To keep track of prices and quantities. But very primitive — I'm sure they're ten or fifteen years behind what you have in the West. Anyway, first they put us on night shift."

"Why night shift?"

"Valuable machines. They cost so much money you couldn't leave them standing. So people had to be there all the time. I hated night shift, I was always tired. And most of the time they didn't even have any work for us to do. They just kept us there for the principle. But I tried to work hard, to be a good worker. Last year they made me leader for my division. I meant that I got a better salary and was supposed to keep the other workers working hard. Last January they wanted our team to come in to work on a Sunday. We had already worked for a few Sundays and nobody wanted to. They don't even give us any special pay. So that time I said to my boss that I wasn't going to come in. And of course all the other workers followed me. Nobody came that Sunday."

"What happened then?"

"Monday they called a meeting of my division. The boss said in front of the group that he had never in his life experienced such fresh behavior. Then he said that he knew I'd been receiving letters from people in West Germany. Had I been influenced by them, he asked. Perhaps I was a spy?"

"What did the other workers think?"

"They wanted to laugh, but they couldn't do anything. They just sat there."

"They didn't participate in the accusations against you or anything?"

"No. They just kept silent."

"So what happened?"

"I lost my position as chief worker in the unit, of course. A week later, I just quit. Who wanted to stay there? I came back to Dresden and moved in with my parents again. You know, the secret police came around this apartment to ask people questions about me. They had to sign an oath saying they wouldn't tell me that anyone had come. But Suzanne told me, of course." He laughed. "Now I'm working in a chemical factory."

"How's the factory?"

"Horrible. Last February, just after I came in, there wasn't enough electricity. So that factory, and all the others in Dresden, had to run at night so that power would be available for stores and homes during the day. It was horrible; people were going around in the streets with flashlights, because there was no street lighting. And there are Party spies in every factory, you know. I know this lady who works as a secretary for the Dresden city government in our district. She once saw a whole directive about these damn spies on somebody's desk. She wasn't supposed to see it, of course, but she did."

"What do the spies do?"

"Overhear what workers are saying. Report on workers. Keep workers scared."

"But supposedly the workers rule in the D.D.R.? Do any workers believe that?"

"Look, everybody here has two faces. In public, you show compliance. You go to all their demonstrations, mouth all their words, because you have to. You know, at our factory we have these horrible things where maybe one night every two weeks all the workers have to meet after work to go to some Russian war movie, or a speech, or a discussion. Their ideal is that you have no free time of your own, just in their groups."

"What do you mean that you *have* to go? What happens if you don't?"

"They have a year-end bonus. It comes if the factory fulfills the plan, but to get it the worker must have a good attitude. Nobody wants to miss his bonus."

"What is the other face?"

"Disgust. People hate the Party. The only people who believe in this system, who really believe in it, are the leadership of the Party. The workers rule? It's more like this: everything is put on the backs of the workers. Workers are supposed to increase production. Workers are supposed to sacrifice for the plan. Workers are supposed to come up with new innovations. And now the latest is that workers are supposed to clean up their own neighborhoods — the city doesn't want to hire clean-up people."

I had seen things around about this so-called "innovator" campaign, and even read an article in *Neues Duetschland* giving the figure of 321,894 innovations — or some such ridiculously exact figure — coming from it. "Just a second," I asked Peter. "What about these innovations? Do workers actually come up with ideas?"

"Sure, we have ideas. We get ideas all the time for eliminating inefficiencies."

"Do people report them?"

"Why should they? What do the bosses do for us? Shit, people save them for themselves, they might come in handy. If they raise the production quota, you can use your idea to help meet it. Look, everybody works for himself, and only himself. When I came to the chemical factory, nobody helped me learn my job." He looked at me, as if he expected me to be shocked. "I hope I haven't destroyed any myths you believed about this place. But I'm just telling the truth."

Suzanne was back with the tea. "You know, Suzanne, I never really asked you anything about *your* job, I mean the one you had at the cosmetics factory."

She snickered. "I can tell you one thing. Don't believe a word they say about how they're going to overtake West Germany. Anyone who works in a factory can tell you they never will."

"Why?"

"Waste, indifference. Nobody cares about anything. In our plant half of everything — raw materials and finished products — had to be thrown out because it was unusable. And the workers don't care."

"But what about the piecework and bonus system they have?"

"Yeah, in some of the factories they're pretty hard with piecework. But the bonus is a joke a lot of the time. They come only if the plan is fulfilled, and there's no reason to go all out for that, because so many times the plan isn't fulfilled, at least at our factory. Or else, if it is fulfilled, it's only at the very end of the year, in November or December, when they start working you Saturdays and Sundays. So you work really hard only then."

"But *Neues Deutschland* said the other day that the plan had been filled for the first half of this year."

"I don't believe them, it's all lies. You know, they said a few years ago that they had introduced a five-day week. That was supposed to be a big thing, right? It was a joke, because people had to work an hour longer each of the other days."

"Steve," Peter cut in, "I hope you don't mind if I ask you to go home now. Suzanne and I are going to bed soon. You know, there are only two things to do in the D.D.R. — drink and fuck. And we're going to do one of them."

"I shouldn't stay too late either. If Frau Luger is still up, she might be wondering. Hey, Suzanne, did I tell you about what else they've done? Bach told me he was going to extend my visa by two days — but he extended it by three, up to the thirteenth. You know what *that* is. Shit, I just don't know what they have planned for me."

"If I were you I'd leave right now," she said deadpan. "I'm worried for you."

"I'm worried for myself."

"What do they *want* from you?"

"Well, you know I've been writing things for them about questions they have about American students and about Harvard."

She snickered once again. "You're doing intelligence work for them, you know."

"Hey, please don't say that, it makes me want to throw up." Suzanne's big round eyes looked at me comfortingly. "You know, it's funny some of the questions they ask. They asked me what Harvard students think of foreign students at Harvard — you know, it's not any problem with us, but I know that it is for *them*, with foreign students being unpopular among East German students."

"You know why, don't you? They get all sorts of advantages we don't get. They get more money, and they can travel to West Berlin."

"Then there was this question they asked that I didn't understand. They wanted to know what kinds of summer activities Harvard arranges for its students. I mean, in fact they don't really arrange any. Students can pretty much do whatever they want during the summer. Is it different here?"

"Yeah, usually students have to go work on a construction project or something."

"Do they get paid?"

"Not really, maybe three marks a day. And usually that all ends up being 'donated' to Vietnam or something."

"You know, I only wish you could meet Waack and Bach. They are so unbelievably disgusting. Waack is even anti-Semitic, you know. I mean, that's hard for me to take, because I'm Jewish — and, you know, with what the Germans did to the Jews. I think it's really dangerous for the government to have this anti-Israel campaign, given the traditional anti-Semitism. Waack once told me some joke about an Arab and an Israeli soldier who are fighting in the desert, and the Arab runs out of ammunition. He yells out to the Israeli that he has no ammunition left. 'Hold on,' the Israeli answers, 'I'll sell you some.' He makes me sick."

Suzanne got up and went over to the sink. "Steve, one thing: I'm not going to Alex much from now on. I don't want to be seen there, it's getting too tight. They have plainclothesmen all over the place now."

"But didn't they always?"

"Yeah. This boy I know named Max just got out of jail — something he said in the grill bar was overheard by a cop and they put him away for a month. Shit, what it did to him. Now he's as quiet as a mouse, never opens his mouth, just slinks around and listens to the radio. I don't ever want to have to be *that* scared, and now the chances for something like that happening have become too big."

"But how will we meet each other?"

"I'll be here most nights. You can come over."

*

It wasn't easy to fall asleep nights, and not only because of the narrow sofa in Frau Luger's living room. Time was getting so short. How I ached to get home to my family. Good, soon I

would be out, soon I *would* see them. Bach would let me go. I
had convinced myself of that. No longer could I even conceive
of being arrested, not after getting so far. They couldn't use the
tenth anniversary of the Wall to announce uncovering an American spy, could they? That was too bizarre. But what *did* they
want from me? Maybe they'd ask for some sort of statement
praising the D.D.R. which they could use for propaganda. I'd
then have no choice but to write something. But I could do
what the American pilots shot down over North Vietnam did in
drafting "confessions" of war crimes, I reasoned. They made
references to their "commanding officers" Major Donald Duck
or Captain Clark Kent. I could write about Professor Arthur
Garfunkel.

But it was hard. You can get used to anything, I had heard
again and again here. You can't keep crying all the time, because eventually you run out of tears. But I couldn't keep from
crying sometimes.

Bach was supposed to come at one to take me to lunch, but he
didn't come before *four,* claiming that the office car had broken
down. (He showed me his oil-greased hands to prove it.)
Meanwhile, I had been sitting in Frau Luger's living room the
whole day, reading Volume Six of the *History of the German
Labor Movement.* By four, I was more than half through the
ponderous volume. The book's basic argument — that the Soviet
Union sought to bring about German reunification after the war,
while the West prevented it — was on the face of it so absurd
that I was incredibly curious to check out other versions of the
"facts" they brought up when I returned home. Occasionally,
the book was grimly funny. In talking about some anti-Communist youth demonstration in 1947 (with which I wasn't
familiar) they spoke of "youthful vandals" who "forced their
way" into the Soviet sector, shouted slogans, tore the red flag

from the top of the Brandenburg Gate, and "defaced" posters put up by "anti-fascist organizations." The police, the account went on, "saw themselves forced to make use of their weapons," and "one provocateur paid for his shameful deeds with his life." It reads like a heavy-handed parody of Spiro Agnew.

Bach and I were to drive into town and meet Waack for dinner. I told him how interesting I found the *History,* and said I hoped to do more research about the period in America.

"If you study these developments back in America," Bach said, looking at me knowingly, "you can be sure your work won't be published. It would be too inconvenient for certain people." This was from a man who also thought *Neues Deutschland* was too dangerous for the West Germans to be allowed into West Berlin.

I asked Bach whether he didn't think that an improvement had taken place in West German policies since Willy Brandt came to power. I know that the official East German view denied any improvement, seeing merely a new strategy to adapt to the increasing strength of the socialist world. Bach explained the official line to me without much apparent conviction. Waack, whom we had picked up near the Neptune fountain on the way, listened attentively but said nothing. Bach concluded by saying that Brandt's great victory had been a propaganda one, in persuading some honest people like myself that West German imperialism had changed faces.

"But Herr Bach, don't you think it's an improvement that West Germany is now led by an anti-fascist like Brandt, a resistance fighter?"

At this point, Waack saw his chance. "Don't believe this crap about Brandt, Steve. We know the real story — we just don't reveal it to the world because it wouldn't solve anything. Brandt left Germany in thirty-three because he was a common criminal the police were looking for, not because he was a so-called 'anti-Nazi.' During the war he was a small-time Nazi spy in Scandinavia."

Some people, I saw, have no shame.

All evening I searched for the right time to bring up my request to visit Schwedt on Monday. I ended up waiting until Bach had driven me home to Frau Luger's. I had discovered during my stay with Bach and Waack that, if I was careful in limiting the number of points I pressed, I could get my way by taking advantage of the fact that they couldn't openly admit that they wanted to prevent me from meeting normal people. This time, I decided, I would press the point. I looked forward with an almost childish curiosity to the explanation Bach would come up with for why he didn't want me to go. It was great to watch *them* have to do some quick thinking sometimes.

When I asked him, a surprised, blank look came over his face, a crazy twisted leer. I had caught him off guard. He was quiet for a few seconds, and then he dribbled out a meek, "Steve, I — I would prefer it if you didn't go."

"Why not?" I asked on a note of triumph.

He hesitated again. "It would — it would please me if you stayed here," he purred. "You've already seen a great deal. There's really no need for you to see any more."

"But I promised Mattias I'd come."

He paused. Finally he perked up: he had thought of something! "Steve, I had planned for you to meet an important administrator at Humboldt University on Monday. He had told me he was willing to take some time out to answer your questions about higher education in the D.D.R."

"But couldn't we do that some other time? Tomorrow, or over the weekend, or Tuesday or Wednesday?"

"Steve, Herr Becker is a busy man. The only day he is free is Monday."

"Wel-l-l, let's hold off a final decision. I would like to meet

Herr Becker, but I also want to go see Mattias." I made a peace offering, and offered to get my remaining can of Pepsi-Cola out of the refrigerator.

Bach smiled. I poured him a little more than I poured myself. He stared at it, held up the glass for inspection, and proposed a "toast" to our continued friendship. He drank the Pepsi slowly, like wine. "Not bad?" I asked.

"Excellent," he replied. "Delicious." He took another sip, and Frau Luger brought out some cake. "You know, once I had Coca-Cola before, at the Leipzig Trade Fair."

✻

Waack was leaving for some unnamed place for a few days, so Friday night was to be our last dinner together. We met at one of our favorite places, the Bulgarian restaurant at the Hotel Sofia on Friedrichstrasse. Waack sipped red wine and looked mellow but spoke with determination in his last words to me.

"Steve, maybe I've been too hard on you during our discussion. I hope you don't think I prevented you from seeing anything you wanted to see. I just want you always to remember one thing: there is a difference between being some sort of generalized critic of society and being a genuine *socialist*. There are any number of people who go around with a few criticisms here and there of bourgeois society without being socialists. You're not a socialist unless you are willing to accept all the elements of genuine socialism — especially Party discipline and the dictatorship of the proletariat. Otherwise, what good are you?" His voice rose in a crescendo, and he took his eyes away from his glass of wine to stare at me coldly. "Let's be honest: tens of thousands of bourgeois social critics aren't worth as much as one single genuine socialist."

I don't know if it was because of the wine, but I almost burst into tears: what if I had actually *believed* the portrait I had given of myself as someone who was trying to be friendly to the "socialist bloc," but just had a few questions? How would I have been cracked by his dismissal as worthless of anyone who deviates even slightly from his line! His torture was terrible. He was terrible. For an imperfect human being he had not even a hint of tenderness.

"Steve," he went on, "I don't know where you got all your ideas about bourgeois freedom and liberalization. Maybe you should read the Marxist literature I gave you more carefully — certainly you won't find any such ideas there. And next time you come to the D.D.R. you should talk with some genuine workers about the dictatorship of the proletariat. I mean, not just any old workers, but genuine, class-conscious workers."

"O.K." I sighed.

"One last thing. I want you to remember me by my motto. It comes from Goethe:

> Rule or serve,
> Win or lose,
> Hammer or anvil."

We shook hands and went our separate ways. I had, I counted to myself, five days left in the D.D.R.

✻

Bach had given me Saturday free to buy a birthday present for my brother and some books for myself. There was naturally nothing produced in the D.D.R. my brother would want, and I planned to use the day to wrap up some loose ends. First I did some more checking in food stores around town, always a depressing experience. Then I walked over to Alex.

It was a sunny Saturday afternoon, and Alex was filled. Most of the long-haired boys and blue-jeaned girls whose faces I now recognized — but very few of whom I knew — were there. I asked if anyone had seen Suzanne, but nobody had for a few days.

"You're Suzanne's friend from America, aren't you?" It was a kid hanging around with two other guys, maybe sixteen or seventeen, with a baby face and long curls. He had a button reading FREE ANGELA DAVIS that had come from America. It was the first such button I had seen an East German wearing.

"How come you're wearing that?" I asked.

"Well, I believe she should be freed." His expression was innocent.

"Do you believe what the government says about Angela Davis? You only get one side, you know."

"I know. But I believe in socialism, even if I don't believe in this government."

"What do you mean?"

"I used to believe in this government. My father believes in it very much. But it's the way the police act here. Were you around when they stopped us from listening to a West German playing songs on his guitar? And the way there are so many plainclothesmen around here, and now they've even forbidden some kids from coming to Alex."

I invited the kid and his two friends to an ice cream in the milk bar. While we were eating, a familiar face came in — the cook's apprentice whom I had met three weeks earlier. He looked surprised to see me, and the rounded, ready-to-whistle expression on his lips accentuated his Pinocchiolike nose and salad-bowl haircut.

"Hey, where were you that night we were supposed to meet in front of the Bowling Zentrum?" I asked.

"I'm sorry. I didn't get your letter until two days after we were going to meet."

"But how's that possible? I sent it four days before we were supposed to meet from Leipzig."

"Yeah, but a letter from Leipzig takes five or six days."

I groaned. The kid joined us at the table.

I turned to the other kid. "You said before that your father believes in the government. What does he do?"

"He's a policeman. Once he was very convinced by the Nazi system, he was active in the Hitler Youth," the kid stated, in a singsong, declarative voice. "But he was captured by the Russians during the war, and while he was a prisoner they persuaded him he had been wrong and that he should believe in socialism. So now he just screams at me all day that I've been corrupted by West German propaganda, and I'm evil. He thinks kids with long hair are mostly West German spies."

"Yeah, but you know, Johnny," the cook's apprentice came in, "they're better with long hair now than they were before. One time two years ago I was walking on Karl Marx Allee with a girl I knew, holding her hand, and this cop stopped me and just told the girl to get lost, we were going to the police station. They took me there and just cut my hair."

"My brother told me," one of the others said, "that when he went to high school a few years ago, two girls were thrown out for dancing the twist."

Outside, we noticed, two policemen were clearing people off the long concrete divider which separated the tables outside the grill bar and milk bar from the rest of Alex. Fountain people often congregated along the divider when the fountain got too crowded, and for some reason they were being stopped now. We saw through the window one girl offering a cop a sip from the large bottle of Coke she and her friends were drinking. The policeman took a small sip, and then shoved them along with the others.

"Hey, let's finish up and go outside to see what's happening," I suggested.

We went up to the girl with the Coke bottle. She greeted one of the kids with a perfunctory kiss on the cheek. The police had told them they were interfering with the view of the café customers, she said. "We asked them if anyone had complained, and the policeman just stood there. An old lady who was sitting there with an ice cream told them to just leave us alone, we weren't disturbing her. She was wonderful."

Having gotten the kids off the divider, the three policemen returned to their beat walking around and around the fountain. Two people, one an adult, followed them for a while around their beat. When they had stopped talking with the policemen and sat down by the fountain, I went up to find out what they had asked about. It turned out the two were Iranians, father and son. The son had been studying in England for five years, and they were on a one-day visit over to East Berlin from the West. They had asked the police why they had been harassing the kids. One of the men spoke English, and answered. "The baker bakes bread because the government tells him to, and I make trouble for these youth because the government tells me to."

Right after lunch I left to visit a new housing project that I had seen along the S-Bahn ride to Frau Luger's. The new apartment buildings I had seen from cars and trains during my stay in the D.D.R. had generally looked rundown, with overgrown weeds and unwatered lawns. Waack had once answered a question on this score by saying that unfortunately people hadn't yet developed the socialist consciousness necessary to take collective responsibility for keeping the areas clean, and with the labor shortage no manpower was available to take care of such things.

One of the three kids I had eaten ice cream with said he had to be leaving too, and volunteered to come with me to look at the project.

"Hey," I asked him, "what do you think would happen if the Wall was opened?"

He laughed. "There's be a real *Völkerwanderung*, I can tell you. If the borders ever opened, this country would become rather empty."

The housing project was considerably worse than I'd expected: in large blocks — which the kid said had been built in 1966 — no grass or trees had been planted yet, and the paths around the complex, plus the center court, were still dug-up mud and dirt, with some cement blocks lying around in piles. There was also a section of student housing in the complex. Outside were some bulletin boards that announced the numbers of the best and worst rooms during the last F.D.J. cleaning inspection. To me it was sickening to think that F.D.J. went around inspecting people's rooms.

"Hey, could I ask you a question about this? This thing with room inspection, and putting room numbers on a bulletin board. I mean, we in the West would think this is an invasion of privacy, that if a kid wants to have a dirty room that's up to him. Do you see it that way, or do you think it's O.K. that the collective concerns itself with whether your room is dirty or clean?"

"We think just like you," the kid answered.

The idea behind getting to the housing project early was to be able to get to Suzanne's early, right after dinner, while she was still likely to be around. She was there alone when I arrived, and said that Peter wouldn't be back until later. She was still wearing her old blue jeans, but her hair was wet from just being washed.

"Suzanne, this might be the last time I see you. I'm hoping to go to Schwedt on Monday, and I think Herr Bach has Tuesday and Wednesday planned out. How about going to that discotheque near Alex tonight and dancing?"

"That place is no good." She frowned. "First of all it's too expensive, and second of all it's mostly foreigners. You know, it's Italian workers from West Berlin who come over here to buy East German girls. In West Berlin they're at the bottom of the scale, but here they're kings. Look, we can dance to my tapes if you want."

"Suzanne, do you know much about East German history? I mean, like, I've been reading in this official book on the history of the German labor movement, and the official line is that it's the *West* that bears the guilt for the division of Germany after the war. That sounds pretty unbelievable. Do you know anything about it?"

"No. We have no way of knowing. That's the only version we can read."

"Haven't you ever talked with your father about the things he's experienced since the war?"

"Sure. He told me that the revolt in nineteen fifty-three was a genuine mass uprising of the people here, like they say on RIAS, not a fascist putsch like the government tells us. And then, also I've heard about a postcard that exists in West Berlin which shows a clip from *Neues Deutschland* in nineteen sixty-one where Ulbricht says that the D.D.R. will never build a Wall."

I had seen that postcard: it showed an article where Ulbricht said, "Nobody has any intention of building a Wall." Suzanne said she had never seen the postcard, only heard about it.

"Suzanne, what about the future? I mean, do you have any hopes for the future, any ideas about how East Germany could be changed?"

She reflected a few moments, and spoke slowly. "I don't know — one hope is if China and America ally against Russia. And then, there was the uprising in Poland last winter — that got them really scared. It was funny: at the beginning, they talked about 'young vandals' rioting, but then when Gomulka had to quit they started talking about 'necessary reforms.'" She smirked, and put her hands on her hips demonstratively. "You know, I was talking to some Party guy the morning the uprising broke out. It was really funny how he told me about it. There hadn't been a thing on Radio D.D.R., but he said he had 'just happened to be playing around with the knob on the radio' and came upon RIAS, and heard a report."

"I bet when there's a big news story, even Honecker listens to RIAS."

She laughed.

"Suzanne, what about diplomatic recognition of the D.D.R.? Should the West do it?"

"I don't think it matters much. On the one hand, it would probably give us some personal advantages. On the other hand, a system which can build a Wall and shoot down people trying to escape should never be recognized."

We danced for a while, and then I said I'd have to be going.

"Steve, I told you: I'll see you again. Within ten years I'll see you in the West." She kissed me on the forehead.

I had four days left in the D.D.R. In five days came the tenth anniversary of the Berlin Wall. Suzanne I would remember long after that.

*

On Sunday Bach took me on an outing to some hills outside Berlin, where from an observation tower one could look down at the city. I had brought along my camera, and twice he brushed off my request for a picture of him by saying, "Later, Steve, later." Then it got dark.

We had come to a compromise about visiting Schwedt. Bach's friend from Humboldt University would come in the morning, and then in the afternoon Bach would drive me to Mattias', stay in Schwedt, and drive me back. I had suggested that I meet Herr Becker at the university, but Bach told me the grounds were closed to the public for "security reasons."

"What happens if, say, you're a girl who wants to visit your boy friend there?"

"Well, you can always apply for a special visitor's pass to come in."

Bach arrived with Herr Becker around ten Monday morning.

Herr Becker was a thin, strait-laced type, maybe thirty-five or forty, who was wrapped up like a gift parcel in a tight-fitting blue suit and tie, which contrasted sharply to Bach's roly-poly shabbiness. Becker also had a fancy black leather folder which was far more snazzy than the briefcase everyone else in the D.D.R. carries around. (All, however, including policemen, have *some* briefcase. The D.D.R. *is* German.)

I was to ask Becker questions, and had jotted down a few the night before. First I asked him to talk about the general makeup of the D.D.R. university system. He spoke for about half an hour straight, chain-smoking the whole way, first about the struggle to produce a "socialist faculty" after the war, one that would orient itself toward research taking place in the Soviet Union rather than the West. "Our scholars were held back by ideological blinders from implementing the Party's slogan 'Soviet standard equals world standard.' All they were interested in was how the West did this or that." The second problem was to make research more "socially useful." What this meant, he proceeded to recount brightly — as if he were reporting on a fantastic achievement — was that scientific research became adapted to the wishes of industry, through research contracts made directly between universities and industries, where the industry footed the bill and got the results. In the social sciences the Party, under whose direct control all social science faculties stood, got to determine all projects.

The way he sat there, chomping on his cigarette and gladly expounding on this shocking system — which if it existed in the West would be branded as fascist by anyone to the Left of Martha Mitchell — seemed right out of Dr. Strangelove.

"Does the individual professor have any time left to do research on his own?"

"No, of course not."

"What about pure research in the natural sciences? The industries don't contract for that, do they?"

"Yes, this is a problem," he reflected. "In fact, it was taken up at the Eighth Party Congress. The complaint was made that no pure research is getting done." I looked at the little Party button on his lapel; Bach and Waack never wore one.

"Herr Becker, another question I wanted to ask you concerns the content of the courses in Marxism-Leninism at the universities. I read a book on Ernst Fischer which Herr Bach's colleague gave me. But he told me that students are not allowed to read Fischer's own books. As a university administrator, you obviously know the way young people think — don't you feel it just creates more sympathy for Fischer's ideas to prevent students from reading him? You know, young people naturally question authority, and if something is forbidden fruit —"

He interrupted me, in a comfortable voice. "Steve, we don't want to create unnecessary conflicts for our students. We want to let them lead a quiet life, and not burden them with the false arguments of a Fischer."

"What about admission requirements to the universities? I understand that there are *numerus clausi* in a number of departments. What about the other departments? Can anyone with a high school diploma come in?"

"No, there is also a test of political maturity for all incoming students."

"Political maturity?"

"Yes, commitment to socialism. After all, we are not just interested in producing unpolitical scholars, but people who will actively engage themselves for our society."

Becker was funny, a rattling incredible-statement machine. It was amusing how little understanding these people seem to have about how to impress a Western audience.

"What about after a student graduates? How does, say, an engineer choose his place of work? Does he work at the place where he is needed most?" I wanted to see if D.D.R. students had free choice of jobs after graduation, or whether the state decided.

"Well, in most cases the student can choose where he wants to work. Of course, the F.D.J. and the university leadership works to influence students to go to those work places where they are most needed."

Herr Becker had a question for me, the standard one about my impressions of the D.D.R. I gave him a standard answer, and he came back with what sounded like his prepared remarks on the subject. "Yes, I think the majority is content here. We have shortcomings — a thousand little annoyances every day — but I think our people are content."

Becker looked at peace with the world. I nodded.

Bach arrived over an hour after he was supposed to. Becker and I had by that time deteriorated into small talk about how the briefcase which had accompanied his fine leather folder had been stolen when he left it unattended in a restaurant, and about how it was hard to get fluid for his cigarette lighter. Bach was obviously trying to delay our departure for Schwedt. When he came, he proposed lunch at a place near Treptower Park, which meant an extra half-hour into town and half-hour back. On the ride in, we passed by the Chinese Embassy, a big corner building on a long street.

"Look at the cars outside," Bach scowled, pointing to two large black Mercedes outside the entrance. "The Chinese prefer to buy West German cars over Volgas from the Soviet Union." He swung his head back and forth in a pompous motion, and pursed his fat lips. "I don't know why we tolerate these Chinese having such a big embassy here in Berlin. It's all spies, you know."

He should know, I thought to myself.

At the first restaurant they told us there would be a forty-five-minute wait, so I insisted we leave. We drove over to a place in Treptower Park that Bach said had been a popular dance restaurant before the war. Now it was decrepit and the service was so slow that at one point Bach moaned about how ashamed he was. A little after three — two hours past the time we had originally agreed on — we left the restaurant for Schwedt, taking a detour on the way out to drop Herr Becker off in some obscure spot at the outskirts of the city.

The mood in the car was jovial. Bach looked like a Rubens angel when he was in a laughing mood, and I occupied the trip by singing American protest songs. As we left the Berlin city limits, the car had to go through the identity check like the one the day Waack and I went to Potsdam. Bach took out some white card rather than the normal greenish-gray D.D.R. identity card, and although I was sitting in the front seat, I didn't even try to look. The car was let through after only a perfunctory stop. "The policeman didn't even look at my card," Bach commented lightly. How did he know, I wondered.

As I expected, Bach asked me the name of my friend in Schwedt. I had thought up a phony name in advance — Mattias Hauptmann — and even a phony address — on Thälmannstrasse. As for the name, only the last part could be made up, because Bach had already heard me refer to him by his real first name. As for Thälmannstrasse, that was the street where we parked our car the day I came to Schwedt with Waack, and it was the only other street name I knew in Schwedt besides my friend's. When Bach let me off, I went up the stairs at the address I gave him, waited in the dark and damp hall for ten minutes, and then sneaked downstairs to look both ways for whether he was there. Bach had said he was going to take a look around town — he hadn't been there since its completion — and he didn't appear to be around when I came out. I walked into the Konsum food store across the street from the parking lot and asked a lady at the counter how I got to my friend's address. I had to take a bus.

"Steve! I never thought I'd see *you* again," Mattias yelled out as he answered the door. "How come you came so late?" His hair was somewhat longer, and he had grown a bit, but I recognized him easily. He had a big broad smile on his triangular face. In both the first and the last days of my trip I was meeting again people I had seen in 1969.

I explained to him about Bach and Waack, and told him I'd given Bach a false name and address. He took me inside to meet his mother, who was sitting knitting, and a friend named Heinrich, who had on a thin autumn jacket even though we were inside. On the jacket an American flag was sewn. Heinrich looked like a figure for a woodcut, with very square and solid features which contrasted to Mattias' almost puffy face. They were friends from the fertilizer factory in Schwedt where they both worked.

Mattias took out some beers that were being cooled in cold water in a basin near the door. They had no refrigerator. "So, Mattias, first of all tell me something about Schwedt. You know, I came here with Doctor Waack around three weeks ago."

His eyes perked up. "What did you see? Did you see the wooden cabins on the road into town?"

"Yeah, Dr. Waack said they were weekend homes for workers."

Mattias erupted in a put-on belly laugh. "Wow, but did he tell you where the building materials came to build 'em?"

"No."

"Stolen, man, all stolen! Workers lifted them from the building sites. Wow, did the Party big shots get angry."

"Waack presented it as a great sign of prosperity."

"What about the war zone, did you see that?"

"War zone, what do you mean?"

"The big new apartment block, the one with bulldozers and mud hills that looks like a war zone."

"No, I don't know which ones you mean. The only big apartment block we saw was this one here. We saw it from the road, and I noticed to myself then how it already looked rundown, and how they hadn't planted any trees or grass here yet. You know, on Saturday I saw the same thing with a housing project in Berlin where they hadn't planted any grass yet either."

"Shit, Steve, if you think *this* block is bad, wait till you see the one they opened last spring. We'll take you there as soon as my pop comes home. It's incredible. Kids have to play in mud hills right next to all these machines that are lying around. And there are no stores even though five thousand people live there. People have to walk over wooden planks to get into the building entrance. And it'll be years before they do anything about it."

"Do you know about the history of Schwedt?" Heinrich came in. "First, they got a famous city planner to do the plans for the city. It was really nice, with movies and places for young people and theaters and all. It was so good they gave the guy an award for his plans. But then the Party boss here decided it cost much too much money. So they scrapped the whole plan and fired the guy. Then they did another plan, and it was too expensive, and finally they came up with what they have now — nothing to do, no place to go at night, no grass or trees anywhere. And the department store they're building is a year late already."

"What about that main street with the fountain and the trees?"

"You mean our 'Street of Grandeur'? The one for the foreign delegations?"

"Well, that grand it isn't. But do you know who lives in those apartments? Is it just higher officials who get to live on that street?"

Neither Heinrich, Mattias, or Mattias' mother knew who lived there.

"Heinrich, how do people *find out* about things like this with the city planner whose plan got scrapped, and so forth. It's not in the newspaper, I assume."

"No, of course not. Nothing's in the newspaper. But everyone gets the real news by word of mouth. I mean, we all know that the factory we work at is going with big losses. A few things everyone can see, and then other things leak out and spread."

"You hear from people who were involved in the thing," Mattias said, starting his second beer, and burping. He burped a lot when he drank. "I mean, like there was a big scandal at the magnetic-tape factory they built at Wolfen a few years ago to supply magnetic tape for all the socialist countries. Well, the conditions were bad, and, you know, the general discontent which exists among everybody — so some workers poured sand in the chemical vats. Production was sabotaged for a long time, and then they put the guys on night shift, and still they haven't fixed it. I heard about it from a kid I met at a discotheque in Berlin who worked at the factory. That's how you hear things."

"Why do people come to Schwedt?" I went on. "In the middle of nowhere with nothing to do? Are there higher wages in the industries?"

"Well, they promised people higher wages in the beginning," Mattias answered. "That's why my dad came here. But it never turned out that way."

"You mean they just lied, or what?"

"Well, they said later that the higher wages were dependent on fulfilling the plan, and somehow the plan never got fulfilled."

We small-talked for a little while, waiting for Mattias' father. Pop music was the best thing they knew. Like some of the other people I had met in the D.D.R., Mattias and Heinrich would have been nonpolitical in a nontotalitarian society. But in a place like the D.D.R. the politicization of everything requires everyone to take a position. And their position, like most everybody else's, was no.

After dinner, Mattias' father took me to look at the "war zone" in his little Trabant car. It seated only two, so Mattias and Heinrich stayed home. The father was gruff-talking and blunt, but open-hearted, a normal middle-aged worker, I imagined, just as his wife, with her tired wrinkles, her knitting, and her smile was a typical working class *Hausfrau*. When we returned we all sat around the dinner table. Mattias brought out more beer. The television was turned on to a West German film, but the volume was low and nobody was listening much.

"What is the feeling among people in Schwedt, or in other smaller places outside Berlin, toward the government?" I asked the group. "In Berlin, some people have told me that in the smaller places everybody is convinced by the system."

"Steve," Heinrich answered, "I think in some of the very poor villages in provinces like Mecklenburg, where the peasants were really almost starving before the war, they have had some improvements and they are convinced. But not many other people."

"Even in these new areas like Schwedt or Halle-Neustadt, where everyone has new housing and so forth?"

"No." Mattias laughed. "You've heard about what it's *really* like in Schwedt. How can you think that? And another thing — Heinrich, you know I visited around the Thüringer Wald last Christmas. The peasants there are really poor, and they weren't at all convinced. They were really angry because the schools had told their children to tell the parents to turn off the Christmas lights to save electricity. You know, they have this special custom with Christmas lights."

"Boys, do you know the old joke about when they collectivized the farms?" Mattias' father crackled, scratching his chest. Collectivization came in 1960, just before the Wall, and collective farms were divided up into LPG 1, LPG 2, and LPG 3. *LPG* standing for *Landwirtschaftliche Produktionsgenossenschaft.* The three grades represented different levels of collectivization, from 1 ("peasants own land, state owns machines") to 3 ("state owns land, state owns machines"). "People asked, 'What is an LPG four?'" Mattias' father continued. "The answer was, 'Land in East, peasants in West.'"

I chuckled. "You mean peasants defected to the West when they collectivized?"

"Whole villages just up and left. We've heard stories about some villages around Schwedt which just suddenly became deserted overnight."

"The problem with the D.D.R. is that you can't buy anything decent here, or else decent things are so expensive." The mother spoke. "It's very nice that they subsidize the cost of bread, but man doesn't live by bread alone. Occasionally, I'd like a piece of chocolate. And who can afford that, except occasionally?"

"Yeah, it's really a problem," I said. "The only decent things around are in the Intershops."

"Oh, don't mention those Intershops," the mother snarled back. "You know, now they're everywhere — I saw one now in some little train station on the way to Berlin. Supposedly, they're only for West German visitors, but what West German goes *there*?"

"You don't have any relatives in West Germany?"

"No, unfortunately," Mattias answered.

"The thing is, it's not that we don't produce some good things, it's only that they're not on sale here. Remember when I had that job as a cleaning lady at the Leipzig Trade Fair? I was astonished to see what we were offering to sell the foreigners. Nylon pullovers, everything! I didn't even know we produced such things."

"Steve," the father began slowly, and with a deep voice, "let me say something. This may sound strange to you, and I don't know if I'm speaking for the boys, but even if the borders were opened I would stay here. I'm the first one to recognize the faults we have, but at least you can walk the streets at night. Here if some kid tries to mug you, the law comes right down on him. But in West Germany you can get away with anything."

The father drove me back to Thälmannstrasse so I could meet Herr Bach in his car by nine. Bach and I had a quiet ride back, with silence in the car after the first ten minutes of perfunctory lies about what had transpired at my friend's house. The problem was that it was *too* silent, and I got to brooding. What had Bach done while I was at Matthias'? Had he perhaps gone to the police station to check out any information on him? Had he found out that no such person existed? Or maybe had he just left the request there, and the police would telegraph him with that information the next morning?

God, save me, I AM SCARED. God, I had lasted out the whole trip, two long months. Now there were just *two days left*. AND I HAD BLOWN IT. Terror reverberated back and forth through my pulsating veins as Bach, seemingly calmly — but deceivingly? — drove the car through the silent and dark farmland along the deserted night road. *Of course*, idiot, Bach had gone to the police and checked. Why didn't you realize that he would do that — what else did he have to do with his time? Shit, why hadn't I *realized* that when he made the offer to drive me, and when he was so precise about getting my friend's name? He would just be checking to make sure my friend was straight, but then he would find out that there was no person bearing the name of my friend, and that *I had been lying*. And he would put two and two together and realize that wasn't the only lie.

IT WAS OBVIOUS HE HAD GONE TO THE POLICE!

Shifting and turning back and forth on that narrow couch in Frau Luger's living room, I got no sleep that night. Maybe an hour or two in the early morning — my watch read a little after 4:30 the last time I glanced at it that endless, weird night. Lord, it was blind terror, my head hot and my belly gnawing, and it would absolutely not go away. What would happen when Bach came in the morning? What would be the expression on his face? I choked and squirmed, as I felt him wringing my neck, strangling me. In my fantasies I told myself that I would have to beg him for mercy. He was old and more understanding, unlike the harsh Waack, and maybe if I just confessed everything and begged to be forgiven? I was ready to weep. I was ready to promise not to write anything, and to keep my promise. PLEASE, JUST LET ME OUT.

Maybe I was paranoid, maybe I was crazy? Perhaps Bach had done no checking at all. I had been wrong in the past with some of my suspicions: they had never searched my luggage, right? Was it so strange that I should become paranoiac, given the environment I was in? Look at how the system had deformed Waack. *There* was an insane man, there was a paranoid. He had an ideology which promised equality and liberation. But he was a privileged member of a society where everyone hated the "liberation" which had been bestowed on them. Maybe he *was*, as he said, a sensitive student once, with ideals. He had been hardened by the contrast between ideals and reality, and, since he had chosen reality, he came to hate human beings and see conspiracies everywhere. Why not, it was a natural response to his situation, to become so hateful. I breathed deeply. Wasn't it a miracle that there weren't many more like him, that millions of East Germans had succeeded in completely tuning out the crap served to them every day, and thus remained human beings in spite of everything, never forgetting that two plus two will always be four? I saw Suzanne's funny, beautiful, long, sad, determined face in front of me.

I thought of those who couldn't tune out politics. Late one night on the S–Bahn I heard some drunk old guy babbling about "Ulbricht and the bosses" and "the role — of — the —

D.D.R. — in world politics." Where else do drunks babble about politics?

Tune out the crap, that's what you had to do to remain sane in the D.D.R. But that's just what I was unable to do. I had my story to get. I had to plod through *Neues Deutschland* faithfully every morning. And I had to keep both hands tied behind my back, damming up all my hatred whenever Waack started spouting his hateful nightmares.

I had to stop thinking about all this and fall asleep! But when I got off thinking about all that I could only think about how narrow the bed was where I was lying.

*

But it was the same bright and smiling "Good morning, Steve" from Bach. I could barely keep my eyes opened, and I must have looked tired to him, but I was so happy by his calm greeting that I wanted to hug him and tell him, this time really meaning it, that I loved the D.D.R., that I wanted to kiss the D.D.R. flag, anything, Lord, *anything*, to show him my loyalty. I hoped, I dared to hope, that he hadn't checked anything yesterday, and that furthermore there was nothing special about the date August thirteenth on my visa. I hoped, I hoped, but I couldn't be certain. I had to flatter Bach, I had to go all out in obsequiousness, I had to be on my very best and most friendly behavior today, hopefully my second-to-the-last in the D.D.R.

"Herr Bach," I said at lunch, "I wonder if it will be possible for me to take back to America information material about the D.D.R. I have a lot of student political friends who would be really interested. They're sympathetic to the socialist bloc and the Soviet Union, but, you know, the information they get is very one-sided." I felt as if I was babbling on like an alcoholic or something. "I think my friends would be most interested in information on the D.D.R. educational system, on D.D.R. support for the liberation movement in Vietnam, on the health system, and, perhaps on the Wall."

"The Wall?"

"Yes, you know, all the misconceptions about the Wall and why it had to be built. I mean, I've gotten a clear understanding of this question through discussions with D.D.R. citizens, but I must confess, before I came here even I had some misconceptions about it. The Wall is probably the major tool of propaganda against the D.D.R. in the West."

"The Wall, yes." Bach mused, still radiating. "Steve, you can't imagine how awful the situation was before. The robber exchange rate they set up. And those horrible border movie theaters right inside West Berlin, where they attracted our youth for their ideological poison. Then of course the kids came back and told their friends about what they saw. How could we build a socialist system under such conditions? I don't know why we waited so long to build it. The leaders wanted to be tolerant, I guess. But we've closed the border now, and it's harder for poison to seep in."

"So do you think you can get me some leaflets like that to take back?"

"Well, we'll see. I'll try."

"Another question," I went on, ass-licking. "I've been so impressed during my stay in the D.D.R., both with what I've seen and learned, and with the hospitality you and Doctor Waack have shown me, that I want to help the D.D.R. in some way when I return to America. Of course, I'm a student and don't have *that* much time, but, well, where do you think I could make the best contribution? Establishing a committee for the recognition of the D.D.R. at my university, writing an article for my student newspaper on the D.D.R., working to counteract West German propaganda? What do you think?"

Bach's reply was curt. "I'll think about it, and give you an answer tomorrow morning."

*

I spent the evening packing my luggage. Making sure that Frau Luger wasn't around, I carefully took out my notebook and tore out my travel notes, putting them into five equal piles. I proceeded to write, on blank sheets from the notebook, one page of notes for the five books I had gotten in East Germany. At the top of the page of book notes I printed the book's title. The page of book notes I placed on top of each of the stacks of travel notes, and carefully folded each in half. Then I put each stack into the pages of one of the books. I would try to smuggle out my notes disguised as notes on the books.

I was all packed, and calm, though filled with a nonnervous excitement, for the morning. My tremors of Monday night I had forgotten; I confidently assumed I would be leaving the next morning on schedule. Confidently assumed! How horrible that sounded, how unworthily privileged I felt. My encounter in East Germany had turned out, despite Waack and Bach, pretty well for *me*. But how could I prattle to myself about "confidence" in a land where desperation, cynicism, and resignation were the prevailing emotions? I remembered how I had told Suzanne that I felt the urge every once in a while to make a run for the Wall. That was true: I *was* gripped by the bizarre urge at times. But for me reality was more prosaic, and luckier. I would show my passport, and my visa, and my currency declaration. Everything would be in order, and I would legally leave the D.D.R. and take the S-Bahn into West Berlin — the very next morning in fact. But meanwhile everyone I met would be left behind. And I would never see them again. Maybe they'll open the border in fifty years, someone had said to me. Are you that optimistic, replied his companion without a trace of irony. Suzanne said that one way or another we would meet in the West within ten years. She could do it, if anyone. But it was bravado nevertheless: she would never succeed.

I would be leaving tomorrow. All my friends would be staying forever.

The big question now was what Bach would come up with this morning, after "thinking about" my question of the previous night — as if he had never thought about it before. I guffawed to myself, I hadn't even seen when I made my ridiculous comment the day before what a perfect lead-in it was to whatever Bach had in mind for me.

Would it be what I now expected it would be?

Bach arrived, and closed the door so that we two were alone in the living room, sitting right opposite each other at the big round table. His voice was slow, hesitant. The taut expression around his mouth and eyes indicated he was having a hard time holding back a gale of laughter, I thought.

"Steve," he began deliberately, "I thought about the question you asked me last night. And I — I, uh, asked several colleagues at the job about it. Now, we've, uh, thought about this first now — you only asked us last night — so it's hard to give a definite reply. But" — he paused in a studied way, and slowed his voice again — "we think the best way you can help the D.D.R. is *not* to work for the D.D.R. in public." *Das Beste ist, in der Öffentlichkeit für die D.D.R. nicht aufzutreten.* The discreet, but definite, accent on *not* was masterful.

It was hard to restrain a gasp of relief and amusement that he had finally let it out of the bag. I had guessed right: *I was now to be a witness to an attempt to recruit me as a spy for the*

D.D.R. What fun it was going to be to see how he did it, what words he was going to use.

"Steve, the reports you have done for us have been excellent. You are a very intelligent young man. We therefore think we should continue our scholarly cooperation. As you know, our countries unfortunately have no diplomatic relations yet, so it is hard for our scholars to get information about America. We are particularly interested in this for our research group of the year two thousand, because, despite different social systems, our societies have certain problems in common."

Didn't he remember he had said the exact same thing two months earlier, on the road from Grosspostwitz to Berlin?

"So, in the spirit of scholarly exchange, we are proposing that you continue to do periodic reports for us on questions we are interested in. In exchange for this, we will frequently invite you to be our guest in the D.D.R., put you up, pay your travel costs over here, make historical documents on the history of the German labor movement available for your own scholarly research, and give you an honorarium for your work."

I bit my lips. Was *that* the word Bach had chosen to recruit his innocent little student — *honorarium?*

"Now, there is one very important condition, Steve. That is that you keep very quiet about our academic exchanges. It is crucial that you not tell a soul."

"Why?" I asked, wondering what wild explanation he'd give.

"Well, you know, our supplies of foreign currency are limited. We're afraid that if knowledge of our offer got out, we'd have thousands of American students coming who would want to help us with scholarly material, and that such foreign currency we don't have."

"What kinds of reports would you like me to do?"

"Well, within the next few months we'd like some reports on

questions involving both America and, since you'll be going back there soon, Sweden. About America, we are very interested in getting a detailed report on the strength of the movement for the liberation of Angela Davis. We want concrete facts — the quality of the organization, its effect on public opinion, and the importance of the Communist Party in the agitation. Also, we want you to do some further investigation of the financing of the student movement. Perhaps you can talk to leaders of the organizations, or former leaders who have now left them, and find out more about where different student groups get money. Finally, we want a report on the influence of the Communist Party in the student movement, the growth of the Young Workers' Liberation League, and also the work of the Communist Party in the peace and labor movements."

"Herr Bach, don't Communist Party delegations from America come to visit the D.D.R? Can't you get this information from them?"

"Steve, what a delegation tells us is one thing and the truth is another. You know how a group of foreign Communists come here, they drink a lot, we show them around, and, well, it's not always the truth that comes forth. And, let's be honest, our American comrades are — well, let me put it this way: the Communist Party is the force that must change America, it is the only force that *can* change America, but we know that Gus Hall has not yet excited the American masses."

"What questions do you have about Sweden?"

"Here, we are interested in two sorts of questions. One is about moves in Sweden to recognize the D.D.R. We want a detailed report about the state of the debate, which politicians and organs of public opinion have spoken for and against. In particular, we want you to investigate the debate within the Social Democratic Party, perhaps by asking around and making contact with government politicians. Also, we want the names of student leaders in Sweden who have expressed sympathy with the D.D.R. The second type of information we want is about the Swedish university system and student movement. We want you to do a report on these similar to the two reports you wrote us about the American student movement and about Harvard."

"Should I send you these reports when I'm through with them?"

"No, no, not through the mails! We want you to *come here* and deliver them to me. In fact, we propose that you come here the weekend of November sixth to deliver your first reports to us. This is the time of the anniversary of the Russian Revolution, and we can arrange for you theater tickets and so forth. You can stay in the luxury hotel, and we'll have Russian caviar and French champagne for you."

"It sounds very nice," I said shyly.

"Any questions?" The tone of Bach's voice seemed uncertain, on edge that I wouldn't accept his offer, fearful that I realized what he was asking me to do.

I had to ask at least one question or he would get suspicious. "Herr Bach, there's only one thing I'm worried about — my independence as a scholar. Wouldn't this be compromised if I entered into such close academic contacts with you?"

"Steve, that's up to you. Nobody has to know about our contacts. If you don't tell anybody, neither will we."

"That sounds all right."

"Then, Steve, do you accept?"

"Sure," I said. "Fine."

"Wonderful! Let's shake hands on it." We did. "Now, just several technical details. The first regards your trip here from Stockholm in November."

"Well, I can just come down the train and ferry via Trelleborg and Sassnitz. That's the shortest way."

"Yes, but we don't want you to come that way. That requires a visa stamp on your passport at our border, and we don't want any stamps in your passport. We think you'll be coming to the D.D.R. quite often, and we don't want your government to get suspicious."

"No."

"What we want you to do is fly from Stockholm to West Berlin, and come into the capital on the normal one-day visit for Westerners. Go directly to Frau Koch's, and she will inform us as soon as you arrive. We will have a visa ready for you — a piece of paper, just like the one you have now, that you can remove from the passport when you leave."

"All right."

"Another thing. I want to emphasize again how important it is not to tell *anyone* in America about your trip to the D.D.R."

"Yeah, I can just tell them that I met many friends, and about all the achievement I saw here."

"No, Steve, not a word of praise for the D.D.R. Don't speak anything, or write anything in any student newspaper, that could in any way identify you as a friend of the D.D.R. Our friendship will be in private. You can mention to your friends you came to the D.D.R., you saw Alexanderplatz and the television tower, but *no more*. Not even to your parents."

"What about the information brochures I asked for?"

"It would be better if you took no brochures with you."

"Anything more?"

"No, that's about it. Of course, you understand that from now on when you visit the D.D.R. you will be our guest the entire time. We will take good care of you, and you need not visit any of your other friends — Manfred or Mattias or whomever."

"You know, one thing I remembered just now: I have to get your address and phone number so I can contact you."

"You will contact us through Frau Koch. You have her address and phone number." He stopped. "Yes, and one more thing — I brought some Western currency with me. I'll give it to you now so you can buy your plane ticket from Stockholm." He took out a hundred-dollar bill, two twenties, and a ten, and laid them on the rough brown wooden table. "When you bring your reports in November, we can give you your honorarium."

Obviously, I couldn't take the money. "Herr Bach," I said hesitantly, "if I take the money now, I'll just lose it. I have a bank account in Stockholm, and I have enough until November. I'll buy the tickets, and you can give me the money when I come back."

I breathed deeply in and out.

*

Herr Bach proposed a festive good-bye dinner — "good-bye but not farewell" — at a place he said was one of the finest in all of Berlin. In the midst of a beautiful wooded area near Wannsee, it served fish which you could choose out of a big tank while they were still alive. They killed them immediately, and served them fresh-cooked. It was, as he said, unique.

As it turned out, the restaurant served these fish out of a tank only on weekends, but the meal was quite good and the place unusually clean. The red-and-white checkerboard tablecloth was the first nonwhite cloth I had seen in an East German restaurant.

"Steve, what was your impression of your political discussions with Doctor Waack? He told me something about them."

"Well," I answered inoffensively, lying to the end, "we exchanged a lot of interesting viewpoints, and I think I learned a lot. But one point I was trying to make I wish I could have gotten him to see. I understand what he says about the reasons for the dictatorship of the proletariat, given the strength of the capitalists and the ideological diversion of the West. But I wish he would have agreed that it is *unfortunate* that these restrictions on freedom have to take place, that in and of itself it's not a good thing."

"Steve, of course! Nobody thinks it's a good thing. But it is necessary, believe me that. And not only because of the capitalists abroad. Exploitation continues to exist in the D.D.R. as well."

I looked at him strangely and asked what he meant.

"I mean that we still have a private sector. It is not dominant, of course, but we have some industries that are privately owned, and plumbers and electricians and bakers who have their own businesses. Why, take this restaurant — *it* is privately owned. There is exploitation here. These waiters are exploited."

I sighed to myself. Bach had picked this restaurant as one that was so particularly good, so unique, so fitting for my last night in the D.D.R. Was the man too blind to see the contradiction between his theoretical words and the practical choice he had made? I had thought back involuntarily to what Suzanne had said that night about how those who were convinced in the D.D.R. had to think not of their daily lives, but of abstract theory. The world of the convinced in the D.D.R. was, I saw now, in many ways worse than that of the millions and millions of normal people below. True, the millions lacked the privileges, but they also lacked the tension between ideology and reality which had made Waack paranoid and Bach pathetic.

For some obscure reason, there was a line of no less than four cars waiting at the checkpoint from Berlin back to Frau Luger's when we drove home from the restaurant. Maybe it was the drizzling rain; maybe it was the unusually detailed checks they seemed to be making. In two of the cases, they had the driver take his identity card out and looked all through it. Then they waved the drivers along with a perfunctory motion of the arm. In preparation, Bach took out his wallet with the white card. Again, I didn't even try to look. When our car came up, the policeman squinted through the slapping windshield wipers. He then proceeded to give Bach a smart salute.

I gulped.

*

The next morning at 11:16 my S-Bahn from Friedrichstrasse crossed above the Berlin Wall, and a few minutes later I was at the Zoologische Garten stop in West Berlin. I rushed out of the train, lugged my luggage downstairs, and went outside into the fresh daylight. There was a small refreshment stand right in front of me, and the first thing I did was buy a bottle of Coca-Cola.

LETTER FROM EAST GERMANY

LETTER FROM EAST GERMANY

Summer, 1971

THE GERMAN DEMOCRATIC REPUBLIC (D.D.R.) is a country whose accomplishments are few. For those which actually do exist the official enthusiasm can be almost boundless. Thus, when the government completed its new town centers — pleasant pedestrian malls with a sprinkling of modern hotels, restaurants, and shops — in East Berlin, Dresden, Leipzig, and a few smaller cities, the impression was conveyed that this event represented no more and no less than the definitive proof of the superiority of the Communist system. Postage stamps and souvenir folders with pictures of department stores and hotels appeared to commemorate the centers. The Schönefeld Airport was entirely redecorated with larger-than-life shots of the rebuilt Alexanderplatz in East Berlin. And newspapers rushed to remind readers that without the Berlin Wall "our new town centers would never have been possible."

The visitor to East Germany cannot help but notice the centers — if for no other reason than that they have almost all been constructed adjacent to the main railroad terminals — and a stroll through them is indeed a pleasant, and surprising, experience for those who have spent some time in Communist cities. The new restaurants and ice-cream parlors feature innovations like polished Formica tables and leather swivel chairs. There are even luxuries like storefronts with bright red, green, blue, and yellow plastic lettering outside, instead of the pallid semi-neon markings which have always created a year-round atmosphere of midwinter dusk across the Communist bloc. (On visiting Paris, Ninotchka, still faithful, sighed. "We have the ideas, but they have the lights.")

Special local features are, of course, not absent. The staff of the service desk at the 36-story Interhotel Stadt Berlin, which dominates Alexanderplatz, has been named the Angela Davis Collective, and next to brochures about theater tickets and guided tours last summer lay a petition to Ronald Reagan. (Almost every East German schoolchild, incidentally, wrote a one-line letter to the California governor, stating, in German, "*Wir fordern die Freilassung von Angela Davis.*") Next door, the corridors of the Centrum Department Store are lined with pictures of exemplary workers in each division. Also in Alexander-platz, a furniture store offers the wonders of Intecta, "an integrated system of interior decoration," with floor models present-ing suggested combinations of modernistic furniture — and bookshelves in the sample rooms filled with volumes like *Under the Banner of Proletarian Internationalism, Proceedings of the Fifth Party Congress of the Socialist Unity Party of Germany,* and *The Struggle of Marx and Lenin for the Proletarian Party.* In the nearby apartment houses, where well-off bureaucrats and professionals live in modern comfort, the entrance to each floor is lined with portraits of Party leaders.

Despite all this, what impresses most is how in building their showcases the authorities have chosen to measure progress by how closely they approach, or how well they ape, the West. Thus the Grill Bar of the Interhotel at Alexanderplatz shows how up-to-date *it* is by introducing pay toilets in the rest rooms. And not only that: the management prominently displays cash registers imported from Sweden and Jet Spray Coolers from the

United States. In normal establishments, they make do with locally manufactured registers, and at the typical restaurant it is considered sufficient for the waitress to sling the customer's portion of juice out of a common bottle. While the menu offers "milch shakes," there is not a single Russian specialty, not even a measly Ukranian soljanka soup, which is usually considered to be any restaurant's minimum gastronomic concession to the Soviet Union.

After a dinner at the Grill Bar one can jaunt over to East Berlin's Bowling Zentrum, the first of its kind in Eastern Europe. (The Soviets recently announced their intention to establish one too.) All the equipment is American-made, and for weekend evenings a lane must be reserved a week or more in advance. There are also two newly opened clothing chains, Exquisit and Boutique 70, selling imported Western fashions at around four to six times what they cost in Western Europe. Blue jeans or Dacron pullovers go for $40, simple suede jackets for $300. And the talk of East Germany this past summer was the new Baltic Sea hotel, the Neptun, erected entirely by a Swedish construction firm under contract with the government. At times the self-consciousness of imitation becomes ludicrous, as when the bar at the modern Interhotel in the port city of Rostock was given the name Boutique.

However, the 17 million inhabitants of East Germany continue with the traditional feeling — literally true since nobody ever bothers to water the lawns there — that the grass grows greener on the other side. A story which began circulating shortly before Walter Ulbricht's "retirement" last May tells of a visit by the East German leader to Mao Tse-tung. "Tell me, Mao," asks Ulbricht, "how many enemies do you have in your country?" Mao thinks for a while and then answers, "Well, I'd guess around fifteen or sixteen million." "Whew, I'm glad to hear that," blurts out Ulbricht. "I don't have any more than that either." And while Western journalists speculate about a liberalization under Erich Honecker, the new Party boss, his subjects remind you that Comrade Honecker's specialty on the Politburo has always been internal security; when he last delivered a speech on cultural policy a few years ago, a number of novels and films which had already been released proceeded to disappear from view.

Mostly, though, life goes on as it has in the past, with the same annoyances as before. A strange mixture of political consciousness and political apathy marks people here. The government's attempts to take credit for every newly opened fruit-and-vegetable market or apartment dwelling as a further proof of the correctness of Party policy, breeds quite naturally a reciprocal attitude of blaming the government for all shortcomings and errors. As one might imagine, the authorities hardly come out ahead in such a weighing process, but it does encourage citizens to reflect on the meaning of politics in their daily lives, and the Party can at least take some comfort in the fact that the people do not ignore it. A simultaneous apathy, however, goes beyond a simple weariness with endless slogans and sermons to an apathy regarding broader questions of the type which have been engaging other nations in recent years. While Americans worry these days about things like, say, hunger in Bangladesh or Consciousness III, people here fret about problems somewhat closer to home. Such as, yes, we have no bananas. Or that the razor blades you buy won't cut your whiskers and the shampoo you get won't clean your hair. America has a silent majority; East Germany has a silenced majority. Minorities have it tough in America; just about everyone has it tough here. Daily life is such a problem that nobody has time for higher considerations. This gives people's political opinions a down-to-earth quality they often lack at, say, a

Leonard Bernstein cocktail party, while at the same time accounting for a level of broad-minded idealism about equal to that of a peanut farmer lobbyist on Capitol Hill.

East Germany officially describes itself as a "modern advanced socialist society," and the East German standard of living is in fact the highest in Eastern Europe. Indeed, while Western outsiders may rank East Germany as the most unappealing country in the Communist bloc, visiting Poles and Bulgarians tend to have the opposite reaction, putting the D.D.R. at the top of the heap. However, there must surely be some unconscious irony in the claim that "the successes of socialist construction in the D.D.R. show that the superiority of socialism applies not only to a country on the road to development, but also to already advanced societies." For in contrast to the Russians, many of whom seem not to know what they're missing, East Germans are acutely aware of what they lack, and will tell you about it on almost any excuse. Items that were common forty years ago — coffee, oranges, apples, bananas, chocolate — are now either luxuries or completely unavailable. "What's the use of having those new buildings at Alexanderplatz, when still none of them sells any bananas?" a matron declared to me one warm afternoon while we were drinking some medicinal-tasting local cola, the somewhat more drinkable lemon soda being at that point sold out in most of East Berlin. Interestingly, Leipzig residents can always find bananas in their markets during the semiannual trade fairs, the authorities apparently being under the impression that the sight of residents actually being able to buy a banana will impress the foreign visitors. But fresh fruits are generally so uncommon that huge lines form whenever and wherever they are sold.

"It's very nice that they subsidize the cost of bread," says a housewife, "but man doesn't live by bread alone. Occasionally

I'd like a piece of chocolate." A stale, crumbling, medium-sized chocolate bar goes for about a dollar — about two hours' wages for the average worker. For reasons nobody can quite fathom, and for as long as anyone can remember, the local specialty beer Berliner Weisse has been largely unobtainable in East Berlin, a situation somewhat akin to a twenty-five-year absence of Jewish rye in New York. One day at lunchtime I made a trip to one of the oldest restaurants located in East Berlin, Zur letzten Instanz, reputed to have the best Weisse in town. I was unsuccessful in finding any. "Precisely *because* we have the best Weisse in the city, we never have any. Whenever some comes in, it's sold out right on the spot," the waitress told me.

Western critics of wasteful advertising, worthless products, and useless packaging might find local attitudes on this subject somewhat surprising. "When I think of cities in the West, it just makes me want to cry with longing," a student rebel told me. "The beautiful advertising, those bright lights. That's where the life is!" Many East German youths eagerly repeat slogans and jingles they have heard on West German radio or television advertising, and one sees more buttons reading PEPSI-COLA than FREE ANGELA DAVIS. Furthermore, it is possible to believe that a product like suntan lotion is useless only until one views the endless sunburned bathers lining East German beaches, where the lotion is unavailable. And one even becomes more sympathetic to the excesses of American packaging after observing the glass jars with dangling labels, syrup bottles sticky all over, or racks of detergent almost invisible amidst the loose powder escaped from the boxes that is a daily experience in groceries here. It should be added that the packaging would also disturb Ralph Nader, since there is rarely even the slightest declaration of the contents.

All that glitters may not be gold, but the same is even more likely to be the case for that which does not glitter, and beneath this surface contempt for the public there lies a deep-going disdain. "In your country, the stores fight with each other for customers," I have heard. "Here, the customers fight with each other for things to buy, and the stores couldn't care less." I got the point upon an inspection visit to East Germany's largest supermarket, in Berlin's new Centrum Department Store. Both in its huge size and in its condition — absent are the standard fading paint and crumbling plaster — the market is, or is supposed to be at any rate, somewhat of a showcase.

The first point to realize about an East German supermarket, as in almost any other East German store, is what is *not* for sale. Basically, this consists of anything out of the ordinary — spices, nuts, canned soups, food with a foreign flavor — and much that is ordinary. The choice of meats the day I came was: pig tails, meat bones, and hearts. There was no specification of from what animal the hearts came. Pork chops, now available somewhat more often than they were several years ago, still unleash good-sized lines when they make an appearance. (In a meat store in the northern resort town of Stralsund, I saw the word *liver* listed under the sign TODAY'S OFFERINGS, followed by three exclamation points.) Canned meats, frequently displaying obviously advanced cases of botulism, lie on the shelves for months, their appearance too sickening to endanger purchase. One afternoon I bought a jar of something called "pig's-head goulash," which gave every appearance of being on the verge of explosion, in a market in downtown East Berlin. The cashier looked at me somewhat peculiarly, as if to say, "How can you buy that?" I felt like asking her how she could sell it.

Other departments in the Centrum supermarket are equally interesting. Milk is left standing out in the open, without refrigeration, and is often sour by the time someone buys it.

Deeming unimportant the effort to develop strains of chickens that will lay eggs the year around, or to speed the delivery of eggs to the stores, those in charge prefer just to freeze eggs during the winter, thus depriving them of all taste. The occasional "fresh" carrots or tomatoes are invariably emaciated and dirty. Jars of honey are about 90 percent crystallized. There is a total of approximately three varieties of cheese. You can buy any kind of cookies you want, as long as they are tea biscuits. Local chewing gum, after several minutes in the mouth, dissolves into lots of sugar and small bits of some synthetic substance which does not coagulate.

Is it any wonder that Consciousness III hasn't come to the D.D.R.?

A private sector in retail trade still exists, and carries more than its share. In Leipzig, a family-run *Konditorei* offers the only genuine whipped cream in town, and a private bakery on the main street has large lines outside, embarrassing the largely empty state-run bakery down the street. Even Wannsee, an exclusive East Berlin suburb where many high Party officials including Ulbricht live, boasts a large and popular combined grocery store and ice-cream parlor which is in private hands. But many older private shops and restaurants are closing as their owners die and no new licenses are granted. "Ten years ago there were five restaurants and about as many bakeries right around where I live," recounts a Berliner. "Today there is one restaurant and no bakeries." The boarded-up shop windows everywhere add, of course, to the general gloom.

In general, gripes divide about equally between bemoaning that things cost so much and complaining that there is nothing anyone wants to buy. Given the quality of East German wares, it is almost easier to sympathize with the latter complaint. In this most industrially advanced of Communist countries, virtually nothing local industry produces is up to international quality — and one would be hard-pressed to come up with a single consumer product which was first *developed* in East Germany, or anywhere in the bloc for that matter. This results in an inability, by and large, to export to world markets, which in turn makes it difficult to import any quantities of the higher-quality Western goods which the people want.

How does one survive in a society where nothing works? In hot weather local traffic lights often go haywire and the telephone system ceases to function properly. In cold weather the new East German trams often break down, the system being saved, some say, only by old prewar Siemens cars. Elevators in public buildings here have only two signs which flash on: THIS CAR UP and OUT OF ORDER. An East German stays on a waiting list for eight years and pays $4500 for his diminutive Wartburg sedan, and then it breaks down after two weeks and is impossible to repair for lack of spare parts. (Months often go by during which it is impossible to obtain even a new battery or spark plug.) During one trip on the East German *Autobahn* I noticed, despite what was at best light traffic, that lots of cars were stopped on the side of the road, usually for overheated engines. There is a saying here that the word *auto* begins with an *ah-h*, ends with an *oh-h*, and has a *t* in the middle for *teuer* ("expensive"). As for the roads, it is said that automobile production cannot be expanded faster because the roads couldn't survive the extra cars.

On one random sample of ten ball-point pens I bought, three were unusable because the click mechanism didn't work. The finest quality East German razor blades give a questionable shave from the first one on, and are dangerous to the skin past the third time around. (Men with heavy beards find no choice but to use imported Gillette blades, costing thirty cents apiece.)

Local shampoo is latherless and basically inoperative. East German shoes, constructed from some sort of plastic, remain hard and uncomfortable throughout their all-too-brief wearing lives. People are even unhappy about the soap (it smells bad) and the toothpaste (it burns the mouth), objections which might be dismissed as trivial except that those with connections rush to supply themselves with Lux and Colgate.

Local clothing design has supposedly moved from the potato-sack look into the world of high fashion, the generous spirit behind this transformation having been expressed best by one editorialist who applauded hot pants because they took up less material. It is hard to tell how much of the dreadful designs is due to a lingering belief that bright colors are really a subtle West German plot, and how much just to incompetence. An American flower child over on a one-day visit from West Berlin felt compelled after looking over the women's apparel section of the Centrum Department Store to ask herself just where all the flowers had gone. "All I saw was rows and rows of the same awful designs." "It is an annoying feeling," says an East German electronics engineer, "constantly to see people on the street wearing the same things you have on." A teen-ager declares, "I can try on fifty pairs of pants in a store without getting one that fits. But a West German girl gives me a pair of old Levi's as a present and they fit fine."

Since the 1970 riots in Poland, easing consumer-goods shortages has become the official order of the day. Erich Honecker laid down the new line at the Eighth Party Congress in June 1971 by informing the delegates that in his humble opinion "the meaning of socialism" could be summed up in the phrase "everything for the people's welfare." Ever since, *Neues Deutschland* has been filled with reports of consumer-goods factories that have actually been attempting to satisfy the demands of customers, together with wrist-slappings for those who continue to operate in the traditional manner. Particular targets have been firms which continue to produce items for which there is no demand.

But despite the new emphasis on consumer goods, shortages are still the order of the day. "If you go into a store looking for ten things, odds are you'll get about five." Surely there is something wrong when one comes across a bar with the sign BEER SOLD OUT on the door — or a gas station with the notice GAS SOLD OUT. A corollary to shortages is waiting. There is a one- or two-year wait for most types of furniture, and a six-month wait for leather boots, just to cite two examples. Repairmen are in such short supply that a year's wait for a plumber or an electrician is typical. The new high-rise apartments often go for weeks without service when the elevators break down, the only exception being the new apartment buildings in the city centers. "A lot of secret policemen live here," explains a resident blithely, "so we never have any problem getting a repairman." Railroad stations constructed before the war with, say, ten ticket windows, generally have around two open, making buying a ticket almost as uncomfortable as taking the ride itself. (Because of a shortage of railroad cars, travelers on popular lines like Berlin-Dresden are often forced to stand during the entire three-hour trip.)

The restaurant situation has recently improved from catastrophic to merely dreadful, but the knowledge that the legendary absence of service in Communist countries has by now been enshrined as part of the local color no doubt inhibits thoroughgoing reforms. The idea of sitting at your own table, rather than packed in at the tail end of another group, is still unknown, and lengthy waits for lunchtime seats are the rule. In all but the very fanciest eating places, setting the tables consists of dumping a pile of silverware and paper napkins in the corner, and often even the napkins are available only by special request. Salt, pepper, or mustard must almost always be specially solicited. Even in Interhotels, fresh towels come to the rooms only every third day, and both times I have stayed in an Interhotel, the room radio has been broken. The finer restaurants, which shun anything so primitive as forcing people to stand up waiting interminably, resort to signs on the door reading TEMPORARILY CLOSED BECAUSE OF OVERCROWDING. The problem is that these signs have a habit of remaining on the door all evening, and the process of making a reservation at some of these places is shrouded in mystery. When I asked a friend whether he had ever tried to get a reservation at a certain one of these restaurants, he replied simply, "*I?* Who am *I?*"

The most popular shops in East Germany are, technically at least, closed to the people here. These are the Intershops, which sell nylon stockings, Marlboro cigarettes, Maxwell House coffee, Lux soap, Johnny Walker whiskey, Tobler chocolates, and other forbidden fruit at prices only slightly above Western levels — for foreign currency. Originally designed to help visiting West Germans buy gifts for their relatives, and for foreign tourists, it was necessary until around two years ago to present one's passport before even entering. It is still illegal for East Germans to hold Western currency, but the profits in hard currency the government makes by buying sought-after Western goods at wholesale and selling them at retail have apparently overcome ideological objections, and in recent times the passport check has been eliminated, and new Intershops have been opened up in nooks and crannies where foreign tourists never venture. The hope is to encourage West German relatives to leave generous sums of cash with their local loved ones, and to flush out black-market money.

To watch an East German shop at an Intershop is to see the expression on the face of a tot let loose in a sweet shop. Junior high school kids wait willingly in line for fifteen minutes to pick up a pack of chewing gum for the fifty *Pfennigs* a West German tourist gave them as presents. Tired-looking old men with two days' growth of beard cart out eight giant economy-sized jars of coffee and a box of laundry detergent. But the problem with the Intershops is that they also tremendously increase the resentment of those who have no West German relatives, who find themselves in the position of the coolie at the door of a "no dogs and Indians" colonial club. Animosity is even greater because people know that there are those who get part of their salary paid in West German marks. Meanwhile the unprivileged are left to wait for the occasional lucky opportunity, such as when, after the Soviet invasion of Czechoslovakia, the hapless Czechs were unable to pay for a shipment of Cinzano vermouth they had ordered from Italy, and the brotherly allies were kind enough to foot the bill. For a time in 1969 Cinzano was thus available, at five dollars a bottle, in East German liquor stores, and it's amazing how many homes here display an empty bottle of Cinzano on their mantelpiece.

✻

One aspect of life in the D.D.R. which might interest Western capitalists — especially the heartless exploiter types among them — is the position of labor. Although theoretically the country's ruling class, the workers here in fact have not only their employers, but the government and the trade unions against them. At the Eighth Party Congress the unions were told, according to *Neues Deutschland*, "to be very careful that improvements in working and living conditions never be made at the expense of higher production," a sentiment which any Western business leader would be happy to endorse, even while being skeptical that the unions would go along. (In what *Neues Deutschland* called "encouraging words," Erich Honecker told the Congress that "a certain amount of obstinancy on this score is also part of the function of a good trade union leader.") Furthermore, wage increases cannot outstrip productivity, since they are determined by the plan, which foresees wages rising about 70 percent as fast as productivity during the next five years. Significant groups of East German workers have received no pay hikes at all for five years, and the average industrial wage, which was about equal the West German level in 1960, is now 30 percent lower. (When I asked an official why it would be wrong for workers in a socialist society to exert pressure to have their vacations increased, he looked stunned for a moment, and then, as if to give the definitive parry to my modest proposal, replied, "First they start asking for more vacations. The next thing you know they'll be asking for more wages.")

Basically, given the ineffectiveness of the economic system, economic growth depends in significant measure on sweating more out of people. Thus in East Germany waitresses work eight or more tables, in New York three to five, a fact which may go some of the way in explaining restaurant service. Recently, the trade unions have encouraged workers to "suggest" that their factories begin working night shifts, so that "expensive machinery" can be amortized more quickly. Grassroots enthusiasm for this scheme can be judged by the effects multiple shifts have already had on family life in a country with Europe's highest divorce rate. Almost all women work, and are given the first shift so they can take care of the children after they return from day-care centers. This leaves most men on the second shift, leaving for work just as their wives come home.

When (as commonly occurs) plan fulfillment is running behind schedule in a factory, a "class conscious worker" magically pops up and is kind enough to volunteer his unit for a Saturday or Sunday of "unpaid labor time." This practice reaches epidemic proportions around November or December. There also come up the occasional workdays where a division decides generously to sacrifice its day's pay to a "Vietnam Solidarity Fund" or some such cause. There is a story about three astronauts who fly to the moon, an American, a Russian, and an East German. The American returns and visits Nixon, who says to him, "You were on the moon for ten days. Would you like ten thousand dollars or a medal?" The American takes the money. The Russian goes to Brezhnev, who says, "You were on the moon for ten days. Would you like ten thousand rubles or a medal?" The Russian takes the medal. The East German comes to Ulbricht, and Ulbricht says, "You were on the moon for ten days. Should we regard it as unpaid labor time or subtract it from your vacation?"

Thus is created what spokesmen here in their lighter moments call the "New Socialist Man."

＊

One should not conclude from all this that complaints here are material ones only. East Germany remains, it is possible to say without fear of exaggeration, a police state. When you talk about repression here, you are talking about people being carted off to jail for a month or so for stray comments the wrong person overheard in a restaurant, or about a student getting several years in jail for unfurling a lonely banner after the Soviet invasion of Czechoslovakia reading RUSSIA OUT OF GERMANY. It is in fact surprising how often one chances across people who have either had political run-ins with the authorities, or who know people who have. In a nothing-special bar nowhere special in Leipzig one evening, I struck up a conversation with a construction worker and his girl friend. The two were not, it developed, specially interested in politics; yet he, it turned out, had almost been thrown out of school at the age of fifteen for calling the class secretary of the Free German Youth (F.D.J.) a "political slut." Somebody else told me how a friend of his had said in class that the material they were taught about West Germany was "lies." Several days later, a policeman interrupted the class to arrest him.

Unless you're talking with family, friends, or foreigners, it takes a spirit of reckless adventure to open your mouth, especially in a public place. Every factory contains paid spies among the workers, and a certain percentage of the delegates at any conference or meeting are secret policemen. Anyone angling for a favor or a reward can always turn volunteer informer, and there is additionally a large net of plainclothesmen, particularly in the central parts of town. One quiet Saturday morning I witnessed a traffic accident in downtown East Berlin, which occurred when the paths of the only two cars in sight somehow managed to cross. What was interesting, I thought, was that of the coincidental passersby, no less than four were plainclothes policemen, who immediately joined the regular police in keeping back the crowd and watching over the scene. When someone began taking photographs of the accident, a plainclothesman approached him. It was not permissible to take pictures of the scene of an accident unless one worked as a journalist, the photographer was told. He was simply interested in taking pictures to show as a warning to his children, came the reply, but the plainclothesman was insistent. Exasperated, the man finally asked under what law it was forbidden to take photos. "I didn't say it was forbidden," answered the policeman with a straight face. "I said it was prohibited." No more pictures were taken.

Taking photos isn't the only thing which is, if not forbidden, then at least prohibited. "There's just so much compulsion," a girls sums it up. Not of the slave-labor-camp variety, mainly just a lot of irritations. And it's not merely what you're *not* allowed to do, but also the rituals you *must* go through. Every child has to join the F.D.J. Factory employees are expected to gather after working hours on occasion for group attendance at some tedious speech, film, or play. You're not fired or arrested if you don't come, but you'll probably lose your year-end premium or something like that. The same is true for attendance at various "mass demonstrations." I once arrived at a rally in Berlin about fifteen minutes late. Since everyone seemed to be leaving already, I thought the whole affair was finished. "No, don't worry, it's just starting," somebody volunteered. "It's just that the factories have finished taking attendance." At a similar demonstration at the Buchenwald concentration camp, where people had to remain because the only way to get back home was with chartered buses, it was literally impossible even to hear the speeches above the noise of chatting, screaming, and frolicking among the "demonstrators."

"As a result of individual changes," begins a warning posted next to the ground-floor elevator in an apartment house for workers of an important export-oriented x-ray machines factory in Dresden, "the appearance of many of the balconies in the building is such that it does not correspond to the level expected of the center of town in a modern socialist city." The announcement went on to complain about individuals who did odd things like put beach umbrellas on their balconies so they could sit outside during the summer. Apparently, what was considered to correspond with the level expected in a modern socialist city was flowers on the balcony, and only flowers. Offenders were warned to remove the beach umbrellas or the matter would be taken up with the building's owner, which was the factory that employed the tenants. In a similar vein F.D.J. committees at universities roam around inspecting students' rooms for cleanliness and orderliness. The names of those with the cleanest and dirtiest rooms then are posted on a bulletin board. One day I was to go out hiking and sightseeing in the Saxon mountains near Dresden. Before we left my hosts told me I'd better tuck in the polo shirt I had on — with it out, the police might object.

Of the many things forbidden in the D.D.R., what rankles most is the inability to travel abroad. Except for excursions to a select list of Communist countries — Yugoslavia is off-limits, Rumania is discouraged, and Czechoslovakia was cut off for a period — it is as good as impossible to leave. For many people, the ban on foreign travel borders on an obsession. It encompasses everything people don't like — the government's non-existent trust for its citizens, the prisonlike nature of the country, the grass growing greener on the other side. Then there is additionally the boundless cynicism revealed in the government's permission of visits to West Germany by people over sixty-five, the reasoning being that if a pensioner defects it just means one less unproductive person to take care of. (About 150,000 pensioners on visit to West Germany have decided during the last ten years to remain there.)

The officially encouraged form of vacationing is group travel, where activities can be programmed and where the group leader is obliged to present a report on the ideological consciousness of each group member. The carefree group vacationer, asking his Bulgarian guide about Georgi Dimitrov's contributions to the socialist construction of that land one day, and playing squash with other members of the group the next, embodies the regime's version of the ideal citizen at leisure. As for those who stay home, *Neues Deutschland* advised last June that with the coming of vacation time "many people will have the opportunity to do things they've had to put aside the rest of the year, and, for example, to read a certain book, to pursue one's hobbies, but this year above all to continue the study of documents from the Eighth Party Congress."

"Everybody here has two faces, public compliance and private disgust," I have been told. Generally direct run-ins with the powers that be are a childhood disease. Soon the boundaries of the permissible become second nature. Since all the advantages lie on the side of going along, one learns very quickly the required routines. "We Germans are not a people which rushes to the barricades. Look, we never rose up against Hitler either. And what's the use of a revolt? The Russians would be here in a minute." Perhaps the single most common expression in East Germany is "you can get used to anything." "You know, man is the most adaptable creature on the earth," a government official observed to me cynically. "Man can live in the Arctic or in the tropics — no other animal can do that. And, you know, as for this freedom you speak of, we think we can make it so that our people gradually get used to living without it."

By now boredom is doubtless a bigger problem than compulsion. "Our people complain they are bored with too much politics in everything," says the same official. "They ask why there always has to be politics in movies and television and the newspapers. The answer is that there has to be because the people are so hard to convince." The result of the current situation? "About the only things you can do here are drink and f—k," they say.

Everybody might be happier, and less bored, if East German propagandists took a few lessons in the art of subtle persuasion. The clumsiness and humorlessness which the world community experienced during the East German attempts to impose their own translations onto the text of the four-power Berlin agreement belongs to the everyday experience of people here. Reflecting the view that West Berlin is a "separate political entity" with no ties to West Germany, while East Berlin is the "capital of the German Democratic Republic," the official term for East Berlin is never simply "Berlin," but "Berlin, capital of the D.D.R." This applies even to exit signs on the East German *Autobahn*. The sign at the Friedrichstrasse checkpoint between East and West Berlin informs the traveler going westward that he or she has come to the place for "Border Crossing from the Capital of the D.D.R. to the Independent Political Entity of Berlin." In fact, among suave East Germans who want to show the proper political attitude, it is customary never to use the actual word *Berlin* at all, but to speak merely of "the Capital."

Such manifestations, and the myriad of posters, banners, and similar exhortations which litter the streets can be, and are, simply ignored. Somewhat more painful are the sleep-inducing work-place "discussions" on the latest directives from on high. "The workers come because their section leader says they have to. The section leader calls the meeting because his boss says *he* has to. *His* boss was told by a higher boss. All these meetings are making somebody up there very happy, but nobody knows at what level people start actually believing in them."

Entertainment not only provides no rest, but is often as awkward as everything else. Films are probably the worst. "Any movie that is pure entertainment takes place a minimum of one hundred years ago, and preferably during the Middle Ages. Their idea of a modern-day entertainment film is a family drama where the factory is moving over to three shifts, and the husband doesn't want to do it, so his wife, a loyal citizen, has to persuade him." Before the Wall, a slew of *Grenzen Kinos* ("border movie theaters") grew up just inside West Berlin which catered to East Berliners. "Ideological poison," grumbles a bureaucrat. "But we've closed the border now, and it's harder for it to seep in." In 1962 an American Western somehow got released, but was closed after large crowds rioted trying to get into movie theaters. Current East German cowboy-and-Indian films are of the type which would please Jane Fonda, politically if not artistically. The latest, *Osceola*, is filmed in Cuba and chronicles an uprising of Seminole Indians and runaway slaves in Florida. Negro slaves appearing in the film are whipped on the average of once every forty-five seconds they are shown on the screen, apparently to drive home the point to people how good they have it in comparison. Of the palefaces who are presented in the movie, their favorite pastime, aside from whipping Negroes, appears to be giving decadent parties. In reviewing *Osceola*, even an East German reviewer felt constrained to comment, "There are dramaturgical weaknesses in the drawing of some of the characters, but it would perhaps be too much to ask if in addition to the film's political strong points deep psychological human portraits were also expected."

The most approved type of film here is of the World War II anti-Nazi resistance variety. Over the past year or so there has gradually unfolded a five-part Soviet film extravaganza entitled *The Liberation*. Part III played all last summer, usually to empty houses, at the giant Cinema International in downtown East Berlin, and Part IV was released in conjunction with the annual Week of Soviet Culture, which coincides with each year's observance of the anniversary of the Russian Revolution. School, factory, and Communist-bloc tourist groups are dragged to films like this, while tickets for a movie like *My Fair Lady* had to be purchased days in advance when it was shown. "About the only people who like these resistance films are a few war buffs who like to see battle scenes or things being blown up," according to someone I asked.

Even normal amusement has to be dressed up with some dull message. Recently East German television began showing some locally produced, more or less standard detective stories. But when one new criminal series began, the local version of *TV Guide* felt it necessary to introduce the show in the following way:

> Crime in the streets — an unfriendly expression, one that doesn't seem at home in our society. For our society's essential features are peaceful labor, carefree learning, unspoiled joy in sports and games. During our country's years of socialist development, the social roots of crime have been eliminated. In our State there exist no immutable conditions causing crime. However there are, even under socialist living and working conditions, factors which do not exclude socially unacceptable behavior. Bad home influences, but above all the attempts at ideological diversion by the class enemy, combined with weakness of character or misuse of alcohol, give crime its chance. And a handful of slackers and lazy bums can succeed at times in escaping social control.

In the early sixties high school students caught dancing the twist got expelled from school. A few years ago a rather pathetic strip-tease at the Moskau Restaurant on Marx-Engels Allee in East Berlin lasted only a few nights. Things have loosened up somewhat since then, but East Germany still has the bloc's harshest policy again Western music and styles. Hair has started growing surprisingly long, even in the small towns — especially when compared with, say, Moscow — and the chairman of the F.D.J. recently went so far as to say that he did not care how a person's head looked from the outside, but from the inside. But border guards still confiscate Beatles albums, which young East Germans bring back from Hungary (where they are for sale), and authorities are always on hand to insure that local pop bands play at least one-half *D.D.R.-Schläger* — local hits — at their performances. (The East German version of pop music leans more toward "I Want to Hold Your Hand" than "Eleanor Rigby," and runs no danger of incurring Spiro Agnew's wrath as a revolutionary influence.)

The large cities now each have at least one dancing spot which plays Western music, although one can only feel pity for the earnest local teeny-boppers who try to make something out of the very limited facilities available. Undecorated and brightly lit, the atmosphere at most of these places is reminiscent of a high school gym. The kids, through lack of exposure and practice, generally can't dance; and the bands, since they can't get sheet music but must rely on what they can pick off Western radio stations by themselves, croon a gobbledygook version of the song texts. Professional "youth" at the doors stand guard against those who might try to come in wearing blue jeans, unshaven, or in any other way failing to correspond to the standards expected of a socialist discotheque. One dance locale in Berlin comes complete with a large banner, placed in back of the bandstand, proclaiming OUR FAITH, OUR LOVE, OUR SOCIALIST FATHERLAND.

While pop music has tentatively been awarded bare toleration in general — after a few drinks in a Dresden pop place, the government representative accompanying me confided that "if I had my way, all these places would be blown up into the air" — rock is exploited on government radio broadcasts aimed at youth. Radio DDR now runs a "youth program," which features sporadic Western songs interspersed with lengthy denunciations of West Germany or sagas of the Arab "liberation struggle." The government also runs an outfit called German Soldier's

Radio directed toward West German draftees. It is about the same, except that it runs much more music and is surprisingly soft-sell. The program has, reports indicate, developed a considerable listening audience in West Germany because it is the only show playing rock late at night. The Soldier's Radio also gives an address in Vienna where one can send letters — no East German address is given because the government refuses to admit that the station broadcasts from East Germany — and the announcers read purported letters on the air. When I asked a young East German whether he thought such letters had actually been written, he paused for a moment and then replied, "Well, I guess there are idiots in every country."

The radio intended for the local population is quite different. That the Central Committee of the Socialist Unity Party of Germany has sent a note congratulating the Polish Communist Party on its fifteenth anniversary, or that a chemical factory in Leipzig has adopted a resolution swearing its full support to the decisions of the Eighth Party Congress are typical "news" items on Radio DDR. To read out long lists of the names and titles of leading personalities taking part in some "fraternal" get-together is also customary. One night I tuned in Radio DDR just as the news broadcast was beginning, and heard the following lead story:

> On Monday there took place in the Crimea a friendly meeting of Communist and labor party leaders of a number of lands who were vacationing in the area at the time. The participants were the First Secretary of the Central Committee of the Bulgarian Communist Party and the Chairman of the Council of Ministers of the People's Republic of Bulgaria, T. Zhivkov; the First Secretary of the Central Committee of the Hungarian Socialist Labor Party, J. Kadar; the First Secretary of the Central Committee of the Socialist Unity Party of Germany, Erich Honecker;

the First Secretary of the Central Committee of the Mongolian Revolutionary People's Party and Chairman of the Council of Ministers of the Mongolian People's Republic, J. Zedenbal; the First Secretary of the Central Committee of the Polish People's Labor Party, E. Gierek; the General Secretary of the Communist Party of Czechoslovakia, G. Husak; the General Secretary of the Central Committee of the Communist Party of the Soviet Union, L. I. Brezhnev; the member of the Politburo of the Central Committee of the Communist Party of the Soviet Union, Chairman of the Presidium of the Supreme Soviet of the USSR, N. V. Podgorny; the member of the Politburo of the Central Committee of the Communist Party of the Soviet Union, First Secretary of the Central Committee of the Communist Party of the Ukraine, P. J. Schelest.

That was the end of that news flash, which contained nothing substantial about what might have gone on at the meeting.

The press is also fun. Reporting on the April 1968 plebiscite on a new East German constitution, for example, *Neues Deutschland* told the story the following way:

Berlin woke up early this morning, wakened by the youth, their songs and their loudspeakers. Precisely at 6 A.M. opened the polling places of the Capital. There were tens of thousands who wanted to cast their free ballots early in the morning. For all those who arrived early the polling officials — true to a custom which has already become a tradition — had flowers ready. Holiday-clad families, many with their children. A holiday which isn't in the calendar. A visit to polling places shows the joy and the optimism of this day.

One wonders how people react to such descriptions, knowing they run counter to the way everybody feels. "What else can the reporter write?" reacted somebody when I showed him the above text. "The truth?"

Among the most ludicrous passages I have ever read in an official East German description of this country comes from a pamphlet, directed at high school students, entitled, "Why Are We Proud of Our Republic?" At one point the booklet states, regarding the "socialist new man" in the D.D.R.: "Let us begin with an observation that to us seems quite everyday, and that we hardly notice. In a streetcar sit workers who are traveling to work. The largest group are reading a newspaper or a book. Some are busy taking notes dealing with training or adult education courses they are taking."

This passage would best have been limited to the brochure's braille edition. Actually, the East German press can at best be described as a huge waste of paper. Party members, and draftees, are required to subscribe to *Neues Deutschland,* the Party daily whose self-advertising describes it authoritatively as "the leading newspaper daily," but even friends of the system concede that there are large numbers of the paper's articles whose readership circle doesn't extend much beyond the author and his family. It is common, certainly, in all countries to wrap things like flowers in newspapers, but only here have I seen people doing the wrapping with the day's editions. Between 10 and 11 A.M. one weekday morning, during which time I took note of the sales at the newspaper stand in front of the always crowded Centrum Department Store in Alexanderplatz, a total of one copy of *Neues Deutschland,* and five of the comparatively more popular *Berliner Zeitung,* were sold.

Probably the two least unread local publications are *Wochenpost* and the satirical weekly *Eulenspiegel. Wochenpost* has "a little less politics than the others," but owes its success mostly to four pages a week of matrimonial classified ads, which many people follow religiously, along with the crossword puzzle. As for *Eulenspiegel,* it is hard to tell to what extent its humorlessness is a function of the traditional shortcomings of the German wit, and to what extent to the straitjacket imposed on it. A typical *Eulenspiegel* joke goes as follows: "I hear that a lot of the Vietnam veterans are demonstrating against the war in Indochina in Washington. But do they have to throw their war medals against the walls of the Capitol?" "Well, I guess they're just trying to give Nixon back a bit of the garbage that he's saying when he always talks about ending the war." Certainly *Eulenspiegel* must be one of the world's few national humor magazines whose primary butts are *other* societies. Nevertheless, their occasional swipe at the bureaucracy, plus some nonpolitical humor, make *Eulenspiegel* popular enough to be sold out usually about a day after each week's issue appears. (This is, incidentally, a situation which makes the never-ending unsold piles of *Neues Deutschland* at the same stands look even more wasteful. For most other weeklies, it is typical to keep the piles of unsold back numbers on display at newsstands for weeks, if not months. At any given time, issues of supposed news weeklies that are two months old are generally available almost everywhere.)

What must of course be added about all this is that the East Germans have West Germany close enough so that virtually nobody needs to, or does, pay much attention to the local media. Most parts of East Germany, except (because of its peculiar geographical location in a valley) for Dresden, can get West German television. From West Berlin there also comes RIAS (Radio in the American Sector, the local version of Radio Free Europe) broadcasting in both AM and a long-range FM with two programs all day and all night. From Bavarian transmitters come several brands of West German radio. It is technically not feasible to jam FM or television broadcasts, and as a result all of the D.D.R. more or less automatically tunes in *drüben* ("over there"). Most of the shortwave radios one sees in East Germany even bear markings of the meter-band locations of some Western radio stations. Wondering whether this represented some official toleration or even encouragement of listening to foreign stations, I asked a schoolteacher about it. "I've often wondered about the same thing. I guess they realize it would look too ridiculous just to mark seven stations." He spoke too soon: new radios I've seen in store windows limit their indications of Western senders to Radio Göteborg, which broadcasts in Swedish.

In fact, although discouraged, it is technically legal for an individual to listen to Western radio and television. It is, however, forbidden to invite friends to join in. This becomes "disseminating foreign propaganda."

The East German educational system has been praised by some foreign observers. It is true that, for example, a greater percentage of youths receive higher education here than in West Germany. This picture should be complemented, however, by some consideration of what the students are taught. Certainly, the antiauthoritarian education methods which have been growing in popularity in chic West German circles have yet to make their first breakthrough in the D.D.R.

As the authorities see it, the young pupil's most important course in *Staatsbürgerkunde* ("citizenship education"), which begins in seventh grade and is often taught by the school principal, who is considered by virtue of his position to be a school's most class-conscious individual. *Staatsbürgerkunde* is good training for anyone who wants to succeed in the educational system as a whole, since it teaches you what you are to believe.*

---

* "I can't understand," says a university student recalling a time he saw Rudi Dütschke, the West German student radical, on television, "how he can say voluntarily the things we are forced to say."

After ten grades of schooling about one third of the students go on to *Gymnasium* for two more years. Depending on the *Gymnasium*, short hair may or may not be an absolute requirement for getting in — but in general, the behavioral standards demanded of, and the supervision practiced over, high school and university students is rather greater than for the general population. One is, for example, expected to continue membership in the F.D.J., something which those leaving school after tenth grade may, and do, give up. (A few years ago there was some concern expressed that somehow it didn't seem right that 95 percent of all youth had joined the F.D.J., supposedly voluntarily, as children, and then suddenly everyone quit as soon as they left school. Rather than groping with the deeper philosophical implications of this drop-off, the F.D.J. leadership decided that the best cure for lagging membership figures was to raise the age of eligibility. As a result, one can now be a member of the Free German Youth through the age of fifty.)

Completion of *Gymnasium* does not, as was traditionally the case in Germany, automatically qualify a person for university training. There is also an acknowledged test of what is called "political maturity." "After all," states a Humboldt University administrator, "we are not just interested in producing unpolitical scholars, but people who will actually engage themselves for our socialist society."

Once a university student has made it in and has chosen his field of study, his course selection is over, the program of study being completely determined from beginning to end. The course program includes no subjects outside the student's major. It is thus not possible for a biologist to study some art history, a historian to dabble in literature. "Are you crazy?" came the reply when I suggested that some room for such sorties might perhaps be made. "Do you think we have the money for that?"

Such a thing might come to pass "in a hundred years, maybe two hundred," I was informed.

Actually, there is one subject outside his field which every student must take, the compulsory courses in Marxism-Leninism. These generally involve about one fourth of a student's total course work. As befits a subject which has been called the "compass" which constitutes a prerequisite for understanding everything else one learns, the universities make sure that nobody takes his Marxism-Leninism lightly. In other subjects there is often a cavalier attitude to examinations, for example, and all tests are written. In Marxism-Leninism all the exams are oral, the theory being that a student can (and will) *write* anything, lack of enthusiasm being more detectable through a tone of voice or a facial expression. Normally, a student with a poor grade average can save himself by agreeing to join the Party or put in some extra work for the F.D.J. But a single failing grade in Marxism-Leninism suffices for removal from the university.

One of the chief concerns in Marxism-Leninism courses — knowledge of the basics being assumed from previous study — is the "struggle against revisionism," which is any brand of socialism which the government doesn't like. In this struggle, the East Germans like to think that they play the leading role in the Communist bloc. Principal current targets include Ernst Fischer, the former leader of the Austrian Communist Party who became enamored of Dubcekism and was later expelled from his party; Roger Garaudy, the renegade French Communist; and, above all, any and all advocates of the so-called convergence theory, which postulates that Communist and democratic societies are gradually becoming more similar. This latter notion, a relatively unimportant rivulet of Western sociological thought in the sixties, becomes transformed in East

German accounts into modern bourgeois ideology's *Leitmotiv*, and is presented in an endless string of largely identical books as part of a strategy to dismantle and subvert the "socialist world."

I got an idea of what the East German student goes through in this regard by reading the book, *Industriegesellschaft und Convergenztheorie* (*Industrial Society and the Convergence Theory*) by one Professor Günther Rose. It is a testimony to the reading interest which this volume awakens that there passed unnoticed through rereading and editing of the book the fact that on two occasions entire one-page or more passages are *repeated* verbatim. (A section on Walt Whitman Rostow's views on American policy in underdeveloped countries appears identically on pages 82 and 204–5. Rostow again, this time on economic growth and the "Buddenbrook Dynamic," comes up word-for-word on pages 143–44 and 201–2.) The index is equally fascinating, containing entries like:

General Crisis of Capitalism, 63 ff., 79, 169
Diversion, imperialist ideological, 74, 260, 282 ff., 298, 304, 312,
    321, 329 ff., 373
Revanchism in West Germany, 159 f., 174, 342, 356

Other index listings include "Great Soviet October Revolution," "Global Strategy of US Imperialism," and "Anti-communism, bankruptcy of traditional."

While students hear endlessly of various revisionists, how the bourgeoisie lured previously trusted sons of the proletariat into ideological decay and why their ideas of a democratization of Communism would strike a death blow to all that is true and good, confrontation with flesh-and-blood revisionists or even their writings is impossible. In Marxism-Leninism classes one reads, say, endless attacks on an Ernst Fischer, but Fischer is never allowed to defend himself. I asked my friend the Humboldt University administrator whether such a policy didn't just make the ideas of Fischer forbidden fruit, thus increasing the student's curiosity for them. "The problem is that these revisionists are very clever. Too many of our students would become too confused if they read them. They wouldn't know the answers right off." Oh. "We want to make life easier for our students. We don't want to create unnecessary conflicts for them," he concluded.

It is difficult for an outsider to observe student life directly, since campuses are accessible by pass only. One hears, however, about random checks of room radios to make sure they aren't tuned in to Western stations, or about F.D.J. meetings discussing the length of hair on certain students. To be fair, one should add that in many ways professors don't have it much better. Research projects in the natural sciences are determined by contracts between the universities and industrial enterprises. This system, according to complaints at the Eighth Party Congress, has led to a total disappearance of pure research. In the social sciences, the faculties stand under the direct control of the Party, which assigns research projects according to its needs. Party membership is also a requirement for any academic post.

Nevertheless, *la trahison des clercs,* like any good *trahison,* does not go without material reward. University professors are among the best-paid groups in society. "At our university," says one student, "the head of the department of Marxist-Leninist philosophy, an uncompromising opponent of all Western influence, drives a Ford Mustang."

*

As they survey their lives, and gaze longingly over to the other side, it is natural that people try to find explanations for the meager results of their work and efforts. "We must create a great deal in this land. Both men and women work here," recounted an old bereted man, painting his fence on a Dresden side street one evening. "The question is why we have so little." His answer was East German aid to underdeveloped countries, a popular scapegoat. ("Have you read about all these African countries that are setting up diplomatic relations with us?" exclaims an East Berliner. "We *bought* every one of them!") People will also point out that anything of decent quality produced in East Germany is immediately carted off to hard-currency countries. West German buyers arrive on East German collective farms and emerge with claims on all the best pigs and beef available. "I once had a job as a cleaning lady at the Leipzig Trade Fair," one woman told me. "And I was astonished to see what we were offering to sell the foreigners there. Nylon pullovers, everything! I didn't even know we produced such things." Even goods designed for export to other Communist-bloc lands are of higher quality than the things kept at home. "If a refrigerator we're supposed to send to Hungary doesn't pass quality inspection, they'll sell it to us."

But an even more significant reason for East Germany's position is her relationship with the Soviet Union. In an era of crumbling alliances and rampant Gaullism, the pristine pattern of East Germany's client state subservience to the U.S.S.R., which has remained unaffected by stirrings in other Eastern European nations, is something to behold. "One's attitude to the Soviet Union and to the Communist Party of the Soviet Union," intoned Erich Honecker in his report to the Eighth Party Congress, "was, is, and remains the decisive test of one's faithfulness to Marxism-Leninism, to proletarian internationalism!"

The only sign outside the main train station in Dresden is a large billboard reading USE SOVIET RAILROADS. Down the street, in the picture windows of a large shoe store in Old Market Square, are pictures of Leonid Brezhnev and Aleksei Kosygin, next to the caption "Long Live the Twenty-fourth Congress of the Communist Party of the Soviet Union!" East German world atlases devote far more space to maps of the Soviet Union than to maps of Germany. East German youngsters all study, although very few genuinely learn, Russian from the fourth grade on. Newspapers here regularly take up entire pages with full-text reprints of lengthy *Pravda* articles. Almost every village boasts a local German-Soviet Friendship Society, and frequent banners on streets and factory gates inform passersby that HE WHO IS ALLIED WITH THE SOVIET UNION IS ALLIED WITH THE VICTORS OF HISTORY.

While Apollo 11 was making the first manned landing on the moon in 1969, East German press and television were concentrating on a Soviet space station which had been launched around the same time. A few still photos of the first men on the moon made it onto East German television several days later. When three American astronauts died in the Cape Kennedy fire the year before, however, this was a big story, the media reacting with barely concealed glee over the lack of concern for human life which, they said, typified capitalism. When three Russian spacemen died on their return to earth last summer, on the other hand, there were only tears.

If the constant obsequiousness toward the Big Brother to the East is a psychological humiliation, East German–Soviet "friendship" rankles even more where it hurts most, in the pocketbook. At the end of the first chapter of the eighth-grade *Staatsbürgerkunde* textbook, the student is asked to "give examples of how the development of our Republic is inseparably connected with all-sided cooperation and friendship with the Soviet Union," which must be a difficult question to answer positively even by the standards of that particular volume. East Germany enjoys an industrial base and a standard of living considerably higher than the Soviet Union's, and it is not hard to guess how the Russian leadership interprets East Germany's resultant proletarian internationalist duties. "The volume of trade between the D.D.R. and the Soviet Union is unique in the world," the booklet "Why Are We Proud of Our Republic?" informs us. Just how unique I began to realize while taking a boat tour of East Germany's international harbor at Rostock, listening to the rasping, droning voice of the captain over the microphone: "And on your left is a Soviet ship . . . Here straight ahead you see another Soviet ship . . . On your right a Soviet vessel." Actually, I later found out, no less than 25 percent of the Soviet Union's total imports come from little East Germany.

In exchange for industrial goods produced in East Germany, the Russians provide the D.D.R. with oil and other raw materials they lack. Who gets the better of the deal? Few official prices are published, but on the day the last East German–Soviet Trade Agreement was signed in 1964, the chief East German economic planner, Dr. Erich Apel, committed suicide, which may say something. The prices the Soviets charge the D.D.R. for raw materials result in a situation where East Germany has escaped from the "international oil cartel" only to have to charge two dollars a gallon for gas.

Of course, a good part of East Germany's problems lie closer at home. In a society where *everything* is planned, energies are of necessity divided up between planning things which should or could be planned, and planning things that can't or shouldn't. The resultant strain often produces mindless planning. In a relatively simple matter like designing some redevelopment in downtown Dresden — the city was destroyed by Allied bombs twenty-five years ago, and already the process of reconstruction is in full swing — somehow a new building at a traffic intersection got constructed twenty meters too long, thus making it jut out into the street. This upset the designs for the entire area, where a new bridge over the Elbe and a pedestrian underpass had been scheduled. These plans had to be completely redone, and when they were finally ready, no building materials could be obtained. Further delays resulted, the work force was put on night shifts, and finally, in order to be able to open the pedestrian underpass in honor of the Eighth Party Congress, the authorities forwent any preliminary safety inspection. (The original offending building, incidentally, bears at the top a large neon sign reading SOCIALISM IS WINNING.)

In Schwedt, a "socialist new town" built on the Polish border as a center for the petrochemical industry, a leading East German architect was hired to plan a showcase city. The plan, it is said, was so imaginative that the man received a medal for it. Then, however, it was decided that the project would cost too much, whereupon the design was not only dropped but the designer was fired from his job. Two plans later, Schwedt emerged as a conglomerate of new housing and not much else. A town of 40,000 in the middle of nowhere, Schwedt has one movie theater and two or three restaurants. Trees and grass are almost nonexistent. New units of housing for 5000 people, already fully occupied, still resemble a building site in the midst of construction. People enter their apartment buildings through planks of wood suspended over muddy holes. Children play amidst huge mounds of soil flanked by bulldozers. Not even a grocery has been erected yet, and people do their basic shopping from mobile trucks that come by the area daily. Residents of the new complex estimate that it will be two years before the situation improves. Meanwhile, the government knows they can get people to move to Schwedt anyway, because it's much easier to get an apartment there than in other parts of East Germany — so they don't care. (The East Germans have built little more than a third as many new housing units per capita since 1950 as the West Germans.)

This government which plans everything nevertheless always seems confounded by things like, say, the change of seasons. Each year "record cold" produces new electricity crises. In the winter of 1970–71 streetlights all over East Germany were largely darkened — even in the best of times only one of the two bulbs in East Berlin streetlights is lit — and people had to get around with flashlights. Many factories began operating at night only because there was insufficient power during the day. In the economically backward areas of the Thüringer Forest, where according to local custom people display special lights outside their houses around Christmastime, schoolchildren were told to tell their parents to turn the lights off. All this despite the official statistical claim that per capita electricity production in the D.D.R. is higher than in West Germany.

In the summer what are officially portrayed as the most heroic efforts still never suffice to insure the production of sufficient soft drinks to last through September. In years past it was often the case that no soft drinks were available for weeks on end. In 1971 supplies held out well until early August, when reports began to appear in the press of factories working all night to keep the stores supplied, and from the time of this alarm signal on, the system came gradually but inexorably puttering to a halt. First the soda started coming into the stores without labels on the bottles. Then bottles began being unevenly filled, and some shipments turned up with the flavoring coagulated at the top. By mid-August, supplies had become irregular, and whenever shipments came in, hoarders bought them all up within a half an hour.

Total planning also displays the inflexibility for which it is justly famous. While all East German household detergents are awful, the best of a bad lot is called Persil. However, since other detergent factories all have their planned quotas, Persil can only be allowed to produce so much, and no more. Because of the resultant shortages, Persil is available only in East Berlin — and one often sees visitors to Berlin from other parts of East Germany lugging around a dozen packages of Persil which they have purchased to take home. Similarly, a complaint about the tastelessness of the orange juice in a Dresden hotel produced the following reply from the waitress: "Well, we have a good brand of orange juice too. It's just that we had to buy some of the bad one also because the government had contracted to buy it as part of a foreign trade agreement." At the same time, stores in Dresden were holding back all brands of cigarettes except for a certain Bulgarian variety. This was the only way to force customers to buy the otherwise unwanted Bulgarian brand, which had to be sold somehow since East Germany had committed itself to purchase them. Firms which produce unsaleable merchandise can only be dealt with through pleas in the press because, it turns out, department stores have targets for how much they should buy, and total production is rarely high enough to allow the stores to pick and choose by canceling the orders given to junk-producing companies. When 100,000 tubes of foot cream produced for export to Russia by a cosmetics factory recently turned rotten even before they could be shipped out, there ensued a general panic among the management, for when something goes wrong on production scheduled for the Soviet Union, sabotage is immediately suspected. It was thus necessary to get up 100,000 new tubes of cream in double time. Coming up with 100,000 empty tubes was not an easy task, but finally, when the management scraped them up from various tube manufacturers, no trucking capacity could be located to deliver them. This required the mobilization of every company car, and the autos of any employees who had them — so that the plant's workers could be sent driving around the D.D.R. to pick up the tubes.

There is a joke about the East German who dies and goes to hell. On arrival he discovers that hell is divided into East Hell and West Hell. Since he had to spend all his life in the East, he naturally decides first to look at West Hell. When he enters, he sees a very unhappy scene — people whining, crying, flagellating themselves. He goes up and asks someone what is wrong. Slowly and dejectedly, the man answers, "We are to be nailed to a wooden cross and burned, and therefore we are so unhappy." Not finding this prospect much to his liking, the East German goes across the hall to take a look at East Hell. Here the scene is exactly the opposite — dancing, drinking, a real party atmosphere. So he asks someone what is going on. "Well, we're supposed to be nailed to a wooden cross and burned," comes the nonchalant reply. "So why are you all so joyful?" the man asks. "Look, when the day comes, there won't be any hammers. And if there are hammers there won't be any nails. And if there're hammers *and* nails, the devil will have a Party meeting."

In addition to the problems of planning, the general discontent makes things worse by lowering job morale and the will to improve things. "The guys in the factories can't find what they want at the stores, or they get lousy service, so they say, 'The hell with it' and slough off on the job," says one worker. The giant D.D.R. photographic film complex at Wolfen, which supplies the entire Communist bloc with ORWO film, received several years ago the assignment to supply the Comecon nations with magnetic tape, which up to then was produced nowhere in Eastern Europe. But production halted when some workers slipped sand into the vats; problems continue to be so bad at the factory that, despite a move over to night shifts, big losses are still being incurred.

A sign of how bad things are in this regard comes from how minute the achievements are which unleash great praise from the authorities. In a store window in the new Dresden town center, for example, there appears the following notice under the rubric BEST INNOVATOR:

> Theodor Leonhard developed, as a result of an Innovator's Agreement in 1970, a coin collector's album. Before his invention there were no coin albums in the D.D.R. Through his own initiative he founded a plant to manufacture his albums. This plant delivered 10,000 albums, of which 9400, with total proceeds of 57,200 marks, were sold. Profits were 30,100 marks. With this Mr. Leonhard has placed himself at the top of all innovators in retail and wholesale trade.

This summer the government celebrated the tenth anniversary of the Berlin Wall, which both the government and many foreign observers have credited with giving new life to the East German economy. Slogans appeared hailing TEN YEARS OF THE ANTI-FASCIST PROTECTIVE WALL — TEN YEARS OF SECURE DEFENSE OF PEACE. A parade was arranged in Berlin. And one perhaps overly zealous pen-pusher came up with the following description of the background to the event:

> A crucial role in the aggressive plans of the West German monopolists was played by the "front city" of West Berlin. With the help of the open frontier to this territory, the DDR's economic structure was to be destroyed and the population held in a constant state of tension and uncertainty. . . . The people of the DDR were aware of the acute war danger which the evil deeds

of the Bonn militarists, in conjunction with provocatory NATO manoeuvers on the DDR border, caused. Among the population anger also grew over the huge material injuries which the enemies of the Republic were causing. More and more voices rose up to demand from the government decisive steps for the safeguarding of peace.

East German rates of economic growth did increase after the Wall, but at the end of the sixties the news came in that the percentage gap between the East and West German standards of living had actually *increased* during the ten years since the Wall — from 32 percent to 45 percent — and recent East German growth figures have been disappointing. A particularly strange confirmation of this came with the fate of the deliberations of the Fifteenth Party Plenum last January. In his speech at this Plenum, Ulbricht made all sorts of optimistic predictions about the economy — yet a few months later all references to the Fifteenth Plenum disappeared from the press, and Fifteenth Plenum documents became unobtainable at bookstores. Finally, on May 11, 1971, *Neues Deutschland* definitively assigned the Plenum to the dustbin of history when it wrote, "When we look at the road ahead, we know that its next big step is the Eighth Party Congress. We go towards that great event, equipped with the decisions of the Fourteenth and Sixteenth Plena."

*

The East German reaction to the announcement of President Nixon's China visit illustrates well the D.D.R.'s special protectorate status, even as against other Eastern European nations. The lead story in the paper that day was "Joint Communiqué Regarding the Visit of the Chairman of the Council of Ministers of the People's Republic of Poland, Piotr Jaroszewicz, to the DDR," and the one-paragraph dispatch "Nixon

Accepts Invitation to China" got less prominence than items like "Meeting Between the Communist Party of Lebanon and the Communist Party of the Soviet Union" and "U.A.R. Proposed Constitution Completed." Nine days of silence followed this modest original notice. Finally, *Neues Deutschland* took up nearly an entire page with a reprint-in-full of a *Pravda* commentary "on Peking's contacts with Washington." The Soviet article cited negative comments on the visit from newspapers in every other Eastern European country, East Germany having been the only one not to make any independent comment on the visit. (An amusing sidelight to these reports concerns the fate of a passage from a New York *Daily News* editorial on this visit, urging Nixon to "play Red China off against Red Russia." *Pravda* took this line up, translating it in the process into "incite Red China against Red Russia," as proof of the anti-Soviet intentions of the visit. The East Germans seemed especially fond of citing this line, the high point coming in one Radio DDR commentary which introduced the passage by saying, "As the well-informed New York *Daily News* reported . . .")

The one area where the East Germans have developed their own line is West Germany. East German opposition to Bonn's *Ostpolitik* has aroused Soviet ire and, many believe, contributed to Ulbricht's fall. Moscow presents Willy Brandt's new policies as a positive adaptation to European realities, while East Berlin sees only anti-Communist, and especially anti–East German, conspiracies in new form.

Official East German historiography has it that it was *West* Germany which sabotaged German reunification. But, it would appear, having once committed this heinous crime, the imperialists will not be offered the easy way out of repenting and trying to unite it again. To emphasize his point that the two Germanies had developed with time into two foreign countries, Walter Ulbricht argued in a 1970 interview that "even the

former commonness of the language is in a process of disinte-
gration," a statement which strikes a responsive chord in anyone
who has been exposed to the tortured prose of the East German
media. (This was, however, not what Ulbricht had in mind:
"Between the traditional German language of Goethe, Schiller,
Lessing, Marx, and Engels, filled with humanism," he said, "and
the language dominated by imperialism and manipulated by
capitalist monopolist publishing houses of West Germany there
is a great difference.") To hear the East Germans tell it, relations between the two Germanies should ideally be of the
character of those between East Germany and, say, Australia.
With West Germany having abandoned its old *Alleinvertret-
ungsanspruch* (the claim that West Germany alone represented
all of Germany), current targets of *Neues Deutschland's* ire are
West German attempts to speak of what are referred to here as
"the so-called 'Unity of the German Nation'" and "a supposedly
'special character' of so-called 'Inner-German Relations.'"

The official position is, naturally, that it is West Germany
which is afraid of the example of East Germany, not vice versa.
"What does the existence of the DDR mean for West German
imperialism? . . . Of enormous importance is the fact that in
the reality of the DDR the imperialists have constantly before
their eyes the writing on the wall of their own eventual disappearance . . . The successful construction of socialism in the
DDR touches the most sensitive nerves of imperialism. These
facts explain the constant outbreaks of undisguised class hatred
in Bonn against the DDR."

But while, if anything, West Germans seem to be simply
forgetting about their fellow Germans on the other side — the
tenth anniversary of the Wall passed even in West Berlin with
only token demonstrations, and West German dailies seem far
more concerned with developments in England or the Middle
East than with the D.D.R. — in East Germany the spreading

of the gospel of hatred against the West Germans is a top and constant priority. Many East German teen-agers regard anti–West German propaganda as the main content of their *Staatsbürgerkunde* classes. Newspapers report extensively on every negative aspect of West German society. Even West German student radicals do not escape the curse. At the beginning of the West German student movement, demonstrations received wide and sympathetic coverage, but this faded as it became clear that not many West German leftists regarded the D.D.R. as their model of socialism. "Socialism already exists today on German soil, here in the DDR," advised *Die Junge Generation,* theoretical publication of the F.D.J. "For West German youth this makes one's political orientation much easier . . . The $64,000 question for a genuine revolutionary in West Germany is thus: What do you think of the D.D.R.?"

But what worries the East German leadership most just now is Brandt's *Ostpolitik*. As they see it, the imperialists, having failed to destroy Communism militarily, have now decided to smother the East with kindness — concessions here and there, mixed in with dangerous reform talk which people will be too confused to understand. The first victim was, in the East Germany account, to be Czechoslovakia: "Under the mask of a 'new *Ostpolitik*,' Prague was to be made a center for anticommunist propaganda, and from there the poison of bourgeois-imperialist ideology was to be spread to Hungary, Poland, and other socialist lands, thus isolating the DDR." Fortunately, with the help of the East German comrades, the Russians came to intervene but, the East Germans will remind you, imperialism never rests. And what do you do when Brezhnev makes nice to Brandt?

✻

Where does all this — the products that don't work or aren't there, the petty interferences, the regimented politicization of everything, what even a stalwart calls "the thousand annoyances every day" — leave people? Surely the average person is not a dedicated champion of personal freedom. But in the D.D.R. there is a discontent for every taste. Those who don't care so much about freedom complain about bananas. Those who admit to being able to survive without bananas complain they can't breathe. The result? In the deadpan words of an anonymous companion on the subway home one night, "If the borders ever opened, this country would become rather empty."

The political jokes — a phenomenon unique to dictatorships — play, as someone commented to me, a functional role similar to sex jokes. When society does not allow the open and free expression of deeply held emotions and feelings, jokes crop up as a sublimation of the longings. With their deadpan humor, these jokes are in many ways the best indicator of the mood here: Ulbricht delivers a speech to a party gathering on the twentieth anniversary of the D.D.R. "Comrades," he begins, "twenty years ago we stood on the edge of a great precipice. Today, I can tell you, we have come one step further." Or another one: Ulbricht goes to visit Brezhnev, and reports that the situation is now fine back home. Everybody is behind the government. Brezhnev is a little skeptical, so he proposes a test — they should go into Red Square and Unter den Linten and ask the first child they see a series of questions to test their loyalty. So first the pair go to Red Square, and Brezhnev stops a little tot. "Tell me, my child, who is your father?" asks Brezhnev. "My father is Comrade Leonid Brezhnev," answers the kid. "And who is your mother?" "My mother is my great Soviet motherland." Finally, Brezhnev asks, "And what do you want to be when you grow up?" "A cosmonaut," replies the child, who has passed the test perfectly. Brezhnev and Ulbricht now go to

East Berlin, and Ulbricht goes up to the first child they see. "Tell me, son, who is your father?" The boy hesitates for a while, and then finally blurts out, "My father is Comrade Walter Ulbricht." "And who is your mother?" Again the kid hesitates, but then he finally says, "My mother is my great socialist motherland, the German Democratic Republic." "And what do you want to be when you grow up?" "An orphan."

The presence of Soviet troops here is strongly felt, and thus there is little prospect for revolt or even active resistance. The feeling instead is one of *Aussichtslosigkeit* — "there's no way out." Cynicism and careerism abound, and so does suppressed hatred. Absent is even the slightest spirit of sacrifice. Last winter some F.D.J. activists stood an entire afternoon in Alexanderplatz collecting money for Vietnam, apparently without getting a single donation. The average Party member joins out of opportunism, or because it's easier than resisting the constant blandishments to sign up. (Almost 10 percent of the East German population are Party members, a figure much higher than most other places in the Communist world.) Ordinary Party members often remove their Party insignias from their lapels before going into stores, afraid that the personnel will take out their resentments on them. A lady who counts East German "election" ballots told me that they are often marked with expressions like *Schlägt die Bonzen tot!* ("Kill the Party bigwigs!") or swastikas. This latter, she felt, expressed the view that the current government is just like the Nazis, rather than approval for Hitler. For years, no major events have been held in the giant Walter Ulbricht Stadium in East Berlin. The stadium lies right near the West Berlin border, and the authorities probably fear mass escape attempts.

❊

It is small wonder that the East German leadership feels isolated, afraid, and perhaps even paranoid. Their subjects seem to be unconvinced and, worse, even unaffected by what they say. People appear to spend an inordinate amount of energy longing for West Germany. As for the West Germans, they are always thinking up new ways to destroy the poor D.D.R., and even the Soviets often seem not to sympathize. Often, the leaders must wonder whether East Germany has anything going for her except Soviet troops. The answer is yes: law and order.

"This may sound strange to you, but even if the borders were opened I would stay here," a middle-aged factory worker told me one evening. "I'm the first one to recognize all the faults we have, but at least you can walk the streets at night. Here if some kid tries to mug you, the law comes right down on him. But in West Germany they can get away with anything."

The government here carefully promotes the view that "socialism," in the eyes of some the source of crime, drugs, free sex, and related signs of moral decay, is in fact the best guard against such influences. West German crime statistics and spectacular individual cases are given detailed press coverage. (East German crimes, if any, are never mentioned.) "Matrimony, Family, and Motherhood," states Article 38 (1) of the 1968 East German Constitution, "stand under the special protection of the State." A lengthy article which recently appeared in *Neues Deutschland,* ambitiously entitled "The General Crisis of Capitalism and the Tasks of Socialism," wrote that "increasing numbers of parents in the West" are being attracted to Communism because of concern over "the spread of dangerous drugs" and "the reduction of the bonds between man and woman to mere physical sex" in Western society. Around the same time a weekly magazine informed its readers that "it is neurologically proven that the consumption of only 4 marijuana joints a week for one

month leads to brain damage." Although there is some hashish
available in East Berlin, and many East German youth seem to
be curious about drugs, narcotics are still a rare thing in the
D.D.R. The police see to it that it remains so.

But even so, and in spite of everything, some East German
youth are beginning to stir somewhat more openly. The first
incident came in 1969, when the wild rumor spread around East
Germany that the Rolling Stones were going to play a concert
in honor of the upcoming twentieth anniversary of the D.D.R.,
in front of the Axel Springer House just on the border between
East and West Berlin. "Thousands of young people came to
Berlin to hear their idols," according to one gushing account,
and the very day of the planned government anniversary festivi-
ties large crowds of strange-looking youth began amassing near
the Berlin Wall. A panicky police force stormed into the crowd,
which wasn't *doing* anything, without warning. Lots of kids
were arrested for *Vorbereitung zur Republikflucht* ("preparing
flight from the Republic"), and a number of university students
in the crowd got expelled.

Now, with a show of poetic justice, the very tentative stirrings
have been concentrated around the regime's showplace of af-
fluence, Berlin's new Alexanderplatz. A magnet for foreign
tourists, the traffic-free square also became a magnet for those
who especially wanted to meet foreign tourists — a mixture of
black marketeers and hippies, with the two groups often over-
lapping considerably. Last spring, as the weather got warmer,
regular groups of long-haired and mod-dressed teen-agers began assembling daily. They sat along the edges of the circular
fountain — whose style is American *kitsch* rather than Stalinist
pomposity — which adorns the square's center. Although most
of the kids hadn't known each other before, they soon began to
feel a sense of group solidarity, which was further promoted

by the predictable police reaction. Soon plainclothesmen began circling for hours on end around the fountain. Policemen
started informing selected people around the fountain that they
should sit up straight or not put their feet in the water. (The
press had previously published loads of pictures showing visitors
to the fountain with their feet in the water, which was felt to be
a symbol of a new spirit of reckless abandon.) Police checked
identity cards without apparent cause, and an occasional "fountain person" was taken into the nearby police station for questioning. A few got *Alexverbot* — prohibition from coming to
Alexanderplatz.

Once last summer Alexanderplatz came close to boiling over.
A West German youth started playing a guitar and a group
quickly gathered around him. Within minutes, several busloads
of policemen arrived, and, after listening to the group's pro-
testations of innocence, a few who continued to argue against
the police decision to end the concert were arrested. The mood
at the time was bitter but nothing happened. With the coming
of winter the fountain people have dispersed, but they will
probably be back again next summer, and the best bet is that
some sort of confrontation is only a matter of time. Indeed, it is
tempting to hope that it is East Germany's proud "prosperity"
that will do her in, except that a few hippies have yet to topple
a government anywhere. Then again, they've never had as an
enemy a government like this.